Building Transcultural Teams

Using Personal Stories to Build Professional Relationships… Across Cultures

(Originally submitted as Interpretive Transcultural Storytelling Method: A Contextual Narrative Approach to Interpreting Transcultural Relationships)

Kent Mankins, Ph.D., M.Ed., N.C.C., L.M.H.C.
Copyright 2007

Preface

This book is an *adaptation* of my Ph.D. dissertation presented at the University of Buckingham, UK in 2007. As such this will not be a typical "commercial" work. Some of the more academic requirements such as the *declaration* and other elements have been deleted. In addition, please forgive some of the formatting issues which were unavoidable in converting this to a different format.

Building Transcultural Teams is offered as a resource for those who may be interested in fields such as: cultural studies, management, multicultural team building, and leadership. If I can be of any assistance, feel free to email me at: kent@leadtosucceed.net

Abstract
Kenneth Mankins
Building Transcultural Teams

Research Question: How can hermeneutic methodology and narrative storytelling identify and enrich cultural differences and enhance communication, deepen understanding and create synergy in multicultural organizations?

As the global economy continues expanding, managers and organizations will be faced with issues that may have gone unaddressed in the past. While opportunities for synergy and creative emergence have increased, so has the potential for conflict. The Interpretive Storytelling Method was birthed from an observation of the growing multicultural climate and the predominantly quantitative nature of multicultural management literature. The purpose of the present research is to develop a model utilizing hermeneutic methodology and narrative storytelling as a protocol for teambuilding in multicultural settings. The project begins with an overview of the global cultural climate and multicultural literature. Hermeneutics and narrative storytelling then provide a backdrop from which the ITSM unfolds. In working with multicultural teams from several organizations, the case studies provide insight into the contributions the Interpretive Transcultural Storytelling Method can make, as well as areas in which further research is warranted.

Table of Contents: Interpretive Transcultural Storytelling Method

- ❖ Title Page — 1
- ❖ Preface — 2
- ❖ Abstract — 3
- ❖ Table of Contents — 4

Beginning

Chapter 1: Introduction to the Method — 7
    1. Research Question
    2. The Problem
        2.1 The Growing Global Economy
        2.2 The Traditional Approach to Multicultural Management

Chapter 2: Literature Review II: — 20
    Multicultural Material in Breadth

Chapter 3: Literature Review III: — 36
Multicultural Material In-depth

Chapter 4: Methodology Part I — 76

Chapter 5: Methodology Part II — 91
    5.1: The Objective of the Present Research
    5.2: The Choice for the present research
    5.3: The Methodological Matrix: Hermeneutics
    5.4: Conclusion

Chapter 6: Method: Narrative Storytelling — 112
    6.1: Narrative Storytelling and Hermeneutics: Method and Methodology
    6.2: Narrative Storytelling within Organizations
    6.3: Narrative Storytelling as a Research Method
    6.4: Overview and Inner-view

Chapter 7: Contextualization: — 132
From Texas to Mexico, via London

Chapter 8: Genesis of the ITSM: 151
M.Sc. Group
    8.1: The M.Sc. Module
    8.2: Final Project for the Module
    8.3: Synthesis and Implications

Middle

Chapter 9: ITSM: Conception, Revision 164
Application
    9.1: In-Spection
    9.2: Expression
    9.3: Interpretation
    9.4: Clarification
    9.5: Understanding
    9.6: Emergence
    9.7: Conclusion

Chapter 10: Fieldwork: An Introduction 179
Chapter 11: Fieldwork Project 1: 185
Mukogawa Ft Wright Institute- The Pilot
Chapter 12: Fieldwork Project 2: Private 203
Investigations Firm
Chapter 13: Fieldwork Project 3: Family 226
Counselling Centre
Chapter 14: Fieldwork Project 4: 250
Investment Group
Chapter 15: Fieldwork Project 5: 262
Pharmaceutical Manufacturer

End

Chapter 16: Summary of Fieldwork 278
Chapter 17: Implications of Hermeneutic 291
Methodology and Narrative Storytelling
Method within Multicultural Management
Chapter 18: Conclusions and 309
Recommendations for Further Research

Bibliography 317

Chapter 1
Introduction to the Interpretive Transcultural Storytelling Method

1. Research Question:

How can hermeneutic methodology and narrative storytelling identify and enrich cultural similarities and differences, enhance communication, deepen understanding, and create synergy in multicultural organizations?

2. The Problem: Growing Global Economy and Traditional Approaches to Multicultural Management
2.1 The Growing Global Economy

As immigration and globalization increase, so will the demand for multicultural fluency. The purpose of the Interpretive Transcultural Storytelling Method (ITSM) is to provide a protocol for building synergy in multicultural teams. Culture, multicultural, and transcultural have varying definitions. In the present work, culture refers to the collective programming of the human mind that distinguishes the members of one human group from those of another. Culture in this sense is a system of collectively held values. (Hofstede, 2001) Culture is an "historically transmitted pattern of meanings embodied in symbols, a system of inherited conceptions expressed in symbolic form by means of which men communicate, perpetuate, and develop their knowledge about and attitudes towards life"(Geertz, 1973). Culture does not necessarily imply different races or nationalities. For example, great cultural differences exist in the United States between the Northern, Southern, Eastern, and Western cultures. Multicultural refers to a community, group or organization with individuals from more than one cultural context. Transcultural refers to an item or philosophy that extends through many cultures. Therefore, the Interpretive

Transcultural Storytelling Method is transcultural because of the contention that storytelling extends to many cultures and in essence transcends cultural boundaries.

Individuals from specific cultural backgrounds may exhibit characteristics different from their general cultural context. While experts, such as Hofstede, recognize this, most of the present research is based on the generalization of cultural populations. By utilizing storytelling and hermeneutics, the participants in the ITSM are exposed to specific cultural characteristics of individuals rather than simply relying on generalized assumptions about an individual based upon their cultural background. The Interpretive Transcultural Storytelling Method is intended to provide a method for building relationships within a group or team by identifying cultural differences and intentionally enhancing these differences to create synergy.

Stephen R. Covey states, "Simply defined, [synergy] means that the whole is greater than the sum of its parts" (Covey, 1989, p.262). He continues, "Valuing the differences is the essence of synergy- the mental, the emotional, the psychological differences between people. And the key to valuing those differences is to realize that all people see the world, not as it is, but as they are" (Covey, 1989, p. 277). During the ITSM workshop, participants are introduced to exercises that assist them in gaining self knowledge so that they can better understand the lenses with which they see the world. I contend that cultural differences are included in the essence of synergy, and in light of the evolving cultural climate, these differences will become more pronounced.

Thomas Friedman (The World is Flat, 2005), and Samuel Huntington (The Clash of Civilizations, 1996, and Who Are We? 2004) have written extensively on the changing nature of the global climate. Friedman offers a broad view of the evolution of the global market place. Huntington places the evolving

American culture in context of an evolving world. Both are prominent figures on the subject, and both present substantially different approaches to addressing this cultural evolution. Thomas Friedman, in The World Is Flat: A Brief History of the Twentieth Century (2005) chronicles the explosion of the global market place in the twentieth century. He begins this prolific work with a personal experience of his journey to Bangalore, India. Friedman (2005) states:

> Outside, some of the traffic signs were also sponsored by Texas Instruments, and the Pizza Hut billboard on the way over showed a steaming pizza, under the headline "Gigabites of Taste!" No, this definitely wasn't Kansas. It didn't even seem like India. Was this the New World, the Old World, or the Next World?
>
> Here I was in Bangalore- more than five hundred years after Columbus sailed over the horizon, using the rudimentary navigational technologies of his day, and returned safely to prove definitively that the world was round- and one of India's smartest engineers, trained at his country's top technical institute and backed by the most modern technologies of his day, was essentially telling me that the world was *flat*- as flat as that screen on which he can host a meeting of his whole global supply chain. Even more interesting, he was citing this development as a good thing, as a new milestone in human progress and a great opportunity for India and the world- the fact that we had made our world flat! (p. 5, 7)

Freidman identifies two forces that "flattened" the world. First and foremost was the fall of the Berlin Wall. This event had major implications for the people of Germany, the Soviet and Communist countries, and it also impacted foreign policy. However, Friedman states that the fall of the Wall had far-reaching philosophical impact that changed the global market. Friedman (2005) states:

> The fall of the Berlin Wall didn't just help flatten the alternatives to free-market capitalism and unlock enormous pent-up energies for hundreds of millions of people in places like India, Brazil, China, and the former Soviet Empire. It also allowed us to think about the world differently- to see it as more of a seamless whole. Because the Berlin Wall was not only blocking our way; it was blocking our sight- our ability to think about the world as a single market, a single ecosystem, and a single community. Before 1989, you could have an Eastern policy or a Western policy, but it was hard to think about having a "global" policy.

Friedman quotes Indian economist, Amartya Sen, who tells a Sanskrit story of a frog who lived in a well, and how his whole world view consisted of that well. After the Wall fell, it was as though that frog was suddenly able to communicate with frogs in other wells. (p.51) Sen states, "Most knowledge is learning from the other across the border" (Friedman, 2005, p. 51). The fall of the Berlin Wall opened up the borders to communicate with others around the globe, and had a significant impact upon globalization. Of course, Friedman acknowledges, the fall of the Berlin Wall did not initiate globalization. In fact, globalization had as much of an impact on the fall of the Wall. With technology such as computers, Windows operating system, the internet, and telephones, the iron hold of information necessary for totalitarian regimes to control masses was compromised.

Netscape's IPO, Friedman acknowledges, was the second factor in flattening the world. Netscape's influence made the internet accessible to the masses, and therefore further changing the way the world communicates and does business. Work Flow Software is the third flattener Friedman acknowledges. This software enables the creation of literal global offices that are not contingent on the boundaries of time or space. People and programs anywhere on globe can be in instant communication at any time. The fourth flattener is Open-Sourcing, which "makes available for free many tools, from software to encyclopaedias that millions of people around the world would have had to buy in order to use" (Friedman, 2005, p. 102). Outsourcing is Friedman's fifth flattener and Offshoring is the sixth. Supply-chaining is number seven, which is a method of collaborating among suppliers, retailers, and customers in order to create better value. (Friedman, 2005) Number eight on Friedman's list is Insourcing, and In-forming is his ninth. In-forming constitutes the information technologies that have dramatically impacted global business, such as search engines. The tenth flattener, Friedman calls the Steroids, which includes the myriads of high technology advancements, such as wireless connections, which are relatively young and maturing with speed.

On a global scale multicultural management issues are increasing, and these issues equally affect the United States. Estimates place the world's Caucasian population at less than ten percent by the year 2010, a dramatic drop from seventeen percent in 1997. In the USA, the populations considered to be minorities today, will be the majority by 2040. In 2005, Texas joined the ranks of California and Hawaii as states where Caucasians are no longer majorities. "In 1970, nearly 99 percent of all Americans were identified as either white or black. Thirty years later, that percentage had fallen to about 87 percent, with the white population declining from 87.4 percent in 1970 to 75.1 percent in 2000, and the black population increasing from 11.1 percent to 12.3 percent over the same period. The change in the white population was offset by the rise in the 'other' population, which increased from 1.4 percent in 1970 to 12.5 percent in 2000" (Singer, 2005). The 'other' populations include all other races. It is estimated that Hispanics, for example, will constitute up to twenty-five percent of the USA population, by the year 2040. (Huntington, 2004, p.224) Samuel Huntington's work, Who We Are?: The Challenges to America's National Identity (2004), addresses what he terms, "The crisis of national identity". In the foreword, Huntington (2004) states:

> This book deals with the changes occurring in the salience and substance of American national identity. Salience is the importance that Americans attribute to their national identity compared to their many other identities. Substance refers to what Americans think they have in common and distinguishes them from other peoples. (p. xv)

Huntington addresses three key arguments:

1. The salience of American national Identity has varied through history. Following the Civil War, national identity flourished until the 1960s when subnational, dual-national, transnational identities evolved and began to deteriorate the national identity. This multi-identity lasted until the tragedy of September 11 when the national identity was given a remarkable boost. Huntington states that the high sense of national identity is a result of Americans feeling their nation is endangered or threatened. "If their perception of that threat fades, other identities could again take precedence over national identity" (Huntington, 2004, p. xv). I agree with his assessment that the rise in national identity has the 9-11 tragedy as its motivator, and that the fear of the enemy, perceived as Islamic Militants, kept that identity intact. However, I have two observations that lead

me to different conclusions. First, as the dissidence over the current administration's foreign policy, in general, and the Iraq War, specifically, continues to boil, the national identity that initially bound the USA together is evaporating, resulting in a defined schism between and within political parties. Although there is no evidence that the threat of terrorism has diminished, the fear of attack is not potent enough to withstand severe discrimination of ideologies. It is apparent that fear is a powerful motivator, but an inadequate sustainer of national identity.

    2. Americans have, over the years, defined the substance of their identity in terms of race, ethnicity, ideology, and culture. "Race and ethnicity are now largely eliminated: Americans see their country as a multiethnic, multiracial society" (Huntington, 2004, p. xv). Huntington asserts that key elements of the original American culture included the English language, Christianity, religious commitment, English concepts of law, responsibility of rulers, and the rights of individuals. Protestant values of individualism, work ethic, and the belief that humans have the right to create heaven on earth were also fundamental elements of national identity. These key elements and the economic opportunities presented by this culture, Huntington states, attracted millions of immigrants to the USA.

    3. The primary force of the Anglo-Protestant culture has been the distinguishing element of the USA national identity, and has been common ground for most American citizens. However, in the late twentieth century, the salience and substance of this culture was challenged by the mass immigration from Latin America and Asia. Huntington states that a politically correct political and academic environment, coupled with an influx, of specifically Hispanic immigrants, could cause the American identity to evolve in a variety of directions. First of these is that

of a "creedal America, lacking its historical core, and united only by a common commitment to the principles of the American creed" (Huntington, 2004, p. xvi). The next would be a split country with two cultures, and two languages, Spanish and English. Third, an Anglo, exclusivist America could return to its racist and discriminatory past. The fourth direction is that of a revitalized American identity, "affirming its historic Anglo-Protestant culture, religious commitments, and values and bolstered by confrontations with an unfriendly world" (Huntington, 2004, p. xvi). The final possibility, Huntington presents is some combination of any or all of the above. I find no amenable option among the possibilities Huntington proposes. The propositions Huntington discusses appear to present his ideal outcome of a return to the "way things used to be," or a disastrous outcome that will virtually destroy any sense of American identity. However, I contend that other possibilities must exist. The American people, with proper leadership, can be foreword thinking and proactive in purposefully evolving into a new paradigm of American identity. Instead of relying upon fear, the American people can strive for understanding and appreciation of those who are culturally different than themselves. A transformed American identity can respect and value differences and the contributions a variety of cultures can make. The ITSM is designed to proactively initiate relationships that would promote understanding and appreciation in the organizational and business setting. While this does not have the scope to influence the whole of American society, grass-root movements have historically had, and therefore potentially have great influence in our culture.

Friedman (2005) closes his book with the following profound statement:

I cannot tell any other society or culture what to say to its own children, but I tell you what I say to my own: The world is being flattened. I didn't start it and you can't stop it, except at a great cost to human development and your own future. But we can mange it, for better or for worse. If it is going to be for better, not for worse, then you and your generation must not live in fear of either the terrorists or of tomorrow, of either al-Qaeda or of Infosys. You can flourish in a flat world, but it does take the right imagination and the right motivation. While your lives have been powerfully shaped by 9/11, the world needs you to be forever the generation of 11/9 [the fall of the Berlin Wall] - the generation of strategic optimists, the generation with more dreams than memories, the generation that wakes up each morning and not only imagines that things can be better but also acts on that imagination everyday. (p. 469)

Huntington proposes a reactive, protectionist approach proposing the USA should return to its historical cultural roots. However, Friedman encourages a proactive, creative approach to dealing with the cultural evolution. The ITSM is an attempt to bring a proactive and co-creative approach to the field of multicultural management. The world is changing, and multicultural management needs to continually evolve to meet the needs of the global economy. The present research developed from an observed inadequacy of the primarily positivistic multicultural management instruments and methods. These methods identify generalizations, degrees of cultural differences, sensitivity, or acculturation, but a general absence exists in practical methods for developing relationships between individuals from different cultures.

2.2 The Traditional Approach to Multicultural Management

Adding to the problem of the growing global economy is the insufficiency of traditional multicultural management literature. Typical research in the Social Sciences is approached from a quantitative, positivist approach. Grounded in the physical sciences, these methodologies assume an objective world which can be studied and measured with scientific, quantitative methods. They seek to predict and explain causal relationships between variables. As the name implies, quantitative research focuses on quantity and is primarily deductive, utilizing statistical methods. It is empirical and emphasizes scientific experimental methods. (Merriam, 1988) While this type of research yields valuable information, I contend it is not sufficient. The addition of a qualitative, hermeneutic approach will address some of the practical elements of building multicultural relationships, adding to the holistic nature of the multicultural management field.

Brian Fay, in his book Contemporary Philosophy of Social Science (1996), emphasizes a multicultural approach to the philosophy of social science. His theory centres on approaching the "philosophy of social science in a new way, one centred on the experience of sharing a world in which people differ significantly from one another" (Fay, 1996, p. 1). The popular positivistic method, favoured especially in the West, is one paradigm for gaining knowledge, but Fay asserts it is not solely sufficient. Fay proposes a new frame of reference for conceptualizing social science research called "interactionism" (Fay, 1996, p. 8). Fay addresses a number of questions throughout his book which are dualistic, that is "either/ or" on the surface. He finds that, often, the presumed either/ or can be answered with "and". He does not blindly disregard positivistic research, but acknowledges the usefulness of qualitative and quantitative approaches. "In a *dialectical* approach, differences are not conceived as absolute, and consequently the relationship between them is not one of utter antagonism. Indeed, on a *dialectical* view, alternatives, while genuinely competing, only appear to be completely "other" to each other. They are in fact deeply interconnected, and the confrontation between them reveals how these differences can be comprehended and transcended" (Fay, 1996, p. 224).

The Interpretive Transcultural Storytelling Method utilizes hermeneutics, a qualitative methodology and is consistent with Fay's dialectical approach. Fay states that multiculturalism poses an "epistemic problem: *if others live within their own framework and we live within ours, how can we understand them?*" (Fay, 1996, p.4). In such a paradigm, we are forced to misunderstand each other. Hermeneutics teaches the researcher to know himself or herself and to interpret the "other" in light of that understanding as well as within the context of the "other". This is, in essence, a dialectical paradigm. While empirical research encourages the researcher to block his or her own prejudices, hermeneutics emphasizes acknowledgement of those prejudices and the interpretation of the other in a cyclical fashion.

Whereas existing quantitative multicultural literature increases an understanding of generalizations, the purpose of this project is to move toward an applicable method for enhancing the synergy of multicultural teams. Informed by hermeneutics and using narrative storytelling, The Interpretive Transcultural Storytelling Method is intended to enhance the working relationships of the members of multicultural teams. The ITSM consists of the following phases:

1. In-Spection: Building self knowledge
2. Expression: Telling a brief story of an event instrumental in personal development
3. Interpretation: The listeners attributing meaning to the story of another, in light of personal context and that of the teller

4. Clarification: Hermeneutic spiral of interpretation, questions, clarification
5. Understanding: Reaching mutual understanding of the story and context
6. Emergence: The identification of new knowledge and its application

The results will positively impact the individuals involved, the teams to which they belong, and ultimately the society at large. Having established the research question within context of the problems of the global cultural climate as well as the traditional approaches to multicultural management, we will now review some of the relevant literature within the multicultural management arena.

References:

Covey, Stephen R. (1989). *The 7 habits of highly effective people.* New York: Simon & Schuster.

Fay, Brian. (1996). *Contemporary philosophy of social science: A multicultural approach.* Cambridge, MA: Blackwell Publishing.

Geertz, Clifford. (1973) *The interpretation of cultures.* New York: Basic Books, Inc.

Hofstede, Geert. (2001). *Culture's consequences: Comparing values, behaviours, institutions, and organizations across nations, 2nd Edition.* Thousand Oaks, CA: Sage Publications.

Lessem, Ronnie & Palsule, Sudhanshu. (2002). From local identity to global integrity. *Leadership and Organization Development Journal UK, Volume 23, No. 4,* 174-185.

McLeod, John. (2001). *Qualitative research in counselling and psychotherapy.* London: Sage Publications.

Palmer, Richard. (1969). *Hermeneutics.* Evanston: Northwestern University Press.

Randall, William Lowell. (1995). *The stories we are: An essay on self-creation.* Toronto: University of Toronto Press.

Rathbone, June. *Components of self.* (Online), Found October 2003. University College, London. http://www.homepages.ucl.ac.uk/~ucjtjur/

Chapter 2
Literature Review: Multicultural Management in Breadth

As identified in the previous chapter, the cultural climate of the globe is evolving. Consequently, multicultural management is increasingly relevant in the global workplace and is concurrently receiving increasing attention among researchers, authors, and organisational psychologists. In addition, the 2006 joint convention of the American Counselling Association and the Canadian Counselling Association highlighted the theme of multiculturalism, with the majority of workshops devoted to that theme. A cursory review of www.amazon.com, an online world leader in book sales, reveals 173 listings for "multicultural management". While the field is not devoid of literature, the same search for other management topics is copious. For example, a search for "leadership" resulted in 18,207 results. While multicultural awareness is escalating, the literature in multicultural management is not quite as prolific.

In the initial stages of reviewing multicultural management literature, I discovered a prevalence of quantitative material such as the seminal works of Trompenaars, Hampden-Turner, and Hofstede. In light of the overwhelmingly quantitative literature available, I have intentionally sought out more qualitative material. Endeavouring to provide a comprehensive literature review, I have identified a spectrum of works that span a continuum from the under-represented qualitative to the predominant quantitative. In the present and following chapters, I will address what I have termed a methodological continuum of multicultural management literature. Within the present chapter is a review of multicultural management literature in breadth. The following chapter will address the works of Trompenaars, Hampden-Turner, Hofstede, and Funakawa more in-depth. The literature, while not exhaustive, represents a general overview of the types of literature available for multicultural managers.

Methodological Continuum of Literature Reviewed in Chapters 2 &3

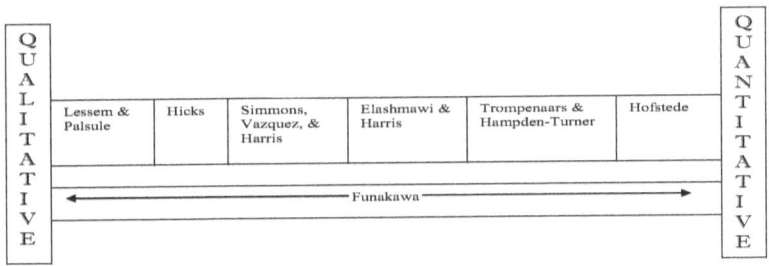

The qualitative pole begins with the work of Lessem and Palsule (1997). While their work references some empirical research, the four worlds model is set in a qualitative approach. The works of Hicks, Simmons, Vazquez, Harris, and Elashmawi progressively become more qualitative and empirical, leading into the seminal works of Trompenaars, Hampden-Turner, and Hofstede. Funakawa brings us almost full-circle as I understand his work to be a bridge between the qualitative and quantitative.

The works Trompenaars, Hampden-Turner, Hofstede, and Funakawa will be covered more exhaustively in chapter 7 because of their stature in the field of multicultural management research. These authors are widely recognized as leaders in the field of multicultural management, and they contribute to the continuum of approaches. While the work of Hofstede is thoroughly empirical, the works of Trompenaars and Hampden-Turner is grounded in empiricism, yet takes on an almost dialectical nature by incorporating some qualitative elements. Specifically, they allude often to hermeneutic principles such as context and reconciliation of opposing values, which resembles the hermeneutic concept of fusion of horizons. Funakawa represents the application facet to the spectrum, and incorporates specific elements of Japanese-American business relationships. His work is valuable because, as Lessem and Palsule point out in the four worlds model, the East is absent from the American cultural paradigm. We begin the journey through the continuum of writings with the work of Lessem and Palsule.

Perhaps the most influential book in birthing my desire to develop the ITSM is Managing in Four Worlds (1997) by Ronnie Lessem and Sudhanshu Palsule. Lessem is an accomplished consultant and academic, as well as my Ph.D. supervisor. Palsule is a talented global consultant hailing from India and living in England. I initially read this book in preparation for my personal interview, with Dr. Lessem, for admission into the Ph.D. programme at Buckingham. In an attempt to familiarize myself with his philosophy, I discovered a new paradigm to approaching multiculturalism. Having been reared in the United States, the concept of the melting pot embodied my understanding of how a variety of cultures can co-exist. The four worlds model challenges the melting pot concept and provides, in my opinion, a more holistic, equitable, and synergistic archetype for understanding multicultural organizations, societies, and even ourselves and others as individuals. Grounded firmly in context and achieving a fusion of horizons, the four worlds model exhibits characteristics of hermeneutic methodology blended with critical theory. Within the four worlds concept, each culture is viewed uniquely distinct and offers a valuable contribution to the whole, such as ingredients in a salad or instruments in an orchestra. In the melting pot concept each individual and his or her cultural distinctiveness is melted together, creating a soup of indistinct flavours. The melting pot concept encourages individuals to try and fit into the mould of the norm, while the four worlds concept acknowledges the value of differences. As in hermeneutics, the context of the world of the self is examined as well as the world of the other. Unique traits from different worlds can be incorporated creating synergy, much like the hermeneutic fusion of horizons.

Lessem and Palsule present the "global businessphere" (Lessem & Palsule, 1997, p. 10) in context of their four worlds model: West, East, North, and South. Drawing from Carl Jung's model of sensing, thinking, intuiting, and feeling, the four worlds model can be observed in "our personalities and in the kind of societies we build" (Lessem & Palsule, 1997, p. 6) as well the world's natural ecosystems. Lessem and Palsule argue that each of the four worlds is distinct, and simultaneously incorporates aspects of the other three. As we will discover later in this chapter, the work of Trompenaars and Hampden-Turner identifies characteristics distinct to individual cultures and simultaneously argue that reconciling these differences is valuable for an organization or society. For them, an organization that operates all individualistically, for example, will miss important contributions that communitarianism can offer. By recognizing the need for reconciled differences, Trompenaars and Hampden-Turner infer that it is quite probable that within an organization weighing heavily with one characteristic lies, however dormant, the other characteristics as well.

For Lessem and Palsule, "the four worlds are the generic principle through which life organizes itself. Whether it is an organism or an organization, the process of individuation must include four aspects: *identity, entity, non-entity, and community*" (Lessem & Palsule, 1997, p. 12). Following is a brief synopsis of each of the four worlds as they relate to organizations.

1. West: The First World of Identity

"To be or not to be." W. Shakespeare, Hamlet

In the West, the USA and England for example, an organization is built upon individuality and "accumulation-through-exploitation of resources" (Lessem & Palsule, 1997, p. 12). Organizations focus upon the accumulation of physical, financial, and human capital as well as growth, dominance, and survival. The doctrine of Manifest Destiny can be readily observed in the philosophy of the West.

2. North: The Second World of Entity

"Cogito ergo sum: I think therefore I am." Rene Descartes, Discourse on Method

The North is exemplified by countries such as Norway, Finland, and Sweden. An organization is focused not as much on survival and growth as it is maintenance and consolidation. Conservation of resources through information and communication technologies is emphasised. This is done by developing efficient cross-functional networks that straddle the "physical, financial and human elements of the company" (Lessem & Palsule, 1997, p. 13).

3. East: The Third World of Non-entity

"Aham Brahmasmi: I am the universe." *The Upanishads*

The philosophy of the East, for example China, Japan, and Taiwan, is the antithesis of the Western individualism. While the West is focused on setting up boundaries and differentiating from others, the Eastern paradigm is to dissolve boundaries and identity in deference to the discovery of an infinite and global non-entity. (Lessem & Palsule, 1997) Within the Eastern context, individuality has little or no meaning. For example, a Taiwanese M.Sc. student in a course I taught at University of Buckingham could not comprehend my questions, "What do you want to do with your life? What are your goals and desires?" His answers were "I will go back to Taiwan and takeover the management of my father's business." As a Westerner I was completely appalled at his lack of personal goals and the pursuit of his dream, not what his family expected of him. It was through this experience that the ITSM concept was born. What I considered wrong was simply different, and both philosophies can be valuable, just as Lessem and Palsule, as well as Trompenaars and Hampden-Turner and Funakawa identify. Lessem and Palsule observe early in Managing the Four Worlds that the East is missing in American culture, even though many people from the East reside in the USA.

4. South: The Fourth World of Community

"I am because you are." Lovemore Mbigi, Ubuntu

Southern community spirit is pronounced in countries such as South Africa or Mexico. The "organization exists as part of a larger family or a community to which it is bound by forces of evolution." The purpose of the organization is, therefore, to continually operate through a communal value-sharing process whereby a dynamic balance is maintained between the entity and the environment" (Lessem & Palsule, 1997, p. 14). The Southern management style is built upon a human-centred concept of the individuals within an organization and the organization within the community.

Lessem and Palsule weave a compelling argument for the value in the development of a new approach to business which will breathe new life into a closed and dying system, built largely in the American management laboratory. This new system would incorporate characteristics of all four worlds, drawing upon useful concepts from each. America is in need of a restructuring in its management philosophy that will include elements of the presently non-existent East.

In reading this book for the first time prior to my Ph.D. journey, I experienced a hermeneutic fusion of horizons. This fusion has been continually emerging as I learn more and more how Western I am. I find myself regularly making statements reflecting my Western nature. With these statements and attitudes becoming more easily identifiable, I am able to reconcile them with those from the other three worlds. As Trompenaars, Hampden-Turner, and Hofstede have identified cultural characteristics, Lessem and Palsule have presented a model for integrating the four worlds which has potential to create a synergistic environment in which organizations can grow. The ITSM is built upon this concept and is intended to provide a practical method for the working-out of such a philosophy through storytelling and dialogue. The work of Douglas Hicks in the following review addresses the issue of religion in context of an organization. As each of the four worlds have an underlying core of religious or philosophical beliefs, Hicks offers a beneficial examination of religion in the workplace.

As the cultural horizons of the globe evolve, religion will play a profound role in multicultural relationships. The realm of business will not escape issues arising from religious practice. While the overwhelming philosophy of the American corporate culture has been to remain religiously sterile, many are experiencing a challenge to this attitude. For example, there have been lectures on the Torah at Microsoft, Islamic study groups at Intel, and classes on the Koran at Boeing.

Douglas A. Hicks, Religion and the Workplace: Pluralism, Spirituality, Leadership (2003), is included in this review because of his concentration on religious differences in the workplace. Hicks is Assistant Professor of Leadership Studies and Religion at the Jepson School of Leadership Studies, University of Richmond, Virginia. He is author of several books and articles on the subjects of religion and leadership and is affiliated with Harvard's Pluralism Project. Hicks, an American, follows in the methodological continuum primarily qualitatively, yet sites more empirical data than Lessem and Palsule. Hicks addresses the American work place and the many challenges that arise from the growing diversity addressed in the previous chapter on the global cultural climate. As demonstrated by the September 11, 2001 attack, the ongoing conflict in Iraq, and the clash of Muslim and Western civilizations, Hicks' focus on religious differences is particularly applicable to contemporary management. Hicks cites Harvard's Diana Eck who points out that the religious landscape has changed dramatically, and that the United States is "now the world's most religiously diverse nation, at least in terms of the number of active traditions and communities" (Hicks, 2003, p. 12).

Consistent with the American melting pot, religion has been de-emphasised in the workplace. Employees are encouraged either through rules or peer pressure to conform to the norm. In the case of the USA, the norm religion has traditionally been protestant. As such, those of the Hindu or Muslim faiths, for instance, do not necessarily fit the mould. As with Lessem and Palsule, Hicks emphasises the uniqueness of the diverse religions found within an organization. Concentrating on religious differences, Hicks differentiates his work from those that seek to find the common ground between the various religious belief systems. Hicks' theory is in concert with that of the ITSM in appreciating differences and the use of dialogue to turn differences from liabilities to assets.

The primary focus of Hicks' work is on the value added to organizations by intentionally identifying and discussing the religious differences employees possess. He articulates the benefits of encouraging discussion between peers and clarifies positive outcomes of such discussions. Hicks presents that even conflicts about religious beliefs can produce positive outcomes such as the breeding of creativity. Lessem and Palsule also make a strong case for the creativity and new life generated when an organization adopts an orchestra versus melting pot attitude. The reconciliation of the dimensions presented by Hampden-Turner and Trompenaars (2000) is similar to what Hicks recommends in his theory. Hicks' model is called Respectful Pluralism, which "means resisting company-sponsored religion and spirituality while allowing employees to bring their own religions to work" (Hicks, 2003, p. 2).

Hicks argues that respectful pluralism should operate in the workplace to encourage citizens and employees to communicate with each other in a respectful manner. Hicks states that he does not believe there is a set of universally shared religious values and morals that can hold a company together. One must look beyond trying to find common ground to finding synergy among the diversity. He contends that employees should be allowed to, or not to, draw upon religious symbols and philosophy, yet do so in a manner that demonstrates respect to other employees. Dignity and equanimity among employees and with the employer is essential. Therefore the institutional hegemony of one religion is discouraged. Hicks (2003) states:

> In respectful pluralism, the organization should not be aligned with any explicit religious, spiritual, or other comprehensive worldview. Rather, in this moral framework I posit that organizations should allow for significant employee expression of various aspects of their identity on an equal basis. When such a condition exists, we say that *diversity*- a descriptive reality reflecting empirical characteristics of the workforce- has been transformed into *pluralism*- a term that reflects a positive quality of relationships among diverse people. (p. 184)

Hicks addresses the potential conflicts that may arise from developing pluralism and states that a leader should not fear conflict; rather it should be utilized to spur on discussion. "The task of leadership is not to impose one set of values upon all followers, but to 'orchestrate' conflict in order to achieve a desirable outcome" (Hicks, 2003, p. 195). Although Hicks encourages management to orchestrate discussions to resolve conflicts and establish respectful understanding, he does not breech the question of "how" to do that. The ITSM provides a method to enable that type of dialogue. As seen in Lessem, Palsule and Hicks, cultural (including religious) differences are valuable resources for an organization. The tendency of managers to overlook differences and find common ground, while possibly easier, does not result in a learning, dynamic, or human-centred organization. Next, Transcultural Leadership: Empowering the Diverse Workforce (1993) by Simmons, Vazquez, and Harris presents an almost hermeneutic approach to multicultural management which emphasises understanding differences among different cultures. While, methodologically, their work exhibits many hermeneutic characteristics, it moves further along the methodological continuum. Simmons, Vazquez, and Harris rely on a greater degree of empirical data in building their case and also utilize qualitative surveys in their research.

George Simmons is principal of George Simmons International, a consulting agency specializing in gender and cultural issues. Carmen Vazquez is an expert in organizational development with over fifteen years of experience. Philip Harris is an international management consultant. Because of the growing multicultural workplace, the authors identify potential breakdowns in communication that could take place and discuss the potential for learning from those breakdowns. The authors' present the "Five C's" (Simmons, Vazquez, & Harris, 1993, p. 195) as a compass to assist transcultural leaders. The Five C's include 1) Continuous learning, 2) Consistent leadership, 3)

Centeredness in one's own culture, 4) Commitment to a vision, and 5) Ceaseless communication.

Simmons, Vazquez, and Harris stress the importance of context, stating that it "is a key concept in understanding how people from other cultures work and behave" (Simmons, Vazquez, & Harris, 1993, p. 43). In chapter 3, language and its context is addressed. The authors draw a distinction between the actual behaviours and words and their potential misinterpretations by the hearer. From a hermeneutic perspective, this is significant. While the authors do not acknowledge hermeneutics, the framework from which they approach communication within context is hermeneutic. For example, the authors' state, "To communicate with others, we must first observe how we talk to ourselves in our own minds" (Simmons, Vazquez, & Harris, 1993, p.50) This is congruent with hermeneutics and the premise that in order to understand others, or the subject, an understanding of one's-self is necessary.

However, the authors do not go into a close examination of how individuals or groups go about discovering context. While the material presented offers valuable information for working cross-culturally, it stops short of offering specific exercises or a model for developing trans-cultural relationships and communication. The authors are in concert with Lessem, Palsule, and Hicks in that they do not stress common ground, but differences. In addition, they stress the power of dialogue in developing understanding of cultural differences. Providing vignettes and observances of interactions between members of American, Japanese, and Arab organizations, the following book to be reviewed offers another pseudo-hermeneutic look at multicultural management.

Another work of relevance in the multicultural management arena is Multicultural Management: New Skills for Global Success (1993). Farid Elashmawi, Ph.D., is a consultant specializing in the management of technology transfer and cross-cultural problems. Philip Harris, Ph.D., is a psychologist and scientist, as well as a co-author of the preceding book. "The text guides management towards success in dealing with cultural differences, and progress toward cultural synergy in business" (Elashmawi & Harris, 1993, p. xi). Elashmawi and Harris specifically address the American, Arab, and Japanese cultures, but they exert that the principles presented will assist many variations of cross-cultural interaction. Due to the contemporary multicultural societies, these cross-cultural interactions may likely occur within a single national organization. The authors present a number of vignettes demonstrating cultural differences that are likely to be encountered in a workplace. In Chapter 3, very useful and insightful tables are presented which demonstrate the top values of various cultures. Some of the top Japanese cultural values include information, harmony, and honesty. American values begin with personal life, wealth, and fairness. The Arab top values are presented as religion, Allah, and the Koran. (Elashmawi & Harris, 1993)

The differences in core values demonstrate how differently these cultures view the world and fits squarely with the four worlds model of Lessem and Palsule. An understanding of the background of people coming from different cultures is important, and again, this background fits in the hermeneutic framework. Although not explicitly mentioned, context is presented as vital. The authors discuss "images of culture" (Elashmawi & Harris, 1993, p. 64) which addresses not only how you view the outside culture, but also how others view your culture, and how you view your culture. This fits with Randall's "The Stories We Are" as he addresses the inside-out, outside-in, and the inside stories.

The authors discuss the importance of language, not only the words used, but their context and accompanying non-verbal behaviour They stress the importance of listening, watching, and feeling. (Elashmawi & Harris, 1993) In addition to national and ethnic cultural values, the authors address the importance of considering corporate values. They describe how even within one corporation, different national branches may have differing values. As an example, the authors chart the top values as surveyed by Apple employees in America and Singapore. This type of empirical data brings the authors' work closer to the quantitative end of the spectrum. Apple's Singaporean branch employees valued teamwork, reserve, long-term gains, analysis, team rewards, and listeners as some of the top values. The American branch listed individualism, openness, short-term gains, zealousness, individual rewards, and talkers. This is an example of how national culture tends to overwhelm corporate culture reinforcing the concept of the four worlds.

The authors of this book present a valuable resource for working cross-culturally. However, again, a specific model for achieving the presented goals is not offered. Information is disseminated, but it is more like a crash course in cross-cultural awareness than a method of mutually reaching cross-cultural awareness. This work correlates with the hermeneutic perspective as it presents the need for knowledge of self and the other, and the importance of context. Although this work incorporates elements of hermeneutic methodology, it is fundamentally couched in the traditional quantitative methodologies. The surveys and self tests as well as the manner in which the results are interpreted represent the over-arching positivistic framework prevalent in much of the multicultural literature. With this being stated, the following in-depth reviews reflect the extreme positivistic and qualitative methodologies utilized overwhelmingly in the social sciences in general, and multicultural management in particular.

Following the reviews of Trompenaars, Hampden-Turner, and Hofstede, Funakawa will round out the final review by bridging the more qualitative work presented earlier in this chapter with the quantitative in an attempt to demonstrate a comprehensive overview of the types of literature available to multicultural managers.

References:

Fay, Brian. (1996). *Contemporary philosophy of social science.* Oxford, UK: Basil Blackwell.

Lessem, Ronnie & Palsule, Sudhanshu. (1997). *Managing in four worlds: From competition to co-creation.* Oxford, UK: Basil Blackwell.

Elashmawi, Farid & Harris, Philip R. (1993). *Multicultural management: New skills for global success.* Houston, TX: Gulf Publishing

Funakawa, Atsushi. (1997). *Transcultural management: A new approach for global organizations.* San Francisco: Jossey-Bass Publishers.

Hampden-Turner, Charles & Trompenaars, Fons. (2000). *Building cross-cultural competence.* Yale: Yale Press.

Hicks, Douglas A. (2003). *Religion and the workplace: Pluralism, spirituality, leadership.* Cambridge, UK: Cambridge University Press.

Hofstede, Geert. (2001). *Culture's consequences: Comparing values, behaviours, institutions, and organizations across nations, 2nd Edition.* Thousand Oaks, CA: Sage Publications.

Simons, George F., Vazquez, Carmen, & Harris, Phillip R. (1993). *Transcultural leadership: Empowering the diverse workforce.* Houston, TX: Gulf Publishing.

Trompenaars, Fons & Hampden-Turner, Charles. (1998). *Riding the waves of culture. 2nd Edition*. NY: McGraw-Hill.

Chapter 3
Literature Review: Multicultural Management In-depth

To this point in we have examined the research question and placed it in context of the global cultural condition and a breadth of multicultural managerial literature. The following works will be reviewed more thoroughly than the previous literature because of the stature they hold within the field of multicultural management. Trompenaars, Hampden-Turner, and Hofstede are influential figures in the realm of multicultural management research, and their works grow progressively more quantitative on the methodological continuum. Their empirical research is extensive and provides a solid foundation of generalized appraisals of cultures. Funakawa has produced a valuable resource for "how to" work with others in a multicultural organization, specifically drawing upon the relationships between Japanese and Americans. While the works of Trompenaars, Hampden-Turner, and Hofstede are decidedly quantitative, and the ITSM research is qualitative, the authors offer a wealth of applicable knowledge. Funakawa's pragmatic and application oriented work is, in essence, a bridge between the two extremes of methodology. Hermeneutics is dialogical, moving between the part and whole, incorporating both. In concert with Fay's concept of the dialectical, hermeneutic methodology does not simultaneously negate the value of empirical knowledge. The ITSM, through the use of hermeneutic methodology, seeks to utilize empirical data in a manner that will provide insight into the individual contexts of the participants.

Trompenaars, Hampden-Turner, and Hofstede each accept the notion that individuals within a culture are unique and that the generalizations found in their research may not always be binding. The works of these three, especially Trompenaars and Hampden-Turner, will be utilized heavily in the ITSM process for gaining self-knowledge and generating discussion to flesh out the individual context of each of the participants. In this way, these works specifically enhance the hermeneutic process of self-knowledge as well as providing a foundation for discussion which is an asset to assist understanding of others. Funakawa, while not formally hermeneutic in his writing, refers strongly to context and dialogue as important factors in the development of productive intercultural relationships, specifically between Japanese and American partners. The works of Trompenaars and Hampden-Turner (Riding the Waves of Culture and Building Cross-cultural Competence), Hofstede (Culture's Consequence), and Funakawa (Transcultural Management) are valuable resources and are examined in this chapter.

Fons Trompenaars studied economics at the Free University in Amsterdam and earned his Ph.D. from the University of Pennsylvania. He is Dutch and grew up in a home speaking French as well. Dr. Trompenaars has worked in a wide range of multicultural careers and is a consultant and author. Charles Hampden-Turner is based at the University of Cambridge Judge Institute of Management. He earned his masters and doctorate from Harvard and is the recipient of numerous awards and fellowships. Dr.'s Hampden-Turner and Trompenaars are renowned for their work in the multicultural arena. For the present project, I will be considering their works, Riding the Waves of Culture (1998) and Building Cross-Cultural Competence (2000).

The work of Trompenaars and Hampden-Turner focuses on the reconciliation of seven dimensions of culture discovered in their research. Their research began with questioning whether or not the predominant American techniques and philosophies of management could be applied in other cultures. This is reflected in the work of Funakawa who devotes much of his efforts to determining how American and Japanese management differs and how to overcome some of these differences. The authors begin with the premise, "It is our belief that you can never understand other cultures" (Trompenaars and Hampden-Turner, 1998, p. 1). They also set forth as a premise that the understanding of "our own culture and our own assumptions and expectations about how people 'should' think and act is the basis for success" (Trompenaars and Hampden-Turner, 1998, p. 2). This assumption is foundational in hermeneutics in which interpretation of the "other" begins with an understanding of the self. While the work of Trompenaars and Hampden-Turner is quantitative, they incorporate elements of qualitative, if not hermeneutic, methodology as well. This brings them further along the methodological continuum, yet not to the degree of the empiricism of Hofstede.

The work of Trompenaars and Hampden-Turner is relevant and complimentary to the ITSM research. They emphasize the human equation, not referring to workers as resources, but as human beings who are involved in relationships. "Culture pervades and radiates meanings into every aspect of the enterprise. Culture patterns the whole field of business relationships" (Trompenaars and Hampden-Turner, 1998, p.16). Trompenaars and Hampden-Turner specify that culture is the "context in which things happen" (1998, p.8), a concept that Funakawa highlights as well. Context is resonant with hermeneutic methodology. Trompenaars and Hampden-Turner also present that the importance of culture is not necessarily the observable topsoil, but the bedrock and core which ultimately determines the way a group of "people understand and interpret the world" (1998, p. 3). Interpretation is the focus of hermeneutics and therefore a foundation of the present research of developing an Interpretive Transcultural Storytelling Method.

Trompenaars and Hampden-Turner state that cultures are not arbitrary or random. Rather they are mirror images of other cultures. "Cultures have always been reflections of the world mirrored in the eyes of members" (Hampden-Turner and Trompenaars, 2000, p.5).

There are certain questions that all cultures must answer, and how these questions are answered determines the way a group of people interprets the world. "Every culture distinguishes itself from others by the specific solutions it chooses to certain problems which reveal themselves as dilemmas" (Trompenaars and Hampden-Turner, 1998, p.8). Trompenaars and Hampden-Turner categorize these into "three headings: those which arise from relationships with other people; those which come from the passage of time; and those which relate to the environment" (Trompenaars and Hampden-Turner, 1998, p.8).

The choices each culture has made in answering the various questions of living are not wrong, they are simply different. In the fieldwork for the ITSM, I have received permission from the Trompenaars and Hampden-Turner as well as the publisher of their material to utilize the questions developed in their research. Because the ITSM is focused upon relationships, only the questions from Trompenaars' and Hampden-Turner's first category, "those which arise from relationships with other people," will be used, specifically, only questions one through four.

Many people have fear of entering a different culture, but once an understanding of other cultures develops, a whole new world appears. It is towards helping others develop an understanding that each of the authors covered in this literature review have devoted their research. To achieve the ability to accept another's culture while still living in your own is essential to a multicultural world. F. Scott Fitzgerald said, "The test of a first-rate intelligence is the ability to hold two opposed ideas in the mind at the same time, and still retain the ability to function"

(Hampden-Turner and Trompenaars, 2000, p.5). In hermeneutics the observer strives to understand what the observed is saying or doing, through his or her framework as well as within that of the other. Brian Fay, in Contemporary Philosophy of Social Science, (1996) advocates moving from a dualistic perspective to a dialectic perspective, or from an "either/ or" to "and".

Riding the Waves of Culture (Trompenaars & Hampden-Turner, 1998) has at its core, seven cultural differences. Building Cross-cultural Competence (Hampden-Turner & Trompenaars, 2000) only addresses six dimensions, omitting "Neutral versus Emotional." These differences are often interpreted as dialectic in nature, or mutually exclusive. In both books the authors endorse reconciliation between the dimensions as a healthy and synergistic alternative, in accordance with Fay's dialectical process.

Trompenaars and Hampden-Turner (1998) state:

> Instead of running the risk of getting stuck by perceiving cultures as static points on a dual axis map, we believe that cultures dance from one preferred end to the opposite and back. In that way we do not risk one cultural category excluding its opposite, as has happened in so many similar studies, of which Hofstede's five mutually exclusive categories are the best known. Rather, we believe that one cultural category seeks to "manage" its opposite and that value dimensions self-organize in systems to generate new meanings. Cultures are circles with preferred arcs joined together. (p. 27)

Trompenaars and Hampden-Turner have hypothesized that cultures which naturally seek reconciliation between seemingly opposing cultures have a better chance of being economically successful. This theory brings the multicultural communication field from being simply social in nature, to direct implications upon economic success.

The first five of the seven dimensions deal with relationships, the sixth deals with time, and the seventh with the environment. They are as follows:
1. Universalism versus Particularism
2. Communitarianism versus Individualism
3. Neutral versus Emotional
4. Diffuse versus Specific
5. Achievement versus Ascription
6. Attitudes to Time
7. Attitudes to the Environment

The questions the authors used for each category can be found in Appendix 3 in the Fieldwork Packet. Because this project utilizes only questions from the relationship category, only those questions are addressed below.

1. Universalism versus Particularism

Succinctly, this can be translated as rules versus relationships. Universalism asserts sameness and similarity. It imposes the same rules for everyone in society regardless of special circumstances. Within Particularism, special circumstances apply. Relationships, for instance, can determine the right or wrong course of action, in contrast to universalism in which the rules are the rules. The consensus of most leading western, specifically American, researchers is that as a society develops and becomes more modern and complex it moves towards universalism. The societies that are less modern and complex and more rural tend to be particularists. Trompenaars and Hampden-Turner do not accept this assumption. They are advocates of reconciling the advantages of each of these cultural perspectives.

The results of their research demonstrated that Americans (Westerners) and Northern Europeans (Northerners) were overwhelmingly universal in their responses. The proportions fall to under 75% for Japan and France, while two-thirds of Venezuelan respondents said they would lie for the friend. (Trompenaars & Hampden-Turner, 1998) In the four worlds paradigm (Lessem & Palsule, 1997) the West and North would be almost completely universal, the East (including France) would be balanced, and the South would be largely particularists in their responses. The authors determined that no culture studied was solely one or the other.

Interestingly, the authors found that predominantly Protestant cultures were universal and predominantly Catholic cultures were particularists. An example of how a protestant culture looks to the law and court system to solve problems is the higher number of lawyers per capita in the United States than in Japan. The United States is credited as the most litigious society in the world.

Trompenaars and Hampden-Turner found that as companies move to a global market place, they tend to adopt universalist paradigms. This expresses itself in contracts, business trip timing, head office role, and job evaluations and rewards. (Trompenaars & Hampden-Turner, 1998) Contracts within a universalist culture are comprehensive legal documents that are meant to keep all parties bound to the same rules, spelling out consequences for breaking those rules. In a particularist culture, relationships are the foundations of agreements, and a contract such as this may be perceived as insulting and rigid. In particularist cultures, business trips may require more time to form relationships than what is necessary to simply do business. In particularist cultures, the relationship with the head office is different, as well, since gratification and loyalty depend greatly upon relationships.

For Trompenaars and Hampden-Turner, the "virtuous cycle" develops as the particularist and the universalist view points work together. This reconciling of the seemingly dualistic paradigms can create a dialectic synergy that has more advantages than either operating independently. Trompenaars and Hampden-Turner stress that cross-cultural competency is based, not on whether or not you are able to grasp the opposite value, but on whether or not you are able to reconcile the opposing values and make them work together. Funakawa (1997) addresses a similar issue by stressing the importance of conversation, or dialogue. He suggests that reconciliation and understanding of opposing values can take place by quality conversation that builds trust and understanding, a concept the ITSM proposes as well.

2. Communitarianism versus Individualism

"Individualism- Communitarianism is a major dilemma for any business unity or any culture. We cannot even define individuality without specifying a group or a social context from which that individual is abstracted and separated. Similarly any group, corporation, or society is constituted by its individual members. The group could not exist but for multiple allegiances" (Hampden-Turner and Trompenaars, 2000, p.68). Individualism is characterized by competition, self-reliance, self-interest, personal growth and fulfilment. Communitarianism is characterized by cooperation, social concern, altruism, public service and social legacy. (Hampden-Turner and Trompenaars, 2000) This dilemma was profoundly manifest in the beginning stages of the development of the ITSM.

I was teaching a Master's class at the University of Buckingham on hermeneutics. While teaching hermeneutics, which included self-awareness, and interpretation within context of self and the other, the differences between the collective and individual cultures surfaced. The students were asked, "What do you want to do with your life?" And, "What are your dreams?" The student from the United States answered the question, and the students from China and Taiwan did not understand. I initially thought it was a matter of interpretation or language gap, but we made a profound discovery. The students from the East did not understand because the question had no familiar context. One Taiwanese student ultimately answered, "I am going to take over my family's business... that is why I was born." His answer was as foreign to us from the West as the question had been to him. It seemed wrong to us (the Westerners) that he had no personal goals or dreams. The one French student was obviously a link between the two worlds as she understood, to a greater degree, the communitarian value. As a Licensed Mental Health Counsellor with a Master's degree in counselling, I have been trained in multicultural issues. However, it became quite apparent that having taken a course on social and cultural foundations had not adequately prepared me for the differences in collectivistic and individualistic cultures. The ITSM had its genesis in the work done in this culturally diverse Master's class.

Individualism does not negate the use of groups. The concept of groups or teams is fundamental in the United States. However, the difference revolves around the types of groups created. "The quintessential American group is the voluntary association: a group formed by the free association and voluntary commitment of like-minded individuals who choose to work or socialize together" (Hampden-Turner and Trompenaars, 2000, p.91). These groups are formed with a motive and they are often characterized as movements. Held together by common socio-political agendas, any disagreements among the constituents may lead to splits or dissolution of the group. In communitarian cultures the group is considered as a family. Again, relationships are revered and the good of the collective is seen as paramount to the good of the individual.

In individualistic cultures, organizations are viewed as instruments assembled to serve the good of individuals such as owners, employees, and customers. The organization is a means to an end. In the communitarian cultures, an organization is a social context members share, and gives meaning and purpose. Organizations are "likened to a family, community, or clan which develops and nurtures its members and may live longer than they do" (Trompenaars & Hampden-Turner, 1998, p. 65). In Japan, the concept of an individual is translated a "person-among-others." (Trompenaars & Hampden-Turner, 1998, p. 65) The group is the context in which the person asks how he or she may serve the others better.

As with the previous values of universalism and particularism, individualism is often presumed to be a characteristic of modernizing societies. However, as seen by the success of Japan, Hong Kong, Singapore, South Korea, and Taiwan, communitarianism cannot be dismissed as the paradigm of undeveloped cultures.

Within a diverse workplace, the values of an organization's employees cannot be assumed to be solely individualistic. In fact, Trompenaars and Hampden-Turner encourage reconciling the two opposing views, recognizing the value of both. As will be seen in each dilemma, reconciliation is seen by the authors as the preferred value approach.

3. Neutral versus Emotional

Spokane, Washington, where I presently reside, is home to a large Russian immigrant population. While visiting the home of a Russian friend, he answered the phone and began, what seemed to me, a very heated and angry discussion with the caller. I sat uncomfortably as he completed the call and hung up.

I inquired about the heated conversation and my friend explained the caller was a colleague at work and assured me they had not had a fight, neither was there any problem between the two. The communication the two had on the phone was simply Russian in nature, or affective in the terms of Trompenaars and Hampden-Turner. The dilemma Trompenaars and Hampden-Turner address presently is that of demonstrating emotions. During their research, they asked "participants how they would behave if something upset them at work. Would they express their feelings openly?" (Trompenaars & Hampden-Turner, 1998, p. 70) The majority (76%) of Russians said they would openly express their feelings. This compared to 74% of Japanese who said they would not express their feelings openly. The USA participants responded near the mid-range with 43% saying they would openly express their feelings.

Neutral cultures tend to conceal what is being thought or felt, often leading to passive-aggressive behaviour. Maintaining a cool and collected composure is admired, and strong facial expressions or gesturing is taboo. Affective cultures reveal thoughts and feelings with transparency and expressiveness. Heated and animated expressions are admired, often including gestures and strong facial expressions.

Differences in demonstrating emotion can be observed in language and par-language as well. Timing within a conversation, tone of voice, eye contact, space, and touch, body language, and other forms of non-verbal communication are important. In fact, research has demonstrated that 75% of all communication is non-verbal.

For communication between cultures to be effective, the communicators should have an understanding of the affective and neutrality dilemmas that exist. "Overly neutral or affective (expressive) cultures have problems doing business with each other. The neutral person is easily accused of being ice-cold with no heart; the affective person is seen as out of control and inconsistent. When such cultures meet the first essential is to recognize the differences, and to refrain from making any judgments based on emotions or lack of them" (Trompenaars & Hampden-Turner, 1998, p. 78). This is consistent with hermeneutics, as the individual recognizes the differences between the cultural styles and interprets the communication of the other in that light. As Trompenaars and Hampden-Turner (1998) write, "Emotions that are expressed without any 'neutral' brake easily verge on the uncontrolled 'neurotic.' An overly neutral person may become an iceman who dies of a heart attack because of unexpressed emotions" (p. 78).

4. Diffuse versus Specific

"Cultures vary considerably in how specific they are, that is, how precisely and minutely they define (put an end to) the constructs they use and to what extent they prefer diffuse, patterned wholes, put together in configurations or systems" (Hampden-Turner & Trompenaars, 2000, p. 123) The results of Trompenaars' and Hampden-Turner's research on this domain demonstrated that generally, the Western and the Northern cultures were quite specific and that the Eastern and Southern cultures were more diffuse. Specific oriented cultures are direct, to the point and purposeful in relating. They are precise, blunt, transparent, and definitive. They value principles and morals above situational factors. Diffuse oriented cultures tend to be indirect and curious. They are typically more evasive, ambiguous and tactful. The situation or persons involved may affect the rules. (Trompenaars & Hampden-Turner, 1998) In a specific culture clear distinctions are drawn between segments of life. For example, a clear boundary lies between work and private life. On the other hand, within diffused cultures, the lines are blurred. A more holistic approach is adopted where one segment cannot be fully segregated from the whole.

Reconciling diffuse and specific cultures "is perhaps the area in which balance is most crucial, from both a personal and a corporate point of view. The specific extreme can lead to disruption and the diffuse extreme to a lack of perspective; a collision between them results in paralysis. It is the interplay of the two approaches which is the most fruitful, recognizing that privacy is necessary, but that complete separation of private life leads to alienation and superficiality; that business is business, but stable and deep relationships mean strong affiliations" (Trompenaars & Hampden-Turner, 1998, p. 99). In the developmental stages of the ITSM, a colleague from Germany expressed concern of the appropriateness of addressing personal stories within a business framework. His view point originated from a specific culture and his point resonated strongly within me. Storytelling, I surmise, can be a potent method in reconciling the specific and diffuse.

Trompenaars and Hampden-Turner describe achievement oriented cultures as using titles only when they are relevant to the competence an individual brings to the present task, respect for hierarchy is based upon their performance, and the senior managers are of varying ages and gender, having proven their proficiency in their specific jobs. Ascriptive cultures use titles extensively to clarify status within an organization, respect for superiors is given out of commitment to the organization, and most senior managers are male, middle-aged, and qualified by their background. (Trompenaars & Hampden-Turner, 1998)

In reconciling ascription and achievement, the authors state that all cultures ultimately do both. However, they begin the cycle with different starting points. Whether achievement or ascription, each eventually leads to the other. For example, a manager may be given respect initially based upon his or her position. After he or she has proven competent, then the status may become based on achievement, and vice versa.

Trompenaars and Hampden-Turner state that cultural competence is grounded in self-awareness and other-awareness. "Genuine self-awareness accepts that we follow a particular mental cultural program and that members of other cultures have different programs... The problem is to learn to go beyond our own model, without being afraid that our long-held certainties will collapse... Both sameness and differences tell us who we are: 'I am like A, but not like B'" (Trompenaars & Hampden-Turner, 1998, p. 201).

Simply knowing a list of cultural rules, such as how to exchange business cards and whether to shake hands or bow, is not adequate. There are literally too many rules to learn. They assert that comprehension of the seven dimensions of culture will aid in understanding the world-view from which the rules emerge, and will provide a better foundation for building relationships. In a discussion (January 11, 2005) with Peter Brew of the International Business Leaders Forum, he spoke of the importance of building relationships: "Business used to be built by relationships, now it is dominated by deals... it needs to come back to relationships."

For Trompenaars and Hampden-Turner, the recurring theme of reconciliation of supposedly opposing views is the foundation of successful relationships. Incorporated in the reconciliation process is mutual respect and mutual empathy. "It is... differences which make relationships valuable. This is why we need to reconcile differences, be ourselves but yet see and understand how the other's perspectives can help our own" (Trompenaars & Hampden-Turner, 1998, p. 204) Trompenaars and Hampden-Turner (1998) believe that, "businesses will succeed to the extent that [this] reconciliation occurs..." (p. 187). An advantage of participating in multicultural organizations is the opportunity to synthesize the strengths of all cultures while avoiding the weaknesses. The synergy created by reconciliation between opposing cultures can be a profound asset to organizations.

Another pillar in the field of multicultural research is Geert Hofstede. He has become a leading authority on multiculturalism. He has served in the military, worked as a factory hand, and has held various management positions. He earned his Ph.D. from Groningen University and has served as professor in a variety of Universities in Europe and in Hong Kong. Hofstede is also co-founder of Institute for Research on Intercultural Cooperation (IRIC).

I will specifically be examining his seminal work, the second edition of Culture's Consequences (2001), which has been re-written and revised from the original which was published over twenty years ago. In the preface, Hofstede explains this volume is written for social scientists, and in scientific language. He recommends his book Cultures and Organization: Software of the Mind (1991) for students and practitioners.

In the present edition, Hofstede explores differences among more than fifty modern nations. He argues as people develop in life, they write "mental programs" adapted in childhood from their family, and reinforced by schools and organizations. "These mental programs contain a component of national culture. They are most clearly expressed in the different values that predominate among people from different countries" (p.xix). Compared to the work of Trompenaars and Hampden-Turner, Hofstede's is decidedly more empirical and positivistic in methodology and methods.

The data was gathered from an existing database "compiled of pen-and-pencil survey results collected within subsidiaries of one large multinational business organization

(IBM) in seventy-two countries and covering, among others, many questions about values" (p. xix). This produced more than 116,000 questionnaires and allowed the respondents to be matched according to gender, age, and occupation. Later, more data were collected from outside IBM. Hofstede's theoretical reasoning and statistical analysis ultimately revealed five dimensions on which national cultures differ. These dimensions include: power distance, uncertainty avoidance, individualism, masculinity, and long-term versus short-term orientation. Some correlation exists between the work of Trompenaars and Hampden-Turner and that of Hofstede (Figure 6.4). As in the review of the work of Trompenaars and Hampden-Turner, we will address specifically the elements of Hofstede's work dealing with relationships.

Hofstede begins by identifying three levels of human mental programming. He presents these three in the form of a pyramid with universal serving as the base, the next level is collective, and the top tier is individual. The universal level of mental programming is shared by virtually all human beings. It includes biological needs, as well as a range of expressive behaviours such as laughing and crying. "The collective level is shared by some, but not all, other people; it is common to people belonging to a certain group or category, but different from people belonging to other groups or categories. The whole area of subjective human culture belongs to this level" (Hofstede, 2001, p. 2). The individual level of human programming is unique to each individual, with no two being identical. This level accounts for the wide range of individual personalities and behaviours within a given culture. Hofstede states that these mental programs can be inherited and / or learned, with the universal being most likely inherited among all humans.

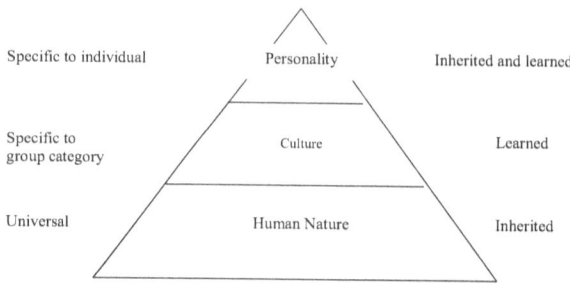

Three levels of uniqueness in human mental programming.

Hofstede states that values and culture are the key construct he utilizes to describing mental software. "Values are held by individuals as well as by collectives; culture presupposes a collectivity. A value is a broad tendency to prefer certain states of affairs over others" (p. 5). Hofstede gives descriptive details of how data on values was gathered and measured. Again, the empirical data are presented.

In defining culture, Hofstede presents the definitions of other scholars, and then presents his own. Culture is "the collective programming of the mind that distinguishes the members of one group or category of people from another" (Hofstede, 2001, p. 9). Hofstede identifies the manifestations of culture as values, practices, rituals, heroes, and symbols. (Hofstede, 2001) He emphasises programming, while Trompenaars and Hampden-Turner emphasise context. This is an example of the more empirical framework of Hofstede, and why the work of Trompenaars and Hampden-Turner is a better fit for the ITSM.

Hofstede (2001) states that information about a population can be considered scientifically valid only when it meets the following criteria:
    1) It is descriptive and not evaluative (judgmental).
    2) It is verifiable from more than one source.

3) It applies, if not to all members of the population, at least to a statistical majority.

4) It discriminates; that is, it indicates those characteristics for which this population differs from others. (p.14)

He asserts that if these criteria have not been met, the statements are unsupported stereotypes.

At the time of Hofstede's research, IBM was one of the world's largest organizations. The dates the data were collected ranged between 1967 through 1973 and utilized the company's human resources located throughout the world. As he highlights, there were mixed reviews from scholars and practitioners alike. Hofstede states that he does not propose his approach to multicultural research as the only way, but as one of many. Like Trompenaars and Hampden-Turner, Hofstede identified different dimensions of cultures. As might be expected, some of these categories overlap, but others are unique. Below is a chart demonstrating the dimensions identified in both works.

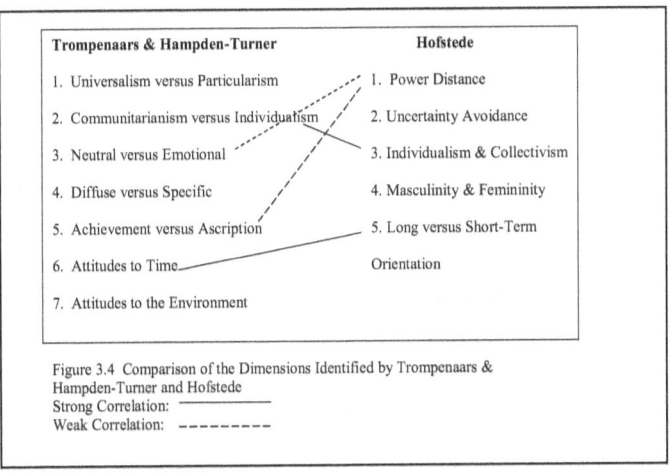

Figure 3.4 Comparison of the Dimensions Identified by Trompenaars & Hampden-Turner and Hofstede
Strong Correlation: ————
Weak Correlation: ‐ ‐ ‐ ‐ ‐ ‐ ‐ ‐

Hofstede (2001) states, "The basic issue involved, which different societies handle differently, is human inequality. Inequality can occur in areas such as prestige, wealth, and power; different societies put different weights on status consistency among theses areas" (p. 79). Hofstede, like Trompenaars and Hampden-Turner utilized questions in researching his dimensions. Regarding his first dimension, he states that power distances are determined, to a great extent, by society. The degree of power distance is assigned as the PDI (Power Distance Index). The PDI was derived by the country's mean score or percentages on three survey questions. "These questions dealt with perceptions of subordinates' fear of disagreeing with superiors and of superior's actual decision making styles, and with the decision making style that subordinates preferred in their bosses" (Hofstede, 2001, p. 79). Cultures differed dramatically in the PDI, as well as did PDI scores across occupations. The author correlated the PDI scores against other data, and then translated into the PDN (Power Distance Norm), as a "value system held by the majority of a country's middle class" (Hofstede, 2001, p. 79).

He asserts that generalizations of a country's or a society's PDI is just that, a generalization, and that exceptions do apply. Hofstede states, "As a one-line definition of Power Distance as a dimension of national culture, I propose: 'The extent to which the less powerful members of institutions and organizations within a country expect and accept that power is distributed unequally'" (Hofstede, 2001, p. 98).

The PDI correlated with a variety of values and attitudes within Hofstede's research. Among some of the Low PDI correlations were "national elites hold relatively unauthoritarian values, commercial airline pilots hold relatively unauthoritarian values, authoritarian attitudes in students a matter of individual personality, freedom more important than equality, positive attitudes toward older people, middle age starts at 40, and top leaders are younger. Correlations among the High PDI results were "national elites hold relatively authoritarian values, commercial airline pilots hold relatively authoritarian values, authoritarian attitudes in students a social norm, students put value conformity, equality more important than freedom, authority based on tradition, negative attitude toward older people, middle age starts before 40, top leaders are older" (Hofstede, 2001, p. 96).

Although both low and high PDI cultures have hierarchies, in a low PDI society, these hierarchies are merely a matter of convenience. In a highPDI society, the hierarchy is "existential: Superiors are seen as superior persons" (Hofstede, 2001, p. 97). Hofstede includes a table (Hofstede, 2001, p.87) that exhibits the PDI for fifty countries and three regions. With a total mean score of 53, the United States had a PDI of 40, Great Britain of 35, Iran and Taiwan both of 58, and Hong Kong of 68. Austria and the U.S. had the lowest PDI with 40, and Malaysia was highest with 104.

Hofstede (2001) states, " It is time now to take a step back from the data and try to describe the general societal norm that is behind the low-PDI and high-PDI syndromes. This is an exercise in induction, which means that I complete the picture with elements of intuition rather than on empirical evidence, much like an archaeologist completes ancient pottery from which shards are missing" (p. 97). The succeeding pages continue in the fashion of empirical dissemination of data with an element of interpretation. While this mostly empirical data is relevant, a hermeneutic approach could have brought a very human and personal application and understanding to Hofstede's intuitive induction. This attests to the appropriateness of both types of approaches in social science research.

Uncertainty Avoidance is the second dimension of national culture found in the data. Hofstede labels the Uncertainty Avoidance domain as the UAI (Uncertainty Avoidance Index), and stresses it is not to be confused with the term risk avoidance. Hofstede (2001) states:

> A basic fact of life is that time goes only one way. We are caught in a present that is just an infinitesimal borderline between past and future. We have to live with a future that moves away as we try to approach it, but onto which we project our hopes and fears. In other words, we are living with an uncertainty of which we are conscious. (p. 145)

In order to help societies cope with uncertainty, humans have developed methods typically stemming from the domains of "technology, law, and religion" (Hofstede, 2001, p. 146). "*Technology* includes all human artefacts; *law*, all formal and informal rules that guide social behaviour; *religion*, all revealed knowledge of the unknown" (Hofstede, 2001, p. 146). Hofstede asserts that technology helps mankind defend itself against uncertainties of nature, law to defend against the uncertainty of the behaviour of others, and religion to help us accept the uncertainties we cannot defend ourselves against. Different cultures adapt to these uncertainties in different ways and incorporate a variety of methods, which may be considered rational or nonrational, dependent upon their values. For example, Hofstede (2001) sites Fromm who suggested that fascism and Nazism "were a result of a need to escape freedom, a response to the anxiety that freedom created in societies with a low tolerance for such anxiety. Freedom implies uncertainty in the behaviour of oneself and others. Totalitarian ideologies try to avoid this uncertainty" (Hofstede, 2001, p. 146).

Different national cultures have developed differing norms for tolerating ambiguity. Tendencies toward "prejudice, rigidity and dogmatism, intolerance of different options, traditionalism, superstition, racism, and ethnocentrism all relate to a norm for tolerance" (Hofstede, 2001, p. 146). Hofstede has labelled these norms the UAI.

Whereas societies use technology, laws, and religion to help avoid uncertainty, organizations utilize technology, rules, and rituals. For example, to alleviate human error, some organizations have replaced employees with computers. Rules are also implemented to reduce variability within employee behaviour. Rituals "keep people together... and appeal to human nature" (Hofstede, 2001, p. 148). These rituals may take the form of staff meetings, management training, accounting, and writing and filing memos. Among the fifty countries represented in Hofstede's research, the highest obtained scores were Greece (112), Portugal (104), and Guatemala (101). The lowest UAI scores were obtained from Singapore (8), Jamaica (13), and Denmark (23). The United States scored 46, Great Britain scored 35, and Taiwan scored 69. The author found a strong positive correlation between the PDI and UAI scores. Some of the correlations with a low UAI are lower work stress, lower anxiety level in the population, more subjective well-being, less hesitation to change employers, less resistant to change, and acceptance of foreigners as managers. The converse can be correlated with a high UAI score. The author statistically relates the relationship of the UAI scores to the way populations are influenced with the family, educational systems, and within organizations. Although Hofstede's data is interesting and beneficial in making generalizations, he does not address practical application such as interpreting the data into meaning that is immediately applicable to interpersonal understanding.

This third dimension describes the relationship between the individual and society. This is reflected in the views individuals take of themselves in context of their neighbours and the way people live together, as in extended families or tribes, for example. These views play a significant role in the development of values and behaviours. This dimension is one of the two strongly correlated dimensions between Trompenaars and Hampden-Turner and Hofstede. Hofstede refers to this dimension as the Individualism Index (IDV). "The central element in our mental programming involved in this case is the self-concept. In Chinese tradition, for example, the "word for 'man' (*ren*) includes the person's intimate societal and cultural environment, which makes that person's existence meaningful" (Hofstede, 2001, p. 210).

In the ranking of IDV scores, the United States ranked highest (91), Australia (90) ranked second, and Great Britain (89) as third. The lowest IDV scores were from Guatemala (6), Ecuador (8), and Panama (11). Japan scored 46, Hong Kong scored 25, and Taiwan scored 17. Unfortunately, China is not included in the research population. Compared to the research of Trompenaars and Hampden-Turner, the United States participants scored only 69% individualist. This is still the majority, but demonstrates the variances among populations.

Hofstede (2001) states:
Individualism stands for a society in which the ties between individuals are loose: Everyone is expected to look after him/herself and his/her immediate family only. Collectivism stands for a society in which people from birth onwards are integrated into strong, cohesive in-groups, which throughout people's lifetime continue to

protect them in exchange for unquestioning loyalty. (p. 225)

In the realm of masculinity and feminism, Trompenaars and Hampden-Turner had no correlating category. "The duality of the sexes is a fundamental fact with which different societies cope in different ways; the issue is what implications the biological differences between the sexes should have for the emotional and social roles of the genders" (Hofstede, 2001, p. 279).

Hofstede's surveys correlate strongly with other data demonstrating that, almost universally, women place more importance on social goals such as relationships and helping others. The same research demonstrates that men place importance on ego goals such as career and money. However, the degree to which respondents answered the survey in favour of masculine or feminine goals varied between countries. Hofstede refers to this dimension as the Masculinity Index (MAS).

The author asserts the only absolute difference between man and woman is the ability to bear children. Although generalities stereotypically apply cross-culturally, there are varying degrees of assumptions which significantly affect the contextual values and behaviours of each society. A common trend across societies is to view the male role as significantly economic and other achievement oriented, while the female cared for relationships and taking care of people. (Hofstede, 2001)

Hofstede noted significant differences in gender trends in his research. For men, advancement, earnings, training, and up-to-dateness ranked high. While for women the highest goals were a friendly atmosphere, position security, physical conditions, manager, and cooperation. (Hofstede, 2001)

Due to the discrepancies in the numbers of women and men in the various countries and other random factors, this dimension must be viewed in light of the statistical data the author presents. The most masculine countries were Japan (95), Austria (79), and Venezuela (73). The most feminine were Sweden (5), Norway (8), and the Netherlands (14). The U.S. scored 62, Great Britain scored 66, and Taiwan 45. The mean score is 49.

Hofstede (2001) defines a masculine society as one "in which social gender roles are clearly distinct: Men are supposed to be assertive, tough, and focused on material success; women are supposed to be more modest, tender, and concerned with the quality of life. Femininity stands for a society in which social gender roles overlap: Both men and women are supposed to be modest, tender, and concerned with the quality of life" (p. 297). In Norway and Sweden, the most feminine countries, "the women scored more masculine than did the men in the same occupations" (Hofstede, 2001, p. 285).

The fifth dimension Hofstede identifies stands independent from his original IBM studies. It was identified from research involving students from 23 countries in 1985. The students answered questions to the Chinese Values Survey (CVS), an instrument developed by M.H. Bond "in Hong Kong from values suggested by Chinese scholars" (Hofstede, 2001, p. 351). On the Long-Term Orientation Index (LTO), the East Asian countries scored the highest, Western countries lower, and Third World countries the lowest. The highest ranking countries were China (118), Hong Kong (96), and Taiwan (87). The lowest were Pakistan (00), Nigeria (16), and the Philippines (19). Interestingly, Canada scored fourth from the lowest at 23, Great Britain at 25, and the U.S. scored 29.

Long-Term orientation emphasizes the future, perseverance, and thrift, while Short-Term emphasizes the past, respect for tradition, "preservation of 'face' and," fulfilling social obligations. Among the societal norms of low LTO are "immediate gratification of needs expected, traditions are sacrosanct, spending, and analytic thinking. Some of the norms associated with high LTO are "deferred gratification of needs accepted, traditions adaptable to changed circumstances, saving, investing, and synthetic thinking" (Hofstede, 2001, p. 367).

Regarding his research findings, Hofstede states, "It shows strong evidence that global solutions to organization and management do not exist. Not only are organizations bound by national cultures, so are the theories that have been developed to explain and direct their functioning; theories betray the nationalities of their authors, and their validity may stop at national borders. (if not before)" (Hofstede, 2001, p. 373).

Hofstede asserts that American management theories do not necessarily apply across borders. He quotes Robert Locke who stated the industrialization of the United States took place because of the historical timeliness and context more than ingenious management practices. Hofstede states that he believes articles written for an international market should include the country and time period in which they were written. He says that "Ideas and theories about management and organization are often exported to other countries without regard for the values context in which these ideas were developed" (Hofstede, 2001, p. 374).

Hofstede addresses various problems that may arise from intercultural contact. One of the primary problematic issues encountered is that of language. Others revolve around social interaction and etiquette. Hofstede states, "Intercultural contact does not automatically breed mutual understanding. Rather, it confirms the groups involved in their own identities and prejudices" (Hofstede, 2001, p.424). This is where one group makes stereotypes about others such as "all Chinese look alike", or "All Dutch are stingy" (Hofstede, 2001, p. 424). The mental software individuals have originates in the early years of childhood and is built upon throughout the lifespan. Mental programming conditions the minds of individuals so that when they are thrust into another culture they generally experience "culture shock."

Culture shock can have profound impact upon individuals, and thereby upon organizations that may be relying upon these individuals for service. "It [culture shock] can lead to expatriate failure and early return... Acculturation and the effectiveness of expatriates can be improved through training in intercultural competence. Such training can raise individual's awareness of their own baggage and provide them with knowledge about intercultural skills..." (Hofstede, 2001, p. 423). An example Hofstede (2001) gives of this type of training is to provide an opportunity for members of the meeting cultures to "meet and mix as equals" (p. 425). For the first time in his writing, Hofstede addresses the interpersonal aspects of intercultural relationships.

Hofstede (2001) states, "A sense of identity provides the feeling of security from which one can encounter other cultures with an open mind. The principle for surviving in a multicultural world is that one does not need to think, feel, and act like someone else in order to agree with that person on practical issues and to cooperate" (p. 454). This statement covertly aligns Hofstede with hermeneutic philosophy which endorses that an inquirer understands himself or herself, in context and with presuppositions. Only in understanding self can understanding others begin.

The work of Hofstede is the most empirical of all the works reviewed. While valuable in many regards, Hofstede's work is geared toward academics. In fact, he has rewritten this work in a more user friendly version. Other than generalized examples, Hofstede stops short of giving a clear model for interacting cross-culturally. The Interpretive Transcultural

Storytelling Method will build upon such empirical work as Hofstede's with a hermeneutic- narrative model of embracing individuals from other cultures based upon self understanding and interpreting the stories of others in context of the teller's culture and that of the interpreter.

Another powerful work in the multicultural arena is Atsushi Funakawa's Transcultural Management: A New Approach for Global Organizations (1997). At the time of writing his book, Funakawa was a seventeen year veteran of multicultural corporate work experience. A native of Japan and educated in an American University, Funakawa brings a rich understanding of the implications and complications spurred by multicultural issues. Funakawa is an international consultant providing global organizational management seminars to assist corporations in building cultural synergy. Funakawa, in essence, provides a bridge between the quantitative and qualitative ends of the spectrum. While his work is empirically based, his Eastern-ness reveals a holistic and human orientation which gives it a qualitative tone. Lessem and Palsule (1997) noted an obvious absence of the East in the West. In a sense Funakawa represents the East in the West discussed in their work.

Particularly focusing on East meets West, Funakawa presents an insightful and practical approach for those who work cross-culturally. The author organizes his material into a transcultural management model for "minimizing and transcending cultural discrepancies" (front cover flap). Funakawa also offers "five core transcultural competencies and seven mental disciplines that help business people transform their mindset- from ethnocentric to geocentric, from monocultural to multicultural, and eventually to transcultural" (front cover flap). This book is a valuable toll for those who work cross-culturally, providing insight into specific business situations as well as powerful perspectives on the emerging global economy.

The author's emphasis of contextual learning and understanding fits closely with the hermeneutic orientation to research. Hermeneutics, in its basic form, emphasizes understanding the context of the researcher as well as the other. In the realm of cross-cultural management, this would translate as the individuals on each side of the cultural gap. Understanding ones' own context and the context of the other is valuable when working cross-culturally. The High Context High Content frameworks Funakawa presents do just that. In addition, the emphasis on introducing key Japanese terms plays a significant role in the understanding of context and prejudgments. Funakawa never identifies hermeneutics as the framework for his writing, but he often makes observations consistent with hermeneutics.

"It is my understanding that the fundamental source of conflict in this new world will not be primarily ideological or primarily economic. The great divisions among humankind and the dominating source of conflict will be cultural" (Samuel P. Huntington as quoted in Funakawa, 1997, p. 3). Funakawa introduces the reader to some significant Japanese words. The first is *kacho* (section managers), the second is *senpai* (more experienced, senior members), and then *kohai* (less experienced, junior members). These terms are valuable in beginning to demonstrate some of the differences in philosophies of Japan and the west, namely the United States.

Funakawa begins the chapter with a case study of Michael, an American employee of a Japanese business located in the USA. The *kacho* informed Michael that he would be hiring a new team member, and wanted Michael to serve as the *senpai* to this new *kohai*. Michael became angry at the request, believing it not to be a part of his portfolio to train new recruits. He resigned his position. Michael did not understand the Japanese corporate culture, although he spoke Japanese and had lived for a number of years in Japan. Michael did not recognize the value of overall good and placing priority on the collective organization over his own inconvenience.

The author introduces the reader, also, to the Japanese business model's three key resources, *hito* (people), *mono* (things, fixed assets), *and kane* (money). (Funakawa, 1997) Funakawa points out that it is easy to make *kane,* and manage *mono,* across borders, but managing *hito* is more difficult. Funakawa also introduces one new term and another concept which exemplify deeper values. *Jishuku,* meaning self-restraint, and the concept of *conflict avoidance* are significant values in Japanese culture. If these are not correctly understood, the tragedy of ignorance, as the author puts it, will be imminent. Here Funakawa begins to address practical applications to the Neutral versus Emotional domain found in the work of Trompenaars and Hampden-Turner.

Funakawa identifies two components of the clash of cultures. First are the real-life incidents resulting from behaviour differences, and the second is that of image. Images can be very negative in some cultures such as the image of economic war between Japan and America. Japanese may interpret this image as a reflection of, for instance, the bombing of Pearl Harbour. (Funakawa, 1997)

The author makes a profound statement that aligns closely with hermeneutics and the ITSM research project, "Mutual awareness, understanding of different mindsets, and effective cross-cultural communication are essential at an individual level. If organizations want to create this more productive cross-cultural working environment, they have to provide appropriate structural support" (Funakawa, 1997, p. 9). The ITSM is intended to provide the appropriate structural support to which Funakawa refers. As Hofstede and Trompenaars and Hampden-Turner have provided the data, Funakawa is suggesting practical application, and the ITSM is providing practical application.

Funakawa defines culture as encompassing the "knowledge, language, values, customs, and material objects that are passed from generation to generation. Culture includes a sense of self and space, communication and language, dress and appearance, food and feeding habits, time and time consciousness, relationships, values, norms, beliefs and attitudes, mental process and learning, and work habits and practices" (Funakawa, 1997, p. 15).

As Hofstede stated, Funakawa also asserts that variations among populations must be accounted for when assigning cultural generalities. He addresses the misuse of stereotypes, which are typically negative, subjective preconceived notions. He states that a better approach would be to approach the subject as "descriptions of national cultures" which are research based and statistically testable societal norms. Funakawa states that although there are national descriptions or norms, there are also many variations among individuals in any society. (Funakawa, 1997, p. 15)

One of the reasons for including Funakawa in a literature review alongside empiricists like Trompenaars and Hampden-Turner and Hofstede, is that he brings an element of practicality to their statistical data. For example, Funakawa addresses the need for consultants and trainers to blend the "soft" Human Resources and the "hard" business segment of corporate organization. He describes four stages of globalization. The first is the *international ethnocentric* stage which upholds the belief that the "home country nationals are superior more reliable, and more trustworthy.

The second stage is the *multinational polycentric* stage which is to go to the other extreme and assume the local people know best for subsidiaries. For example, an American corporation will hire Japanese managers for the Japanese office. The third stage is the *multiregional regiocentric* corporation. This stage is represented by the message, "Regional insiders know what neighbouring countries want" (Funakawa, 1997, p. 39). And the fourth stage is the global geocentric which requires "collaboration between subsidiaries and headquarters in order to establish universal standards and permissible local variations, on the basis of which key decisions are made" (Funakawa, 1997, p. 39). The final stage is optimum for creating an environment of synergy and interdependence.

Funakawa outlines five core competencies for transcultural management. The geocentric mindset is the first of these competencies. This is an attitude in which business is approached from a global perspective, not from an egocentric one. The second is Strategic focus, which incorporates the Six C's Model. The six C's are, corporation, customer, competitor, community, communication, and the over-arching culture.

Cross-cultural communication is the third competency and it incorporates not only language, but the frames of reference behind the language as well as behaviours and other non-verbal forms of communication. The fourth competency listed is culturally sensitive management processes. In this section the author presents the equation: Actual productivity = Potential productivity – Losses due to faulty process. (Funakawa, 1997) Synergy learning systems is the fifth competency. The author states that, "Synergy in teams must be learned... [it] is a dynamic process that involves two often-opposing views that must be brought together after both parties mutually conclude that they need to unite their efforts to achieve their goals and create an integrated solution" (Funakawa, 1997, p. 58).

Funakawa presents seven practical disciplines needed to work effectively with other cultures. The first discipline he presents is to observe situations without judgments. The second is an ability to tolerate ambiguity. Style shifting, which is the ability to expand personal views, styles, and thought processes and apply them to situations at hand, is listed as the third discipline. The fourth is to flip your perception which entails assuming another person's point of view before criticizing it. Reprogramming your question is the fifth discipline. It proposes the need not to assume a question from someone of another culture is negative, but to objectively examine the meaning behind the question.

    The sixth discipline is to work interdependently, and the seventh is to keep mental stability and growth. Funakawa provides an examination of the importance of understanding communication and rules of communication in different cultures. The author introduces the readers to two new Japanese words, *tatemae*, the façade of what is supposed to be said, and *honne*, reality. "A high context conversation is one in which most of the information is already encoded within the person, while very little is coded in the explicit, transmitted part of the message" (Funakawa, 1997, p. 84). High-context communication is deeply engrained in Japanese culture. Some Japanese proverbs which exemplify this are, "silence is golden" and, "still water runs deep" (Funakawa, 1997, p. 86).

    Handling duality and dilemmas is an issue challenging emerging global organizations. Dualities found in working cross-culturally between America and Japan include individualism and collectivism, risk-avoidance and risk-taking, and vertical and horizontal thinking. Trompenaars and Hampden-Turner as well as Hofstede address similar characteristics as well. Finding a "zone of complimentarity" (Funakawa, 1997, p. 101) helps the organization achieve balance between dualities and is dynamic and cooperative. The zone of complimentarity is similar to Hampden-Turner's concept of reconciling differences. Funakawa states, "It is crucial for a cross-cultural team to share their common understanding of two different values. Especially when each party sees its own core value as positive and the value of the other party as negative, it is important to show that the two values are not isolated but interrelated" (Funakawa, 1997, p. 103).

Hofstede's PDI and Trompenaars' and Hampden-Turner's Universalism versus Particularism and Neutral versus Emotional have strong correlations. What Funakawa suggests is that dialogue, rather than dictation and disguising of feelings and thoughts, may be much more beneficial to relationships. In addition, the notion of Universalism could be discussed. If two values are discussed and the relationship between the people involved is one of understanding, the possibilities to find interrelated and synergistic conclusions may indeed surface. This is precisely the focus of the ITSM. In the telling of personal stories understanding can be reached that will enable individuals to find a dialectic and synergistic agreement.

Funakawa presents two paradigms developed by Japanese and Americans to aid in the cross-cultural communication process. The first is the Knowledge-creating company which is, according to Japanese scholar Nonaka, "the process of converting tacit knowledge into explicit knowledge" (Funakawa, 1997, p. 113). Within the knowledge-creating company exists four patterns of interaction between tacit and explicit knowledge. These patterns can be summed up as socialization (from tacit to tacit), articulation (from tacit to explicit), combination (from explicit to explicit), and internalization (from explicit to tacit). Nonaka states that although Japanese companies are good at developing "the process of exchanging tacit and explicit knowledge… they are good at it in their own cultural context" (Funakawa, 1997, p.116). Bridging the gap between the Japanese and American contexts is the key to working effectively in a cross-cultural setting.

Another contribution that has developed to help work within a dichotomous context is Senge's (American) contribution of the Learning Organization. Learning organizations are "places where people continually expand their capacity to create the results they truly desire, where new expansive patterns of thinking are nurtured, where collective aspiration is set free, and where people are continually learning how to learn together" (Funakawa, 1997, p.117). Funakawa states that these paradigms have developed as frameworks for turning potential obstacles into learning opportunities. In harmony with the concepts of the Knowledge –creating company and the Learning Organization, the ITSM also focuses upon knowledge and learning. However, the ITSM seeks to intentionally take the organization past the accumulation of knowledge and learning to emergence, the application of new knowledge.

Funakawa notes two critical gaps in the U.S. and Japanese business environment. First is a "gap in the flow of information". This gap exists because of the communication styles of the two cultures. Americans are outspoken and Japanese more reserved causing an unbalanced flow of information. The second is closely related as it also relates to communication. A "cross-cultural communication gap" specifically between American researchers and Japanese employees exists because of the American's perception of a lack of feedback by the Japanese. Again, this is due to differences in styles of communication. These gaps have a strong correlation to Neutral versus Emotional and the PDI.

Funakawa (1997) sites Nancy Adler's list of key factors in enabling managers to effectively lead multicultural groups:
- Differences are recognized rather than ignored.
- Members are selected for task-related abilities rather than ethnicity.
- There is mutual respect rather than ethnocentrism.
- There is equal power rather than cultural dominance.

- There is a superordinate goal rather than individual goals.
- External feedback is given to individuals and the group as a whole. (p. 132)

Funakawa introduces the term *gaishi* which means foreign capital. American gaishi experience a number of challenges. "Different perceptions of the Japanese market by American headquarters and Japanese operations and poor communications are the root causes of problems in managing gaishi in Japan" (Funakawa, 1997, p. 139). Again, Funakawa addresses the issue of communication as a primary problem within multicultural settings. The ITSM is focused upon building healthy communication through storytelling.

Whereas American companies in Japan are called gaishi, Japanese companies operating in the U.S. are called, *nikki kigyo*. American manager working for Japanese companies listed the top four factors for success as quality of products and services (32%), quality of managers and employees (14%), distribution and price (12%), and management ability (10%). Some of the main complaints Americans working for Japanese companies listed were in regards to their lack of communication skills. This can be attributed to a lapse in cross-cultural communication, since the Japanese managers described the American employees as having to have everything spelled out. There is an obvious lack of understanding in the context and content of communication. The author identifies three cultural variables that contribute to what he calls the "leadership gap" (Funakawa, 1997, p.155). Communication style, management style, and language comprise these variables.

Although U.S. - Japanese alliances have grown over recent years, Funakawa quotes a 1994 *International Business* article that over half of them fail. He states his belief that most of these failed relationships stem from an inability to effectively communicate and operate cross-culturally. Funakawa lists three specific situations he terms the "triple culture gap" (Funakawa, 1997, p. 162) that contribute to the failure of U.S.-Japanese alliances. The first gap is the national culture referring to, for example, the individualistic versus collectivistic frames of reference, as Hofstede, Trompenaars and Hampden-Turner found. The second gap involves the industry culture which surfaces when different industries develop alliances. Each industry has its own protocols and cultural norms. The third gap is in corporate culture "which reflects the norms, assumptions, and values about business practices that corporate members share" (Funakawa, 1997, p. 164). These culture gaps can be sources of conflict, but when managed well, can become great resources.

As Funakawa bridges the gap between the quantitative and the qualitative, he also acknowledges the advantage of "bridge persons" in multicultural settings. Bridge persons are those who bridge the gap between cultures. (Funakawa, 1997) Funakawa, in essence, is a methodological bridge person. He, in many regards, takes the data presented by researchers such as Hofstede, Trompenaars and Hampden-Turner, and applies it in context of Japanese- American relationships. He acknowledges a gap between academics and practitioners in the cross-cultural realm. American managers have a tendency to underestimate national cultural differences and overestimate universal rights, just as Trompenaars and Hampden-Turner have found. Funakawa states that in this regard, European companies are ahead of American. He attributes the European success to the implementation of management training based upon the work of Trompenaars and Hampden-Turner and Hofstede.

Beginning with the more qualitative works of Lessem and Palsule, Hicks, Simmons, Vazquez, Harris, and Elashmawi, I have presented a continuum of literature. This continuum progresses through the more quantitative works of Trompenaars,

Hampden-Turner, and Hofstede. Funakawa, a Japanese living in America, provides a bridge between the East and West as well as between qualitative and quantitative methodologies. While Trompenaars, Hampden-Turner, and Hofstede have provided varying degrees of solid empirical data for helping to understand cultures, Funakawa has provided a more practical interpretation of the application of knowledge.

In each of the works reviewed, the authors stop short of bringing this knowledge into the practical realm of building multicultural relationships. Even Funakawa, while offering examples of Japanese and American interaction does not breach the grass-roots level of the small team environment addressed by the ITSM. Therefore, building upon the reviewed literature, the ITSM will provide a complimentary dimension of micro-level multicultural management application. By placing the ITSM in context of the global cultural climate in general and multicultural management specifically, the stage is set to begin examining the methodological approach to the present research project.

References:

Fay, Brian. (1996). *Contemporary philosophy of social science.* Oxford, UK: Basil Blackwell.

Lessem, Ronnie & Palsule, Sudhanshu. (1997). *Managing in four worlds: From competition to co-creation.* Oxford, UK: Basil Blackwell.

Elashmawi, Farid & Harris, Philip R. (1993). *Multicultural management: New skills for global success.* Houston, TX: Gulf Publishing

Funakawa, Atsushi. (1997). *Transcultural management: A new approach for global organizations.* San Francisco: Jossey-Bass Publishers.

Hampden-Turner, Charles & Trompenaars, Fons. (2000). *Building cross-cultural competence.* Yale: Yale Press.

Hicks, Douglas A. (2003). *Religion and the workplace: Pluralism, spirituality, leadership.* Cambridge, UK: Cambridge University Press.

Hofstede, Geert. (2001). *Culture's consequences: Comparing values, behaviours, institutions, and organizations across nations, 2nd Edition.* Thousand Oaks, CA: Sage Publications.

Simons, George F., Vazquez, Carmen, & Harris, Phillip R. (1993). *Transcultural leadership: Empowering the diverse workforce.* Houston, TX: Gulf Publishing.

Trompenaars, Fons & Hampden-Turner, Charles. (1998). *Riding the waves of culture. 2nd Edition.* NY: McGraw-Hill.

Chapter 4
Methodology of Research: Part I
Quantitative vs. Qualitative

Because the multicultural management field is heavily weighted in the quantitative methodologies, I have posed the question of how might a method founded in hermeneutics contribute in a practical manner. The initial stages of research require the researcher to choose a methodology as the framework for his or her work. While some use the two terms interchangeably, I make a distinction between methodology and method. Methodology refers to the philosophical framework or paradigm through which I approach research and method refers to the strategies or methods I employ to conduct the research.

The methods, then, are chosen in light of the methodology. In addition, the methodology determines the writing style of the work. While empirical, classically scientific writing avoids the use of the first person when possible, hermeneutics, for instance necessarily requires the use of the first person. Therefore, the chosen research methodology impacts the entire project form beginning to end.

This chapter contains elements of the characteristics of both qualitative and quantitative methodologies, compared and contrasted, in an effort to present my research in a back-drop of my methodology of choice, hermeneutics.

I have chosen to utilize hermeneutics for several reasons. First, hermeneutics is a relatively new methodology in the social sciences. It was developed as a methodology for Biblical interpretation and evolved into the field of literature in general. Recognizing the value of interpreting a literary work in context of its authorship and intended audience, as well as the context of the reader, some social scientists began utilizing hermeneutics as a methodology for interpreting others. Among those who have greatly contributed to the field of hermeneutics within the realm of social sciences are Cushman (1995), Geertz (1973),Gephart (1999), Maloney (1993), McLeod (2001), Palmer (1969), Rabinow and Sullivan (1987), Ricoeur (1981), and Taylor (1994). These contributors will be referenced throughout this thesis.

Clifford Geertz, The Interpretation of Cultures (1973), significantly contributed to evolving the field of hermeneutics into the study of culture. He asserts that hermeneutics is a viable methodology for cultural study because of the innate roles interpretation plays in the field of anthropology. Geertz (1973) reasons that by using hermeneutics, "we are seeking, in the widened sense of the term in which it encompasses very much more than talk, to converse with them, a matter a great deal more difficult, and not only with strangers, than is commonly recognized... If speaking for someone else seems to be a mysterious process that may be because speaking *to* someone does not seem mysterious enough. Looked at in this way, the aim [among others] of anthropology is the enlargement of the universe of human discourse" (p.13). According to Geertz, cultural analysis is, "guessing at meanings, assessing the guesses, and drawing explanatory conclusions from the better guesses" (1973, p.20). His emphasis on discourse and interpretation aligns Geertz's theory closely with the intent of the Interpretive Transcultural Storytelling Method. The ITSM emphasises dialogue and interpretation of the dialogue or story.

Because the nature of a Ph.D. is to produce new and useful knowledge, using hermeneutics for research of this nature can contribute to the field of knowledge of this methodology in the social sciences. Another reason I have chosen hermeneutics is the emphasis placed upon interpretation of a text, in this case, another person and his or her story, the method employed in this research, as a "text". Hermeneutics recognizes that understanding "self" is instrumental to understanding "others". Trompenaars and Hampden-Turner, as well as Hofstede, recognize the importance of understanding our own cultural framework when entering into a relationship with those from another culture. Hermeneutics will be discussed in more detail in the following chapter on methodology.

The quantitative, positivist approach is grounded in the physical sciences and assumes an objective world which can be studied and measured with scientific, quantitative methods. It seeks to predict and explain causal relationships between variables. As the name implies, quantitative research focuses on quantity and is primarily deductive utilizing statistical methods. The methods utilized in the physical sciences are useful in certain arenas of the social sciences, however, a number of scholars have found them to be inadequate when studying social phenomena. Social scientists with a bias towards the qualitative approach argue that the positivist, empirical approach does not allow for the nuances found when studying living, thinking, evolving human beings who do not live in a static cultural environment. Robert Gephart (1999) [University of Alberta] writes:

> Positivistic methods strip contexts from meanings in the process of developing quantified measures of phenomena. In particular, quantitative measures often exclude members' meanings and interpretations from data which are collected. These methods impose outsiders' meanings and interpretations on data. And they require statistical samples which often do not represent specific social groups and which do not allow generalization to or understanding of individual cases. Finally, quantitative

and positivistic methods tend to exclude discovery from the domain of scientific inquiry.

Rabinow and Sullivan, Interpretive Social Science: A Second Look (1987), present an anthology of "papers exemplary of the interpretive, or hermeneutic, approach to the study of human society" (p. 2) In addition, Rabinow and Sullivan (1987) express, "As long as there has been a social science, the expectation has been that it would turn from its humanistic infancy to the maturity of hard science, thereby leaving behind its value, judgment, and individual insight" (p. 2). The authors argue, along with Weber, that this dream that is supposedly freeing and liberating is in essence an iron cage. Rabinow and Sullivan, along with others such as Geertz and Gephart, have greatly contributed to the field of hermeneutic methodology in the human sciences.

The quantitative approach to research is empirical and emphasizes scientific experimental methods. (Merriam, 1988) Quantitative research also requires an objective researcher who is unbiased and brings no, or at least minimum, interpretation to the study. Qualitative research, specifically hermeneutics, recognizes the inability of the researcher to remain completely unbiased and by its very definition is interpretive in nature. Quantitative researchers posit that the social sciences, like the natural sciences, can strive for testable theories to explain phenomena by demonstrating how they are derived from theoretical assumptions. In this attempt social phenomena are approached as dependent and independent variables and examined in a controlled environment. It is concerned with prediction, control, description, hypothesis testing, and confirmation. In quantitative research, the data is generally gathered using structured research instruments, large samples that are representative of a population, and the results are presented in such a manner as to enable the replication of the research. (Merriam, 1988) Some typical quantitative techniques are observation, experimentation, and surveys.

Qualitative research is descriptive, holistic, and concerned with phenomenology and symbolic interaction. It generally utilizes subjective fieldwork where the researcher is the primary instrument, often utilizing interviews and observations. (Merriam, 1988) In qualitative research, such as hermeneutics, the researcher is expected to recognize his or her biases and incorporate them into the research.

In contrast to quantitative research, qualitative attempts to answer "why" more than "how," and addresses the meaning behind the behaviour over simply the behaviour. The overarching goals of qualitative research are achieving understanding, developing a thick and rich description, discovery, and hypothesis generation. (Merriam, 1988)

Quantitative and qualitative research designs often diverge in their settings. Quantitative research often occurs in a structured, artificial, unfamiliar, and controlled environment such as a laboratory. Conversely, qualitative research is often conducted in the natural environment, unstructured, and familiar to the subjects. Quantitative research is primarily predetermined while qualitative is generally flexible, evolving and emerging.

In the fields of social science and psychology, quantitative research is the traditionally favoured design. However, some scholars argue that, while quantitative methodology has its place, qualitative research is more conducive to the study of humans.

Philip Cushman (1995) argues that the dedication to the "philosophical frame of reference of the physical world has helped us develop power to manipulate the physical world in undreamed of ways. But that same point of reference has a built-in paradox: By conceiving of a world that is based on doubt and

irrevocably separates 'inner' from 'outer,' body from mind, science from superstition, the physical science framework makes it nearly impossible to use traditional ideas, philosophical thinking, and a sense of moral understandings that would help us cooperate in using our newfound power for the betterment of humankind.
The very power that has made it possible for us to develop our power has made it difficult for us to determine how to use it wisely" (p. 9).

In addition, philosopher Charles Taylor (1985) [McGill University, Montreal] writes:

> A social science which wishes to fulfil the empiricist tradition naturally tries to reconstruct social reality as consisting of brute data alone. These data are the acts of people (behaviour) as identified supposedly beyond interpretation either by physical descriptions or by the descriptions clearly defined by institutions and practices; secondly, they include the subjective reality of individual's beliefs, attitudes, values, as attested by their responses to certain forms of words, or in some cases their overt non-verbal behaviour. What this excludes is a consideration of social reality as characterized by inter-subjective and common meanings. (p.40)

Qualitative research "is a process of careful, rigorous inquiry into aspects of the social world. It produces formal statements or conceptual frameworks that provide new ways of understanding that world, and therefore comprises knowledge that is practically useful for those who work with issues around learning and adjustment to the pressure and demands of the social world" (McLeod, 2001, p.3). McLeod (2001) identifies three areas in which qualitative research can generate new forms of knowledge. The first, and most common, is knowledge of the "other". This knowledge is generated by research which takes a category of a person (such as psychotherapy client, hospital patient, gang member) who is of interest to members of a professional group, and seeks to describe, analyze and interpret the world-view, experiences and language of a sample of people who represent that category. (McLeod, 2001)

The second area of knowledge development is in regards to knowledge of phenomena. This field is directed at categories of events that are of interest to a professional group. The third and least frequently used field is directed towards reflexive knowing. "Reflexive knowing occurs when researchers deliberately turn their attention to their own process of constructing a world with the goal of saying something fresh and new about that personal (or shared professional) world... This is research which is intended to subvert everyday ways of seeing" (McLeod, 2001, p. 5).

Contrary to the flexible characteristics which make qualitative research a viable option for the psychologist and social scientist, empirical quantitative research is rigid, unbiased and reductionistic. This type of research has value, but when complemented by qualitative approaches presents a more holistic picture.

Trompenaars and Hampden-Turner as well as Geert Hofstede have produced seminal works in the field of cross-cultural studies. Their works present invaluable information that aids in the building of multi-cultural competencies. These scholars, as well as the majority of others in this field, work primarily within the design scheme of empirical methodology.

Although Trompenaars and Hampden-Turner are rooted in empirical perspective, they are considerate of a basic principle in hermeneutics of understanding the self. In the introduction of Riding the Waves of Culture (1998), Trompenaars states, "I believe understanding our own culture and our own assumptions and expectations about how people 'should' think and act is the basis for success" (p.2). This statement eludes to the principle that self reflection and understanding is necessary before one can have an understanding of another. This could be perceived as opposing the empiricist view of researcher as an objective, unbiased observer. Instead of being bound to a rigid empirical paradigm, it is apparent in the reading of Trompenaars and Hampden-Turner, that their perspective is dialectical in aspects. For example, in the following comment from Trompenaars and Hampden-Turner (1998), the authors expand the purpose of their research from simply presenting various cultural competencies, to acknowledging the importance of understanding the ways people interpret the world.

> There are, indeed, many products and services becoming common to world markets. What is important to consider, however, is not what they are and where they are found physically, but what they mean to the people in each culture. As we will describe later, the essence of culture is not what is visible on the surface. It is the shared ways groups of people understand and interpret the world. (p. 3)

Trompenaars and Hampden-Turner, in this statement, refer indirectly to hermeneutics when discussing understanding and interpretation. Hermeneutics emphasizes reaching understanding through interpretation. Involved in interpretation is the cycle of moving between self-understanding and the attempt to understand the other within his or her context. In doing so, the interpreter recognizes the value of static knowledge as well as the dynamic knowledge that is created through moving back and forth between the other and the self. While the actual research conducted by Trompenaars and Hampden-Turner is framed within the empiricist scheme, the application of the knowledge is clearly intended, (as in the above quote), to be applicable within a framework of self-understanding and interpretation. Trompenaars and Hampden-Turner (1998) state:

> Peters and Waterman in *In Search of Excellence* hit the nail on the head with their critique of "the rational model" and "paralysis through analysis. Western analytical thinking (taking phenomena to pieces) and rationality (reckoning the consequences before you act) have led to many international successes in fields of technology. Indeed, technologies do work by the same international rules everywhere, even on the moon. Yet the very success of the universalistic philosophy now threatens to become a handicap when applied to interactions between human beings from different cultures. (p. 4)

Trompenaars and Hampden-Turner openly acknowledge the inadequacies of a rigid framework for knowledge creation. They (1998) denounce the mindset that "regards emotionally detached rationality as 'scientifically" necessary. Trompenaars and Hampden-Turner (1998) state:

> The mistake is to assume that technical rationality should characterize the human element in the organization. No one is denying the existence of universally applicable laws with objective consequences. These are, indeed, culture-free. But the belief that human cultures in the workplace should resemble the laws of physics and engineering is a cultural, not a scientific belief. It is a universal assumption which does not win universal agreement, or even come close to doing so. (p. 4)

Therefore, while the research conducted by Trompenaars and Hampden-Turner is in its core analytical empirical, the essence of their research is dialectical in nature, valuing and incorporating both, quantitative and qualitative, philosophies. Specifically, due to the emphasis Trompenaars and Hampden-Turner place upon interpretation and self-understanding, their framework is at least in approximation to hermeneutics. In essence, Trompenaars and Hampden-Turner have adopted the Japanese philosophy of, "When in Rome, understand the behaviour of the Romans, and thus become an even more complete Japanese" (Trompenaars and Hampden-Turner, 1998, p. 4).

While recognizing that culture incorporates a variety of elements such as social class, religion, region, and gender, and is not necessarily determined by political boundaries, it is specifically with national culture that Hofstede concerns himself. "Using nationality as a criterion is a matter of expediency, because it is immensely easier to obtain data for nations than for organic homogeneous societies. Nations as political bodies supply all kinds of statistics about their populations" (Hofstede, 1997, p. 12).

The generalizations which can be made from such exercises as the one above are helpful in understanding how different macro-cultures approach answering the problems to Hofstede's specified dilemmas. On a micro scale, however, Hofstede proposes that individuals may vary greatly. As an example, I have had extensive training in cultural foundations as a Licensed Mental Health Counsellor, as well as having done much reading on multicultural issues for the present project. When performing my first fieldwork exercise with a group of Japanese and American participants, I approached the session with preconceived ideas of what to expect from the Japanese participants. I assumed, for example, the Japanese would be highly collectivistic and non-confrontational as well as have a high degree of respect for their elders.

While the Japanese participants demonstrated these traditional characteristics, they also demonstrated elements of individualism. In addition, they exhibited the freedom to politely confront and disagree with others, including their elders. This fusion of cultures has not been statistically accounted for in Hofstede's work, but it is in fact a main focal point in hermeneutics, within which, the experience is called a "fusion of horizons" (McLeod, 2001, p. 28). This fusion of cultures had not been addressed in my prior education, or any of the reading I had done to that point.

In debriefing my experience with an executive staff member from the institution, we discussed possible reasons for the fusion of Eastern and Western cultural characteristics. We discussed how the Japanese media is profoundly impacted by Western, specifically American, music, movies, commercials, and television programmes. The continual exposure to these and other sources of influence may partially account for the participants' fusion. In addition, the participants have lived in the United States for several months, purposefully attempting to learn American culture. Another possible influence may have been the students' unintentional acquiescence demonstrated by a desire to answer as an American would be expected to answer.

In any case, the generalized, statistical information I had learned about Japanese culture did not account for the fusion of cultures in each participant, and in each participant to varying degrees. In addition to the Japanese participants' fusion of cultures, the American participants also exhibited a fusion of cultural traits. Most were highly collectivistic, and demonstrated a high regard for authority. This fusion of cultures highlights the difficulty in stereotyping individuals based on generalized cultural typologies, demonstrating the need for a method that will enable individuals to probe into the different layers of a culture, both micro and macro, on an individual basis, in contrast to general analysis. The goal of the Interpretive Transcultural Storytelling Method is to promote transformation, fusion, and mutual team emergence by utilizing narrative as a means for exploring the different layers of micro and macro culture.

Hofstede is considered by many to be the industry standard, however, his purpose is not to specifically address actual relationship building between individuals from different cultures. Within the new global economy, where media, travel, and multinational organizations are prevalent, these statistics can be used as a good place to start interaction, but inadequate as the sole source for interpersonal relationship building.

While some continue to who hold unswervingly to either the quantitative or qualitative fields of inquiry, others recognize the value in both. Because the nature of this research rests strongly upon contextual awareness, interpretation, and understanding, I will be utilizing qualitative hermeneutic methodology. The purpose is two-fold. The first purpose is to maintain a uniform structure in approaching the project. The second is to contribute to the field of hermeneutic research in the arena of the social sciences. The following chapter will address hermeneutic methodology more in-depth.

References:

Abbey, Ruth. (2000). *Charles Taylor*. Princeton: Princeton University Press.

Blaikie, Norman. (1993). *Approaches to social enquiry*. Cambridge: Polity Press

Cushman, Philip. (1995). *Constructing the self, constructing America: A cultural history of psychotherapy*. Reading, MA: Addison-Wesley publishing Company, Inc.

Dostal, Ricahrd. (2002). *The Cambridge companion to Gadamer*. Cambridge: Cambridge University Press.

Dreyfus, Hubert L. (1991). *Being-in-the world: A commentary on Heideggar's being and time*. Cambridge, MA: MIT Press.

Gadamer, H. (1976). *Philosophical hermeneutics*. (D.E. Linge, Trans). Berkley: University of California Press.

Gadamer, H. (1975). *Truth and method (2nd edition)*. New York: Continuum.

Geertz, Clifford. (1973) *The interpretation of cultures*. New York: Basic Books, Inc.

Gephart, Robert. (Summer 1999). Paradigms and research methods. Academy of Management, Research Methods Division. Research Methods Forum, Vol.4. Retrieved May 10, 2004 from Http://www.aom.pace.edu/rmd/1999_RMD_Forum_Paradigms_and_Research_Methods.htm

Grondin, J. (1990). *Hermeneutics and relativism*. In K. Wright (Ed.) Festivals of interpretation: Essays on Hans- Georg Gadamer's Work. New York: State University of New York Press.

Hampden-Turner, Charles & Trompenaars, Fons. (2000). *Building cross-cultural competence.* Yale: Yale Press.

Heiddeger, Martin. (1962) *Being and Time.* Translated by John Macquarrie and Edward Robinson. New York: Harper.

Hirsch, E. D., Jr. (1967). *Validity in interpretation*. New Haven: Yale University Press.

Hofstede, Geert. (1997). *Cultures and organizations: Software of the minds:Intercultural cooperation and its importance for survival.* New York: McGraw-Hill.

Hofstede, Geert. (2001). *Culture's consequences: Comparing values, behaviours, institutions, and organizations across nations, 2nd Edition.* Thousand Oaks, CA: Sage Publications.

Koch, T. (1995). *Interpretive Approaches in Nursing Research: The influence of Husserl And Heidegger*. Journal of Advanced Nursing, 21, 827-836

Laverty, S. M. (2003). *Hermeneutic Phenomenology and Phenomenology: A Comparison of Historical and methodological considerations.* International Journal of Qualitative Methods, *2*(3). Article 3. Retrieved May 11, 2004 from http://www.ualberta.ca/~iiqm/backissues/2_3final/html/laverty.html

Maloney, M. (1993). <u>Silent strength: A Heideggerian Hermeneutical analysis of the stories of older women</u>. Unpublished doctoral dissertation, Georgia State University, Atlanta. Retrieved April 2, 2004 from http://www.coe.uga.edu/quig/proceedings/Quig98_Proceedings/byrne.html

McLeod, John. (2001). *Qualitative research in counselling and psychotherapy.* London: Sage Publications.

Merriam, S.B. (1988). *Case study research in education: A Qualitative approach*. San Francisco: Jossey-Bass Publishers.

Palmer, Richard. (1969). *Hermeneutics*. Evanston: Northwestern University Press.

Rabinow, Paul & Sullivan, William M. (1987). *Interpretive social science: A second look*. Berkley and Los Angeles, CA: University of California Press.

Taylor, Charles. (1994) *Multiculturalism.* Princeton, NJ: Princeton University Press.

Trompenaars, Fons & Hampden-Turner, Charles. (1998). *Riding the waves of culture.*
    2nd *Edition.* NY: McGraw-Hill.

Chapter 5
Methodology of Research: Part II

The previous chapter provided an overview of research methodologies and a basic presentation of the methodology chosen for this project. The present chapter is intended to provide a more comprehensive examination of the relationship of hermeneutics to the Interpretive Transcultural Storytelling Method as well as an orientation to hermeneutic methodology.

The Objective of the Present Research

The selection of a research methodology is equivalent to selecting the materials for the foundation and construction of a building. The foundation is laid to establish a solid base on which to build. The frame and construction materials determine the shape and the style of the new construction. Likewise, within a research project, the methodology not only forms the foundational approach of the research, but determines framework as well. The philosophical approach, writing style, and methods of the research are all affected by the chosen research methodology.

In building new construction, one of the primary questions is the use or objective of the new facility. The same question can be asked when constructing a research project. The objective of the present research is to develop a method for bringing about understanding between cultures, specifically between growing minority cultures and the predominant white culture in the United States. As the United States continues to experience dramatic increase among diverse cultures through immigration and the expanding global economy, understanding between these cultures, including the majority white culture, will become more imperative if a cohesive, synergistic society is to emerge.

This research project approaches the cultural issues from a religious, spiritual, and philosophical point of reference. Although many factors are involved in developing and defining a culture, the religious, spiritual, or philosophical aspects are often foundational. As demonstrated by the September 11, 2001 attack on the World Trade Centres and Pentagon, the resulting invasion of Iraq, the subsequent uprisings between Iraqi Muslim forces and the occupying coalition forces, as well as the ongoing Israeli and Palestinian conflict, religion plays a complicated role in the world. In the pursuit of understanding, an attempt will be made to determine how very different cultures may conjointly and harmoniously exist, and a framework will emerge of how to lead organizations in a trans-cultural setting.

The Choice for the Present Research

Based upon the prevalence of quantitative methodology in the field of multicultural management, I determined to utilize hermeneutics, a qualitative approach. Evaluation of various qualitative and quantitative methodologies was made concerning epistemological and ontological questions. McLeod (2001) writes:

> The process of knowing involves employing a practical method, which is derived from an epistemology (theory of knowledge) which is in turn grounded in ontology (set of assumptions about the nature of life). Routine decisions made by qualitative researchers, for example relating to sampling strategies, ways of collecting data, ways of analyzing data, and selecting a format for communicating findings can only be resolved by recourse to underlying epistemological and ontological principles. (p. 55)

McLeod (2001) identifies three key questions that reflect the interconnection of methodology, epistemology, and ontology. These include:

> 1 The ontological question. "What is the form and nature of reality and, therefore, what is there that can be known about it? 2 The epistemological question. What is the relationship between the knower and what can be known? 3 The methodological question. How can the inquirer (would-be knower) go about finding out whatever he or she believes can be known? (p. 55)

McLeod continues to say that the positivist scientists have addressed these questions, but those of the qualitative approach have not done as well in this regard. He states that phenomenology and hermeneutics (often used interchangeably) are the roots of all qualitative research. (McLeod, 2001, p. 56) McLeod writes:

> Ontological hermeneutics is a way of understanding that views people as existing within multiple horizons of meaning, as striving to make sense of their experience, as constituted by their cultural and historical context, as engaged in dialogue.... Epistemological hermeneutics is a body of philosophical writing that has examined the value and limitations of an interpretive approach to knowledge creation. For example, the notion of the hermeneutic circle is an important element of epistemological hermeneutics. A hermeneutic methodology for social sciences relies on both ontological and epistemological hermeneutic principles. (p. 28) ...In hermeneutics, understanding is always from a perspective, always a matter of interpretation. The researcher can never be free of the pre-understandings or 'prejudices' that arise from being a member of a culture and a user of a language. We can

> never get beyond our language- all the questions we ask and words we use to articulate our understandings are embedded in culture. What we can do in research is to extend the horizon of our culture-based understanding, or achieve a fusion of horizons through allowing ourselves to learn from our immersion in the 'text' being studied and thereby permitting the world expressed by the text to speak to our world. (p. 56)

The hermeneutic emphasis on interpretation, understanding, history and context is congruent with the objectives of this research. The subjective researcher plays a vital role in hermeneutic research and is viewed as part of the process of understanding. Since hermeneutics places an emphasis on the role of the researcher and his or her emergence in the research process, the writing style departs from traditional objective, third-person voice commonly found in other scholarly and scientific literature. In keeping with the core philosophies of hermeneutics, this dissertation will be written in the first person.

Historical Overview of Hermeneutics

The word, *hermeneutics*, can be traced back to the Greek, wing-footed messenger-god, Hermes. "Significantly, Hermes is associated with the function of transmuting what is beyond human understanding into a form that human intelligence can grasp. The Greeks credited Hermes with the discovery of language and writing- the tools which human understanding employs to grasp meaning and to convey it to others" (Palmer, 1969, p.13). Hermeneutics simply means "to interpret". (Palmer, 1969)

As a methodology, hermeneutics was developed to aid in the interpretation of Biblical texts. An emphasis is placed on understanding the language and the context of the writings under scrutiny. In addition, the prejudices and cultural context of the examiner is seen as important. Hermeneutics has evolved from a methodology solely for interpreting written texts, to include texts in the broad sense, including art, human relationships, sociology, and psychology. Palmer (1969) describes the general context of hermeneutic interpretation as follows:

> Consider for a moment the ubiquity of interpretation, and the generality of the usage of the word: The scientist calls his analysis of data 'interpretation'; the literary critic calls his examination of a work 'interpretation.' The translator of a language is called an 'interpreter'; a news commentator 'interprets' the news. You interpret- or misinterpret- the remark of a friend, a letter from home, or a sign on the street. In fact, from the time you wake up in the morning to the time you sink into sleep, you are 'interpreting.' Palmer (1969) continues, stating that hermeneutics is "fundamental to all the humanities- all those disciplines occupied with the interpretation of the *works* of man... it's principles should be required fundamental study for all the humanistic discipline" (Palmer, 1969, p.10).

Hermeneutics, therefore, has transcended the literary arena and enveloped any field in which the study of humanity is the focus. Hermeneutics emphasizes interpretation of the world by a biased, as opposed to an unbiased, observer. The researcher acknowledges his or her own prejudgments and interprets the world reflexively, in a way that brings about new knowledge. This new knowledge is dynamic, not static, and is understood to be valid within context. "Implicit in any form of qualitative inquiry is the realization that, ultimately, we can never really know how the world is constructed. We can never achieve a complete 'scientific' understanding of the human world. The best we can do is to arrive at truth that makes a difference that opens up new possibilities for understanding" (McLeod, 2001, p.4). Understanding is the key concept in this approach.

Some of the Significant Contributors

Historically, hermeneutics has been influenced by a number of renowned scholars, each having made his own impact upon the philosophy. Dilthey (1833-1911), Husserl (1859-1938), Heidegger (1889-1976), and Hans-Georg Gadamer (1900-2002) are among some of those who have made a significant contribution to the field hermeneutics. Each of these individuals, as well as many others, have contributed consequentially to the literature of hermeneutics, therefore each will be addressed briefly.

Dilthey distinguished the cultural and social sciences from the natural sciences on the basis of their objects and the appropriate means for knowing them. The natural sciences could be studied by an objective, distant observer. In this realm causal relationships could be tested. He also observed that social science involved a different set of phenomena, such as texts, verbal communication and actions which could be observed from an insider's, the researcher's, perspective. This observation distinguished the positivist and phenomenological or hermeneutic approaches to research. An interpretive or hermeneutic methodology could more reliably account for these objects by reconstructing the internal cognitive processes which motivated and gave meaning to each of them. Richard Palmer (1969) writes:

> It was Dilthey's aim to develop methods of gaining 'objectively valid' interpretations of 'expressions

of inner life.' At the same time, he reacted sharply to the tendency in the humane studies simply to take on the norms and ways of thinking of the natural sciences and apply them to the study of man. (p. 98)

Dilthey also rejected the idealist tradition, determining that concrete experience and not solely speculation must be the starting point for a theory of the social sciences and humanities, or *Geistewissenschaften*. (Palmer, 1969) Dilthey held that the subject of investigation and the investigator can communicate with each other, and that the methods used in the natural sciences were unable to accommodate such a methodology. Dilthey taught that, "Concrete, historical, lived experience must be the starting and ending point for the *Geistewissenschaften*. Life itself is that out of which we must develop our thinking and toward which we direct our questioning... Behind life itself our thinking cannot go" (Palmer, 1969, p. 99).

Husserl, a phenomenologist philosopher, as well as a mathematician, sought a logical method of discovering the experience of consciousness. He adhered to a concept he termed bracketing. Bracketing assumes an individual is able to separate his or her pre-conceived ideas from their lived experiences. This philosophy is in close conjunction with that of positivistic experimental research. Phenomenological hermeneutics also assumes that in order for the object to be fully interpreted, a mental framework is needed. However, instead of considering the surrounding historical and cultural contexts, Husserl argued that the text reflects its own mental frame. Husserl's theory focused on addressing the things themselves, considering objects as complete in themselves. To interpret a text, according to Husserl, means to methodically isolate it from all extraneous things including the subject's biases and allow it to communicate its meaning to the subject. "The aim of phenomenology is to produce an exhaustive description of the phenomena of everyday experience, thus arriving at an understanding of the essential structures of the 'thing itself', the phenomena" (McLeod, 2001, p. 38).

Heidegger, a colleague of Husserl, theorized that an individual cannot be separated from the context in which he or she lives. Heidegger's philosophy offered an alternate world view from Husserl's belief of a subject-object split. As a human or *Dasien*, our meaning is co-created through being born human and through our life experiences and culture. Heidegger, unlike Husserl, did not believe it was possible to bracket our prejudices of the world. However, awareness of our prejudices or assumptions is important to valid interpretation. "Heidegger regarded understanding as being fundamental to human existence and therefore, the task of ordinary people. He argued that there is no understanding outside of history; human beings cannot step outside their social world or historical context in which they live. Prejudgments shaped by our culture are the only tools we have." (Blaikie, 1993, p. 35). Heidegger's approach can be defined as a way to "interpret the shared meanings and practices that we have for our experiences within a context" (Maloney, 1993, p. 40). "For Heidegger, understanding is no longer conceived of as a way of knowing but as a mode of being, as a fundamental characteristic of our 'being' in the world" (Koch, 1995, p. 831).

Heidegger is attributed with the development of the hermeneutic circle which is a method of building an interpretation by "moving back and forth between the part and the whole. This involves gaining a sense of the whole text, and then using that as a framework for understanding fragments of the text; carrying out micro-analysis of the possible meanings of small sections of text, and using these to challenge or interpret the overall sense of the total text" (McLeod, 2001, p.26). The hermeneutic circle is an important concept within the scope of hermeneutics, and will be addressed later in this chapter.

Hans-Georg Gadamer was another significant contributor in the realm of hermeneutics. Gadamer understood our pre-judgments to have a powerful influence in our interpretation of the world. "For whomever pronounces himself or herself free of prejudices is all the more blindly exposed to their power. Prejudices will exercise their underground domination all the more strongly, and potentially distortingly, when denied or repressed" (Grondin, 1990, p. 54). The prejudices of the researcher originate from his or her own historical background and context. Prejudices are not viewed as an impediment to knowledge, rather a tool for gaining new insight. A common principle in psychotherapy is that individuals interpret the world in light of their own experiences; this is in congruence with hermeneutic philosophy. Explicitly understanding the lens through which the world is viewed becomes a vital part of the hermeneutic process. The researcher does this by keeping a research journal, documenting the process of the hermeneutic circle. Gadamer also proposed the concept of the clearing and the horizon to be discussed later in this chapter.

Hermeneutics has a long history with many philosophers and scholars having made profound contributions. The preceding contributors are only a sampling of the significant individuals involved in the evolution of the art of interpretation.

Overview of Hermeneutic Concepts

Hermeneutics was originally developed as a philosophy for understanding and interpreting texts. As the philosophy evolved it began to be valued as a paradigm in the social sciences. In order for hermeneutics to be useful in the humanities, certain adjustments to the approach were needed. Cushman (1995) says, "The process of studying humans is not the same as 'reading' persons as 'texts,' but more like standing behind them and reading over their shoulder the cultural text from which they themselves are reading" (p. 23). Some criticisms of the hermeneutic approach in social science research are the lack of set guidelines, theory and methods. Due to the heavy emphasis on the interpretation of the researcher, validity, generalizability of the research, is suspect. Charles Taylor "contends that humans can never be fully or finally understood: as self-interpretations change, so theories of human behaviour must alter to accommodate this" (Abbey, 2000, p. 155).

Hermeneutics is a philosophical way of gaining understanding, and a variety of approaches may be utilized within this framework. Every author who has contributed to the literature on hermeneutics adds his or her own interpretation of how study should be approached. Cushman (1995) concisely describes the hermeneutic perspective as:

> "...a determination to focus on the everyday, lived *context* of whatever, or whoever, one is studying. This approach focuses on situating one's object of study in the cultural and historical context in which it is embedded. People and things exist only within a certain political and moral context, and they are not understandable outside of it. Studying humans by abstracting them from their cultural context and observing them in a dispassionate, putatively objective manner in the psychological laboratory is more akin to removing a fish from water than picking up a rock from its resting place. Studying people in a scientistic way renders them lifeless. Individuals and their context form a dialogical, interpenetrating *unit*. By studying one, the researcher

inevitably studies the other. Also, in undertaking a research project, the researcher brings his or her own cultural frame of reference into the picture, which continually and unavoidably frames and shapes the process. (P. 17)

An important aspect of the hermeneutic perspective is that it is holistic, a departure from the dualism found in traditional research. The researcher emerges or evolves as a result of the study, as does the object of the study. Relationships and interaction between human beings continually change those human beings. In an attempt to find understanding, the researcher necessarily becomes a significant component in the study, both learning of the other as well as learning of himself or herself.

Understanding

For Heidegger, understanding has its origin in his concept of a human being's ongoing encounter with the world. This involves an individual's questioning of the world, questioning of others, and questioning of one's own being. Heidegger refers to *Dasein* as "a 'human way of being,' which he [Heidegger] calls 'being there'" (Dreyfus, 1991, p. 14). He argues it is impossible to separate one's human consciousness from his or her encounter with the world. In other words, it is impossible to separate the subject from object. Further, for Heidegger, it is understanding which is the ongoing manifestation of *Dasein*. He also notes that understanding, like Dasein, is never static, rather it is continually transformed. Heidegger posits that understanding is always dependent upon and shaped by the world that the human being encounters.

For Gadamer, understanding is a social activity, a "sharing in a common meaning" (Gadamer, 1977, p.292).

Gadamer posits that the human being is always involved in understanding, and understands by participating in a conversation with what he or she experiences. To understand (*verstehen*) means to grasp something or to see more clearly, to integrate a meaning into a larger frame of reference.

Interpretation

Hermeneutics itself means to interpret, to bring about understanding. Gadamer is clear that interpretation is a special kind of understanding, but he is equally clear that it is not a tool for understanding. In *Truth and Method* he notes, "Interpretation is not a means through which understanding is achieved; rather, it enters into the content of what is understood" (Dostal, 2002, p. 398). For Gadamer, to call interpretation a tool for understanding is to distort and simplify its much more intimate relationship to understanding. Gadamer's avoidance of the term *tool* reflects his consistent distrust of methodizing any reading or writing activity. To make any interpretive activity a tool is to destroy the conversation which is unique to each reader's understanding of a text. Gadamer's position here is significant, for it shows how any hermeneutical term for him is constantly re-seen in the activity of interpretation.

Gadamer agrees with Heidegger, who says that interpretation is simply "the working-out of possibilities projected in understanding" (Dostal, 2002, p. 189). Interpretation is articulating the meanings of experience so that one can say that interpretation makes understanding more explicit. It can be seen as the linguistic manifestation of understanding which is always contextualized, always an understanding in relationship to something else. Abbey (2000) discussing Charles Taylor's position writes:

> Taylor has argued that there is a double hermeneutic at work in the human sciences compared to

the natural sciences. This is due directly to one of the ontological features he ascribes to persons. As outlined in Chapter 2, he believes that humans are self-interpreting beings and any attempt to explain their attempt must take this into account. This is necessary for two reasons. Firstly, how humans understand themselves and their world is an essential or primary property of their existence, not one that can be bracketed out in the quest to explain them. Secondly, because humans' self-interpretations influence their actions and behaviour, any account that excludes this variable can not be adequate. So, appreciating how the persons under study view their situation is an essential component of understanding them. As Taylor puts it, the demand "that we confront our language of explanation with the self-understanding of our subjects, is nothing else but the thesis of hermeneutic theory." (p.154)

Taylor does not suggest that the social scientist take these self-interpretations as the final word or as empirical evidence, but that they must be taken into account whenever the study of human beings is being conducted. (Abbey, 2000)

Application

Application for Gadamer is what locates the interpreter and the text within the historical moment, so that application allows the interpreter to appropriate what he or she reads into his or her present historical situation. Because of the temporal nature of application, Gadamer can conclude that a text must be understood continuously, concretely, and in a new and different way. (Dostal, 2002)

Horizons

Gadamer maintains that hermeneutic thought merges the horizons of the past and present, giving it an open horizon. A horizon can be defined as conscious awareness, underlying assumptions about the way the world works, a world view, or an order of things. Hermeneutic consciousness has a horizon which is in motion and which is continually changing as our consciousness of the present continually merges with our consciousness of the past. Cushman (1995) writes:

> Martin Heidegger and Hans-Georg Gadamer argued that it is not possible to exist as a human being outside of a cultural context. People can exist only within a cultural framework that is carved out of the sensory bombardment of potential perceptions and possible ways of being… The bombardment of perceptions and possibilities is like a forest, and the carved out space is like a 'clearing' in the forest. The clearing of a particular culture is created by the components of its conceptual systems and transmitted from one individual to the next and one generation to the next through their communal traditions of shared understandings and linguistic distinctions. It is only within the clearing that people 'show up' in certain shapes and with certain characteristics. The paradox of the clearing is thought to be caused by its horizontal nature: Horizons are created by the culture's particular way of perceiving… That is, the clearing is both liberating, because it makes room for certain possibilities, and limiting, because it closes off others. Horizons are thought to be perspectival, and therefore moveable. (p. 21)

True hermeneutic inquiry requires both the researcher and the object of the study be changed. As the two interact, a fusion of horizons occurs, in which both emerge transformed. "The emphasis on fusion of horizons and arriving at consensus over meaning reflects the *dialogical* nature of hermeneutic work" (McLeod, 2001, p. 28).

Dialogical Reasoning

Gadamer stressed the importance of reflection and conversation in knowing. Conversation assumes mutuality of question and answer (Gadamer, 1976). Gadamer proposed that through conversation with one another, understanding, that can not be predicted nor controlled, will occur. He believed that true conversation is when people are open, equally participative, and interested in achieving common understanding. Gadamer believed conversation to be an important function in crossing cultural or personal borders, leading to new discovery and understanding.

Contextualization

Hermeneutics relies heavily upon contextual analysis. The context of the researcher as well as the object of the research is important to consider. Developing a mutual understanding of these contexts aids in the emergence of new understanding and meaning. Context involves, among other things, reflecting upon historical and socio-cultural factors. This is often addressed utilizing the hermeneutic circle. The individual parts of context are revisited in context of the whole. "Hermeneutics is all about context, about placing the topic of inquiry into historical and cultural perspective" (McLeod, 2001, p. 56). McLeod (2001) continues:

> Hermeneutics can be understood as 'tradition-informed' inquiry, in the sense that questions that are being investigated are always viewed not only in their cultural-historical context or tradition of the researcher. We cannot step outside culture and history. We can only

make sense of action in terms of the value, virtues and story of the good life that prevail within our cultural world. Hermeneutics insists that we accept and embrace these realities, rather than pretending that we can achieve a knowledge of human affairs that somehow transcends culture and history. The way we can achieve useful understandings of human affairs is to enter fully into dialogue. (p. 23)

Hermeneutic Spiral

The hermeneutic spiral is considered fundamental to the interpretation process. This principle suggests that understanding is achieved through iterations in a dialogical reflection. The researcher iterates between considering the interdependent meaning of parts and the whole that they form. McLeod (2001) states:

> Inquiry proceeds by building up an interpretation, through moving back and forth between the part and the whole. This involves: gaining a sense of the meaning of the whole text, and then using that as a framework for understanding fragments of the text; carrying out the micro-analysis if the possible meanings of small sections of text, and using these to challenge or re-interpret the overall sense of the text. (p.27)

The hermeneutic spiral is sometimes called the hermeneutic circle. I have chosen to use the term spiral in order to diffuse confusion of continually retracing one's steps as connoted in the term circle. To maximize the effectiveness and efficiency of the hermeneutic spiral, constant alternating between and merging into another world and linking back to our own is required. The spiral not only helps one interpret the other, but it also helps in understanding self. Ricoeur said that we can make sense of ourselves only in and through our involvement with others. (Ricoeur, 1981)

Prejudice

Prejudice, defined by Gadamer (1976), is prejudgment. Prejudices are our preconceived notions of things, emanating from our past experience and socialization. In the positivist/empirical and Husserlian views of truth, the way to eradicate prejudice was to maintain objectivity by "*bracketing*" experiences. However, Heidegger and Gadamer believed this was impossible. To understand another we cannot shed our past experience, because it is this past experience that actually facilitates understanding the other. Gadamer advocated continual striving to explicate our prejudices. Gadamer (1975) writes:

> Long before we understand ourselves in retrospective reflection, we understand ourselves in self-evident ways, in the family, society, and state in which we live. The focus of subjectivity is a distorting mirror. The self-reflection of the individual is only a flicker in the closed circuits of historical life. (p. 245)

Understanding and awareness of our prejudice is vital in the hermeneutic process for it impacts the whole hermeneutic process. "Every act of hermeneutic understanding begins with a pre-understanding, which orients the inquirer to the text or topic. One of the tasks of the hermeneutic scholar is to become aware of and reflexively explicate this pre-understanding in a way that creatively feeds into the process of understanding itself" (McLeod, 2001, p.23).

Conclusion

Originally uttered by Schleiermacher (1768-1834), and popularized by Dilthey, the phrase, "there is no understanding without pre-understanding" is central in hermeneutic thought. However, when striving to find understanding, we must be careful not to understand it only in terms of our own prejudices, or only in terms of the prejudices of the author and agent. Hermeneutics offers a rich philosophical starting point from which to begin a study into human interactions. As in the case of this research, some have ventured to utilize hermeneutics in studying cross-cultural relationships. For example, Clifford Geertz has made great strides in helping hermeneutics evolve from a predominately historical literary methodology to the cross-cultural realm.

  With the introduction of hermeneutics into the story of the ITSM project, the next component to the story is an introduction to a suitable method. The following chapter introduces narrative storytelling as a logical method to partner with hermeneutic methodology given its literary history.

References:

Abbey, Ruth. (2000). *Charles Taylor.* Princeton: Princeton University Press.

Blaikie, Norman. (1993). *Approaches to social enquiry.* Cambridge: Polity Press

Blaikie, Norman. (2000). *Designing social research.* Cambridge: Polity Press

Cushman, Philip. (1995). *Constructing the self, constructing America: A cultural History of Psychotherapy.* Reading, MA: Addison-Wesley publishing Company, Inc.

Dostal, Richard. (2002). *The Cambridge companion to Gadamer.* Cambridge: Cambridge University Press.

Dreyfus, Hubert L. (1991). *Being-in-the world: A commentary on Heideggar's being and time.* Cambridge, MA: MIT Press.

Gadamer, H. (1976). *Philosophical hermeneutics.* (D.E. Linge, Trans). Berkley: University of California Press.

Gadamer, H. (1975). *Truth and method (2nd edition).* New York: Continuum.

Gephart, Robert. (Summer 1999). *Paradigms and research methods.* Academy of Management, Research Methods Division. Research Methods Forum, Vol.4. Retrieved May 10, 2004 from Http://www.aom.pace.edu/rmd/1999_RMD_Forum_Paradigms_and_Research_Methods.htm

Grondin, J. (1990). Hermeneutics and relativism. In K. Wright (Ed.) Festivals of
   interpretation: Essays onHans- Georg Gadamer's Work. New York: State University of New York Press.

Heiddeger, Martin. (1962). *Being and Time.* Translated by John Macquarrie and Edward Robinson. New York: Harper.

Hirsch, E. D., Jr.(1967). *Validity in interpretation.* New Haven: Yale University Press.

Koch, T. (1995). Interpretive Approaches in Nursing Research: The influence of Husserl and Heidegger. Journal of Advanced Nursing, 21, 827-836

Laverty, S. M. (2003). Hermeneutic Phenomenology and Phenomenology: A comparison
   of historical and methodological considerations. International Journal of Qualitative Methods, *2*(3). Article 3. Retrieved May 11, 2004 from http://www.ualberta.ca/~iiqm/backissues/2_3final/html/laverty.html

Maloney, M. (1993). Silent strength: A Heideggerian Hermeneutical analysis of the
   stories of older women. Unpublished doctoral dissertation, Georgia State University, Atlanta. Retrieved April 2, 2004 from http://www.coe.uga.edu/quig/proceedings/Quig98_Proceedings/byrne.html

McLeod, John. (2001). *Qualitative research in counselling and psychotherapy.* London: Sage Publications.

Merriam, S.B. (1988). *Case study research in education: A Qualitative approach.* San Francisco: Jossey-Bass Publishers.

Palmer, Richard. (1969). *Hermeneutics.* Evanston: Northwestern University Press.

Ricoeur, Paul. (1981). *Hermeneutics and the human sciences.* Cambridge: Cambridge University Press.

Taylor, Charles. (1994) *Multiculturalism.* Princeton, NJ: Princeton University Press.

Chapter 6

Method: Narrative Storytelling

Having established hermeneutics as the methodological framework of the ITSM project, the natural unfolding of the storyline reveals the need for the adoption of a research method. In selecting a method, I relied heavily upon the historical literary nature of hermeneutics and a M.Sc. course I taught on hermeneutics at University of Buckingham. The students were part of a Socio-economic Transformation cohort which emphasised a team approach in the pursuit of the M.Sc. degree.

The participants were from China, Taiwan, USA, France, and England. In the module I addressed the importance of self knowledge, utilizing the Components of the Self worksheet as part of the process. In reviewing the worksheets, the students from the East presented completely different responses than the Western students. We investigated this phenomenon and the students illuminated using personal stories. Throughout the course, personal stories emerged as a valuable resource for helping others understand a variety of cultural dynamics.

In the end, the group presented a class project on which they worked together. The students unanimously agreed that the module had helped them to better understand each other and to work more effectively together. Observing the transformation of this group during a one week course illuminated the value of a hermeneutic and storytelling approach in building a synergistic team.

As a follow up to the module, I reflected upon the elements that had contributed to the transformation of the M.Sc. group. Among the contributing elements present in the M.Sc. course were exercises for increasing self knowledge, personal storytelling, dialogue, an emphasis on interpretation and fusion of horizons, in context with a multicultural team of students working towards a common goal. As demonstrated in their final project and their comments regarding the more synergistic team work in the final project, the utilization of hermeneutics and storytelling dramatically improved the team's cohesiveness. This was the birth of the Interpretive Transcultural Storytelling Method.

Narrative storytelling is utilized in sociology and psychology, but I have been unable to detect its evolution into the field of transcultural relationships specifically. Narrative storytelling in conjunction with hermeneutics achieves an element of the goal of a Doctorate of Philosophy by contributing new knowledge to the field of study. Paul Ricoeur (1981), a significant contributor to hermeneutics argued that because personal identity is a narrative identity, we can only make sense of our own lives through our involvement with others. This chapter expounds on the use of narrative storytelling and its relationship to hermeneutics in context of the ITSM.

Narrative Storytelling and Hermeneutics: Method and Methodology

Narrative storytelling, as a method, and hermeneutics, as a methodology, provide a rich framework for understanding self and others. Hermeneutics was developed, and evolved, as a methodology for studying the Bible and later, literature in general. It is now being used in the social sciences as a methodology for gaining understanding between human beings. As hermeneutics has its foundation in literature, utilizing narrative storytelling as a method for interpersonal, multicultural team building is a natural progression. As a methodology for interpreting literature, hermeneutics has served as a framework for emphasising the importance of the reader understanding his or her personal contextual framework. Only when having attained a clear understanding of self, (the *inside story*) can a reader understand the literary work (the *other*). In understanding self, the reader or listener can interpret the other in light of the differentiating factors as well as those where common ground exists.

Hermeneutics, as a methodology, purposes to cultivate a fusion of horizons where distinct individuals can emerge in new ways of knowing and understanding. Due to the unique frames of reference of individuals, especially those from diverse cultures, a completely accurate understanding of another's story may be impossible. Denzin (1989) writes:

> "A story that is told is never the same story that is heard. Each teller speaks from a biographical position that is unique and, in a sense, unshareable. Each hearer of a story hears from a similarly unshareable position. But these two versions of the story merge and run together into a collective, group version of the story that was told. Because there are always stories imbedded in stories, including the told story and the heard story, there are only multiple versions of shareable and unshareable personal experiences. (p.72)

Blending the cultures of the listener and the storyteller is not the object of hermeneutics, rather facilitating understanding which leads to a fusion where differences remain, generating new, transforming knowledge and a co-creative cultural context. Hermeneutics, from its creation, has been concerned with facilitating the fusion of horizons between differing cultural contexts, originally the modern reader and an ancient text. Utilizing hermeneutics for multicultural integration is consistent with its original purpose, and using narrative storytelling is a natural method for the implementation of such.

In social science generally, and specifically within the present research, the person listening to the story of another is the "reader". The storyteller, and his or her story, is the "literary work". The use of narrative storytelling naturally unfolds from hermeneutics as a method of understanding the other. In clarification, most scholarly literature classifies storytelling as narrative. In defining narrative and storytelling, Randall (1995) writes, "Narrative is the genus of which story is but one species. Accordingly, while all stories are narratives, not all narratives are stories" (p. 85). Therefore, as a method, I have chosen to utilize the term, "narrative storytelling," in order to encompass the general and specific uses of the concept.

William Randall's seminal work titled, The Stories We Are: An Essay on Self-Creation, "explores the links between literature and life and speculates on what may be called 'the range of storytelling styles' according to which people compose their lives, transform the events of their lives into experiences, and seek coherence amid the diversity of the inner world of self" (Randall, 1995, p. 0). In doing so, he draws on a variety of fields including psychology, psychotherapy, theology, philosophy, feminist theory, and literary theory. Randall presents that each of us makes sense of our lives by constructing a story in which we are the author, narrator, main character, and reader. The "stories we are," are the stories of our lives as we interpret them. Robert Atkinson, professor at the University of Southern Maine and author of The Life Story Interview (1998), states, "Historical reconstruction may not be the primary concern in a life story; what is, is how people see themselves at this point in their lives and want others to see them" (Atkinson, 1998, p. 24). This story can be re-written consciously or subconsciously as the novel unfolds, and includes categories such as plot, character, point of view, and style.

Each story contains a beginning, middle, and end. Randall (1995) quotes Sartre, "We live our lives *through* our stories and we understand ourselves, others, and our world in terms of them" (p.330). Charles Taylor states, "Thus my discovering of my own identity doesn't mean that I work it out in isolation, but that I negotiate it through dialogue, partly overt, partly internal, with others" (Taylor, 1994, p. 34). Therefore, based upon its use within the social sciences, storytelling is valuable in helping the teller understand himself or herself, as well as an aid for others to understand the teller.

Narrative Storytelling within Organizations

In context of the present research, which focuses on intercultural relationships within organizations, Randall states, "Unless we hear each other's side of [that] story, however, and get the story straight, distrust is likely to grow, and the relationship itself unroll rather rockily, if not completely unravel" (Randall, 1995, p. 107). In developing relationships with others, Randall recognizes the importance of "getting the story straight," in other words, interpreting, clarifying, and understanding while communicating. Jack Maguire (1998) states, "Sharing real life stories [in human history] was an essential element in forging friendships, alliances, families, and communities. It brought individuals a greater intimacy with each other and, simultaneously, a stronger sense of self" (p. xiii). Maguire continues, quoting Jimmy Neil Smith, "We're all storytellers. We all live in a network of stories. There isn't a stronger connection between people than storytelling" (Maguire, 1998, p. xiii). Atkinson adds his conviction, stating, "People telling their own stories reveal more about their own lives than any other approach could" (Atkinson, 1998, p. 90).

Although we are living in a time of unprecedented communication technologies, the very use of such technologies has deleted an element of personal interaction and has inhibited the ability to communicate in a meaningful manner. Maguire (1998) asserts that in light of such technologies, "the world has grown alarmingly less personal" (p. xiii). Although it is understood that storytelling may not be appropriate in all corporate environments, the premise of the present research is that storytelling can play a productive role in establishing relationships among co-workers, specifically those of different cultural backgrounds. As Peter Brew of the International Business Leaders Forum stated, "Business used to be built by relationships, now it is dominated by deals... it needs to come back to relationships." (Peter Brew, 1-11-05). For purposes of the present research, we will be specifically addressing the usefulness of storytelling to build relationships within transcultural businesses and organizations. Storytelling has been shown to have a profound impact in the workplace. As an example, Maguire (1998) writes:

> Call her Harriet: in the early 1980s, the harridan of my daylight hours, and an all too frequently recurring harpy in my nightmares. During those years, I was scripting video programs for a large communications company. She was my immediate supervisor, and her management style was driving me crazy. At staff meetings she appeared to be democratic, good-natured, and supportive, but on a one-to-one basis she proved to be exceptionally autocratic, abrasive, and undermining.
>
> One of Harriet's most irritating habits was to communicate her orders or complaints by surreptitiously leaving a typewritten memo on the seat of her intended recipient's empty chair. My office was not visible from hers. It was far away, through a maze of corridors. But many times I would sit down unwittingly on a fresh Harriet dropping. I couldn't help but picture her lurking

behind some wall or cabinet near my door, clutching a newly drafted memo, ready to pounce the moment I vacated the premises.

Then one afternoon I was in Harriet's office reporting on the day's taping. A discussion of camera angles somehow prompted her to begin talking about the first time she thought she might need eyeglasses. She was in the second grade, she told me. From her seat at the back of the classroom, she couldn't see her teacher's lips move, and the white a's,e's, and o's on the black-board all looked the same. She confessed her problem to her parents, and the three of them nervously consulted an eye-doctor. It was a dark, clear night when she rode home in the back seat of the car after picking up her new glasses. She stared out the rear window, and for the first time in her life she saw the stars burning white in the black sky. (p. 4)

Maguire describes how the simple three or four minute picture of Harriet's story "humanized the situation" and transformed the whole atmosphere surrounding their relationship (Maguire, 1998, p.4). His perception of her changed, and therefore, his response to her management style changed. (Maguire, 1998, p.4) Maguire demonstrates the power of storytelling within the workplace. This simple glimpse into the story of a co-worker can "humanize" a relationship and change the perspective from which individuals view each other. In considering the above story, the lack of multicultural issues is apparent. In researching relevant literature on narrative storytelling and multicultural team building, I found no correlating references. In lieu of multicultural equivalency to Maguire's Harriet story, I have rewritten the story, based upon the neutral versus affective dimension of Trompenaars and

Hampden-Turner (1998), as it may conceivably be experienced in a multicultural workplace.

Call her Hidemi: in the early 1980s, the harridan of my daylight hours, and an all too frequently recurring harpy in my nightmares. During those years, I was scripting video programs for a large communications company. She was Japanese, and my immediate supervisor. Her management style was driving me crazy. At staff meetings she appeared to be good-natured, and supportive, yet simultaneously stand-offish and evasive. She never answered my questions directly and never demonstrated how she felt. She never showed emotion, and that was foreign to my way of thinking as a second generation Italian-American.

One of Harriet's most irritating habits was to communicate her orders or complaints by beating around the bush. She seemed weak and afraid of her authority as a boss by the way she would rebuke her employees. For example, instead of just saying, "This is the third time you were late meeting a deadline this month, next time you lose the project." Hidemi would say, "If you could please see your way to kindly troubling yourself to try and have your project on time, I would be most appreciative." It drives me crazy that she won't just come out with it.

Then one afternoon I was in Hidemi's office reporting on the day's taping. A discussion of camera angles somehow prompted her to begin talking about when the company first moved her to the US. She was thirty years old, she told me. Her immediate supervisor was an older American gentleman. She confessed her horror and embarrassment the first time he yelled at her for making a mistake. She had never been spoken to like that before. In Japan, her experience at work had always been respectful and to demonstrate emotion was highly frowned upon. She was faced with the choice of becoming like her boss, or hold closely to her Japanese values. She chose to hold to her Japanese culture and did not fight back. Her boss berated her and crushed her spirits. She considered quitting and moving back to Japan. Soon after that incident, her supervisor had retired, and she was promoted to his position. She consciously chose to conduct herself as a Japanese person, and even though she has received a few complaints that she is too abstract, she feels content knowing she has been true to herself and to her Japanese heritage.

Presumptively, if storytelling has been proven beneficial in the workplace, within a multicultural workplace it could be valuable as well. The purpose of the present research is to develop a method that facilitates the forming, telling, and hearing of stories which will in turn create a cohesive transcultural team.

Quoting Donald Polkinghorn, Randall writes, "Narrative… is the primary form by which human experience is made meaningful" (Randall, 1995, p. 90). Jungian psychoanalyst, James Hillman states that patients are in search of a new story, and that it is the story that needs doctoring, not the patient. Freudian Analyst, Roy Schafer posits that "each analysis amounts in the end to retelling a life in the past and present- and as it may be in the future. A life is re-authored as it is co-authored" (Randall, 1995, p. 90). The use of narrative storytelling, then, is utilized in the field of social sciences as a viable concept for developing understanding of oneself and others. Robert Atkinson, researcher author, and university professor, (1998) states:

> Storytelling, in its most common everyday form, is giving a narrative account of an event, an experience, or

any other happening. We can tell of these happenings because we know what has happened. It is this basic knowledge of an event that allows us to tell about it. What generally happens when we tell a story from our own life is that we increase our working knowledge of ourselves because we discover deeper meaning in our lives through the process of reflecting and putting the events, experiences, and feelings that we have lived into oral expression. (p. 1)

Demonstrating the correlation of hermeneutics and storytelling, Atkinson highlights the importance of developing self-knowledge, a core value of hermeneutics. Atkinson continues, stating that the life story interview is a "qualitative research method for gathering information on the subjective essence of one person's life" (Atkinson, 1998, p. 3). "In the process of telling our life stories, we share important truths, as we see them, and in so doing, create vital links with those who participate in the exchange. Telling and listening to life stories is a powerful experience… The life story, then, is very much an interdisciplinary approach to understanding not only one life across time, but how individual lives interact with the whole" (Atkinson, 1998, p. 3-4).

Validating the use of storytelling in a variety of disciplines, Atkinson (1998) notes a number of uses:

> Psychologists now see the value of personal narratives in understanding development and personality (McAdams, 1993; Runyan, 1982). Anthropologists use the life story, or individual case study, as the preferred unit of study for their measures of cultural similarities and variations (Langness & Frank, 1981; Spradley, 1979). Sociologists use life stories to understand and define

relationships and group interactions and memberships (Bertaux. 1981; Linde, 1993). (p. 6)

Consistent with the variety of uses of storytelling, the present research places it within the context of business and organizations. David Boje, associate professor of management at Loyola Marymount University and editor of the Journal of Organizational Change Management, states, "Think of an organization as a big conversation. People are conversing all day long. An organization is an ongoing storytelling event" (Maguire, 1998, p. 202). Author and vice-president of Armstrong International, David Armstrong advocates storytelling as a valuable means to forge partnerships and teams, and has developed a reputation world-wide as a leader in storytelling on the corporate environment. (Armstrong, 2002) Maguire (1998) writes of another advocate of storytelling in the workplace:

> John Ward, a corporate consultant in what he diplomatically calls 'creative communication' rather than 'storytelling,' believes that stories develop a businessperson's 'peripheral vision.' … Ward's theory is that stories set in motion a different way of thinking that can result in workplace breakthroughs: 'Stories can potentially support thinking beyond the dots by arousing emotions and awakening the imagination.' He believes that storytelling is particularly effective in helping resolve those problems in a corporation that somehow relate to communication. (p. 204)

The "workplace breakthroughs" of which Ward speaks are analogous to the "fusion of horizons" of hermeneutics, and the use of the term "emergence" I have chosen to utilize in the ITSM. The breakthrough, fusion of horizons, or emergence requires the conjoint effort of two or more participants, synergistically creating new knowledge. This new knowledge will inherently involve valuable inter-personal understanding and relationship building, and will theoretically lead to other productive ends as well, such as more efficient protocols, co-creation, operating procedures, and innovative ideas.

Academic and practical anecdotal evidence exists that supports the use of storytelling as a means of enhancing corporate communication and camaraderie.

However, an obvious gap exists when translating storytelling into the specific realms of multicultural communication. While there is no shortage of literature on multicultural communication or management, the bulk of the literature addresses the stereotypical differences. Trompenaars and Hampden-Turner, as well as Hofstede have provided valuable works on multicultural competencies, but the questionnaires and results obtained are not designed for facilitating emergence between individuals who are a part of a team. These individuals will most assuredly have varying levels of acculturation and characteristics that are too complex for the generalizations such as collectivistic, universal, or low power distance.

Through storytelling, dialogue can occur which will promote understanding of self and the other. As demonstrated in the first fieldwork exercise of the present research, the students from Japan and the American faculty members shared certain qualities generally attributed to the other culture. The Interpretive Transcultural Storytelling Method will contribute to the field of storytelling as an organizational device by specifically addressing the multicultural arena in a manner that will take individuality into consideration.

Narrative Storytelling as a Research Method

In congruence with hermeneutic methodology, the narrative method is best described by Atkinson (1998) as follows:

> The position here is that the life story interview can be approached *scientifically*, but it is primarily carried out as an *art*. Though there is a structure (a set of question or parts thereof) that can be used, each interviewer [researcher] will apply this in his or her own way. Tough theories may come into play to varying degrees throughout the process, the interview and the interpretation of it is highly subjective... Because the life story interview is primarily an artful endeavour, it should be interpreted as an art form. The life story interview has its own standards of reliability and validity, distinct from quantitative research methods... Qualitative research (including life story interviews) can be determined reliable or valid on its own merits... based primarily upon subjectivity, flexibility, and inevitable human variables.... A life story is first and foremost a text to be read, understood, and interpreted on its own merit and in its own way. (p. 21)

The texts, the stories of the participants, are interpreted by other participants and me, the researcher. The evolving story is that of the individuals, the interpersonal relationships, and the team to which they belong. The validity and reliability, as well as the perceived value of the ITSM is interpreted as well, by the individuals, the team, and by me, as Atkinson stated, subjectively.

Each ITSM workshop approximately lasts between four to six hours and is typically done in one or two hour intervals on consecutive days or weeks. The workshop begins with an overview of hermeneutic philosophy. This is done in layman's terms, avoiding technical detail. Primarily, the emphasis is placed upon self-knowledge, or personal context, which dictates the frame of reference from which each individual views the world in general, and others, specifically. The participants are then briefed on the importance of understanding the context, specifically the cultural context, of the other.

This is analogous to understanding the context of the literature one is reading. Finally, the hearer interprets the message, purposefully considering the storyteller's context and his or her own context. The ITSM stages in which this process takes place are Interpretation and Clarification. The outcome of the interpreted story is understood to be a culmination of the process resulting in new knowledge and understanding. This takes place in the ITSM stages of Understanding and Emergence. This process is presented by Webb as the X-Y-Z Principle. (Webb, 2001) While Webb's terms will not be explicitly utilized in the ITSM, his concepts present a valuable backdrop for understanding the hermeneutic process within the ITSM model. Succinctly, the X-Y-Z Principle as applied to the ITSM process is as follows, accompanied by examples from the first field work exercise:

> **X:** The cultural context from which the storyteller, and therefore the story itself, originates.
> **Example:** Lisa is a twenty-one year old Japanese woman. She is in the United States for the first time, and she will be in the USA for four months. Lisa's family holds to traditional Japanese values, of special relevance to her story, is the value Japanese places upon elders.
> **Y:** The actual text, or message, being conveyed.
> **Example:** Although Lisa's family highly regards the traditional Japanese cultural values, Lisa could not tolerate the demands her grandfather placed upon her. She refused to talk to him, unless absolutely necessary, for approximately one year. To compound the stress of

this relationship, Lisa lived with her grandparents during that time.

Z: The interpretation of the story by the hearer, in light of X, Y, and his or her own context. This ultimately leads to new knowledge and understanding between the storyteller and the listener, from the evolved relationship emerges.

Example: As an American with an understanding of the value Japanese culture places upon elders, I found it incongruent that Lisa would consider herself a traditionally Japanese person, and yet break communication with her grandfather. My mother and grandmother had a similar relationship for several years, yet we lived in different towns, and our culture is much more independent and individualistic. In our discussion as a group, Lisa explained how she never treated her grandfather with disrespect; she simply did not pursue communication with him. She said she still "acted" respectfully. Through following the ITSM process of Clarification, as a group, we came to a mutual understanding.

Following the overview of hermeneutic principles, the participants are given the opportunity to complete the Components of the Self worksheet as well as the Trompenaars and Hampden-Turner questions. The purpose of these exercises is to promote In-Spection, or self-knowledge, as well as to spur discussion which illuminates cultural differences.

The participants are encouraged, but not required, to consider a story that helps others gain insight into their personal and cultural foundations. As the participants take turns sharing their stories, the listeners are encouraged to be aware of a number of processes taking place. The story tellers are encouraged to begin with a brief overview of their cultural background, especially illuminating cultural nuances affecting the story they will be sharing. This allows the participants to place the story, at least to a small degree, within a context, fitting with the "X" phase of the process identified above. As a primary level of Interpretation, the listeners are then encouraged to listen to the facts, trying to hear the pure message, congruent with the "Y" stage.

Next, the listeners are asked to attempt Interpreting the story in light of the context of the teller, the message, and their own context. The participants are asked to clarify what they have interpreted by asking questions and re-stating certain key elements. The discussion in this phase will cycle back and forth until a measure of mutual understanding is achieved. This moving back and forth between the teller and the hearer is known as the hermeneutic cycle, or spiral.

In addition, the participants are asked to subjectively be aware of the different levels at which the stories and subsequent dialogues rise and fall. This is outlined for the participants in the handout they each receive, and includes the general categories of Surface and Depth, and specifically breaks down into the topsoil, subsoil, bedrock, and core. Surface includes the topsoil and subsoil, while Depth incorporates the bedrock and core. (Lessem and Palsule, 2002) The Topsoil, according to Lessem (2002) includes our personal, instinctive attitudes and behaviours, or inclinations. Attitudes toward time, the manner in which business cards are exchanged, and other social and etiquette phenomena are considered topsoil. As the name implies, topsoil is a superficial level of communication. Subsoil takes us deeper into understanding institutional frameworks, systems, and models, and includes the way individuals and groups within a society relate, forming a collective intelligence. Included within Subsoil are economic, political, and legal systems.

Styles or philosophies of business and management styles are also included in this level. "At the bedrock level of culture, we are dealing with the holistic philosophies and policies, that is the *ideologies,* that lie well below the everyday surface, stimulating insight" (Lessem and Palsule, 2002, p. 175). According to Lessem (2002), this level incorporates ideological orientations, philosophies and policies. An example of an ideological framework is the cultural impact of Confucianism in China. The Core, then, represents the depth of cultural understanding and includes "*images* drawn from the sciences, the humanities or indeed from the depths of religion, inclusive of language in its original context, informing our imagination" (Lessem and Palsule, 2002, p. 175).

The participants are encouraged to enter into dialogue regarding the stories shared, specifically exploring differences and similarities between different cultural nuances. The listeners and the storyteller then agree, after cycling through the previous stages as often as necessary, upon a shared understanding and how this new and information can spawn mutual, synergistic Emergence, for example, a new way of thinking and behaving.

Utilizing storytelling is an established practice for building teamwork within organizations. However, the literature is lacking regarding the use of storytelling specifically in building teamwork within multicultural settings. The present research will contribute to the field of management by examining the use of storytelling for specifically this cause.

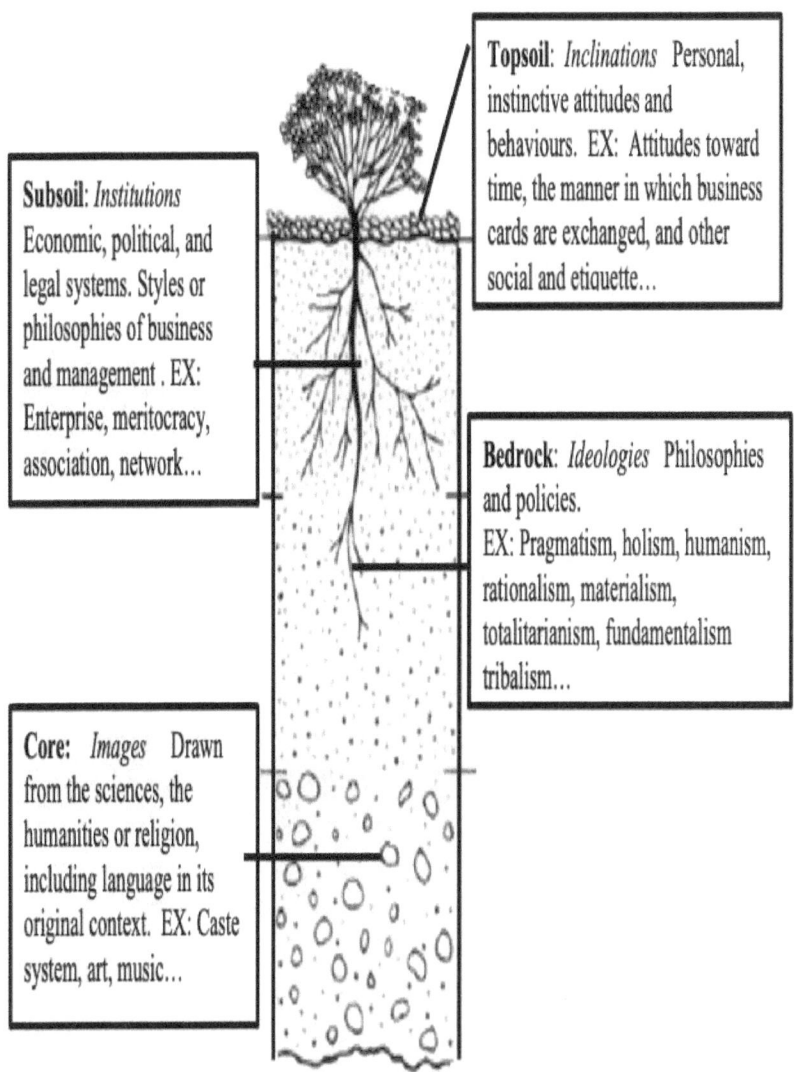

Figure 1: Cultural Topography

References:

Armstrong, David. (2002). *Chief storytelling officer: More tales from America's foremost corporate storyteller.* Three Rivers, MI: Armstrong International.

Atkinson, Robert. (1998). *The life story interview.* Thousand Oaks: Sage Publications.

Brew, Peter. (Jan. 11, 2005). Personal communication, University of Buckingham.

Denzin, Norman K. (1989). *Interpretive biography.* Newbury Park: Sage Publications.

Friedman, Thomas L. (2005). *The world is flat: A brief history of the twenty-first century.* New York: Farrar, Straus and Giroux.

Lessem, Ronnie, & Palsule, Sudhanshu. (2002). From local identity to global integrity. *Leadership and Organization Development Journal UK, Volume 23, No. 4,* 174-185.

Lessem, Ronnie & Palsule, Sudhanshu. (1997). *Managing in four worlds: From competition to co-creation.* Oxford, UK: Basil Blackwell.

Maguire, Jack. (1998). *The power of personal storytelling: Spinning tales to connect with others.* NY: Jeremy P. Tarcher/ Putnam.

Randall, William. (1995). *The stories we are: An essay on self-creation.* Toronto: University of Toronto Press.

Reissman, Catherine K. (1993). *Narrative analysis.* Newbury Park: Sage Publications.

Ricoeur, Paul. (1981). *Hermeneutics and the human sciences.* Cambridge: Cambridge University Press.

Taylor, Charles. (1994) *Multiculturalism.* Princeton, NJ: Princeton University Press.

Webb, William J. (2001). *Slaves, women & homosexuals: Exploring the hermeneutics of cultural analysis.* Downers Grove, IL: InterVarsity.

Chapter 7
Contextualization: From Texas to Mexico, Via London

With the ITSM placed in context of literature and methodology, the stage is set to begin the practice of hermeneutic research. Before embarking on a journey into the study of others, it is necessary to begin with a solid foundation of one's own perceptions, beliefs, biases, prejudices, and general culture. The cornerstone of Socrates' philosophical teachings was, "Know Thyself". The Tao Te Ching proclaims, "He who knows others is wise, He who knows himself is enlightened". It is difficult to study a foreign culture and truly understand that culture.

However, it is equally difficult to step out of one's indigenous culture and study it from an objective view point. Presuppositions must be challenged with a critical evaluation of veracity and validity. For Socrates, the beginning of knowledge is doubt. As Will Durant summarizes Socrates, "There is no real philosophy until the mind turns around and examines itself" (Durant, 1953, p. 6). Genuinely examining one's own religious faith, opinions, values, and other cherished beliefs requires a willingness to reject those beliefs if warranted. As well as internal beliefs, the cultural context must be examined. A critical evaluation of one's culture requires the same willingness to challenge the pillars of that culture.

Hermeneutic methodology requires a researcher and interpreter to have a sense of self-knowledge prior to interpreting another's story. This chapter on Macro-contextualization is included as part of my personal journey in gaining self-knowledge. As the primary researcher in this project, a solid grounding in my personal history as well as that of my cultural context is necessary. William Randall, in "The Stories We Are" (1995), addresses the metaphor of our lives as stories, and the various manners in which our stories unfold.

This chapter describes the beginning of a purposeful process of transformational emergence. The present exposure to literary, cultural, spiritual, political, and ethnographic frameworks outside of my norm, have propelled me from the status quo into a new world awaiting discovery. The process has included, and will continue to include, wrestling with long held traditional beliefs and pre-judgments in a variety of arenas, most significantly in the field of spirituality and religion.

"From Texas to Mexico, via London" is the slogan printed on the back of a souvenir t-shirt I purchased in a Tex-Mex restaurant located near Trafalgar Square, in the heart of historic London, England. Beginning my second year at the University of Buckingham, I arrived in London a few days early in order to do some sight-seeing. Leaving my hotel near Victoria Station early the first morning, I strolled past the New Scotland Yard, over to Westminster Abbey, and stood in awe as the early morning sun reflected off of Big Ben. My journey led me to the National Gallery, St Martin-in- the-Fields Cathedral, and the fountains of Trafalgar Square. As I walked past the Canadian Embassy, something out of place caught my attention. It was a Texas flag flying outside of a restaurant called the Texas Embassy. It is located just behind the Canadian Embassy, and a few blocks from where the historic Texas Embassy stood from 1835 to 1846. I was intrigued and purposed to return that evening for dinner. I felt an impending sense of guilt for eating at a restaurant that was so closely related to my own culture while in a city filled with food from around the world. After all, I was there to learn and explore. What I received that evening was more than a meal and a souvenir t-shirt. What I received that evening I would only discover about six months later while reflecting on the experience.

"From Texas to Mexico via London" has become a metaphor chronicling my journey to this point in my story.

Texas has come to represent the historical, ethnocentric me. London, (more specifically the University of Buckingham), is representative of the present where I am in process of evolving. Mexico represents the future and a Transcultural, world-centric me. In a story, there are a variety of themes the author may choose to highlight. In my story, for this context, the theme I have chosen is that of my world-view.

    As the t-shirt implies, Texas is where my personal journey began. I am a Texan, and proud of my heritage. During the U.S. presidential campaign of 2000, I had an opportunity to meet and chat with the future President of the United States, George W. Bush. He was then the Governor of Texas and he was on a campaign stop in Washington State, where I now reside. I greeted him that morning with, "Hello Mr. Bush, I am a fellow Texan." Immediately he stopped, put his arm around me and asked where I was from. The hundreds of people gathered around him waited impatiently as we talked about Texas, where my family members live, and about his recent trip to the area where my grandparents live.

    There is a strong element of American patriotism in the U.S., but my experience is the patriotism of Texans goes deeper. There is even a saying that goes, "Don't ever ask a man where he is from. If he's from Texas, he'll tell you, if he's not, you don't want to embarrass him." I am a Texan and an American. I am also white and a Christian fundamentalist. As such, I have had a very concrete way of perceiving the world, other cultures and religions. I have not been ignorant of these prejudices, but they are growing evermore apparent as I continue to delve deeper into the philosophies and beliefs of the "other."

    My story begins in the small West-Texas town of Floydada. Located in the panhandle, Floydada is an unimpressive community supported by agriculture. It is arid and flat, with only an occasional oasis of trees, usually planted strategically as wind blocks. The extent of multicultural experience afforded me in those early years was the strong Mexican-American population and to a lesser degree an African-American population. For the most part each group stayed to themselves, segregated into sub-communities.

The Mexican-Americans lived in one area of town, and on the west side of the railroad tracks was an area populated mainly by African-Americans we called *"Nigger Town"*. During my childhood, this term was as normal sounding to me as any town's name. What I realized only as a young adult, is that this type of labelling created within me the sense of the "other". The "other" is someone, or a group of people, who do not fit in the same mould. This can be because of language, skin colour, religion, or other factors. The "other" is different. I learned early on that the "others", at that time Mexican-American and African-Americans, were different. Not only not the same, but not as good.

In elementary school I had a childhood girlfriend who happened to be African-American. Although at that age I certainly had no potential of marrying her, my grandparents strongly rejected the idea saying, "You will have children that are zebras". Prejudice was being programmed into my logic. Later in my childhood, my Grandfather purchased a gasoline station. As a boy, I spent many hours helping him at his gas station, working alongside his only employee, *"Nigger Willie"*. This, quite unfortunately, was how I was introduced to him, and the name by which I addressed him. Willie was one of only a handful of African-American people living in our small town. These individuals with dark brown skin were considered by most whites as dirty, dishonest, and of sub-normal intelligence. Their place was that of service to the white man. Although slavery was abolished, the lingering attitudes prevailed and people of colour were not allowed to use the same restroom, or drink from the same water fountain as a Caucasian.

Another non-white group of people with a larger population in Texas is the Mexican-American. The Mexican-American population also resided in an area of town segregated from the majority whites. While not despised to the extent as the African-Americans, Mexican-Americans were definitely considered far less than equal. They were the ones who worked in the fields, lived in migrant houses, and did all the jobs that were too dirty for, or below, the white population.

These prejudicial attitudes were not held by my family, or by me, with any maliciousness or ill-will, they were simply the undisputed facts, as we knew them. Not until my adult years did I begin to recognize the influence this early programming had on my view of the "other". Geert Hofstede (2001) calls these types of attitudes Mental Programmes which can be "inherited (transferred in our genes), or they can be learned after birth" (p.2). My brain was programmed with this prejudice which I have now reprogrammed as intolerable.

I was reared in a fundamental, Christian family, a heritage of which I am fond and appreciate. I grew up going to church on Sundays and Wednesday evenings, attended children and youth camps, and even attended fundamental Christian colleges for my undergraduate education. In our small West Texas community, when we asked, "What religion are you," we meant, "Are you Baptist, Methodist, Church of Christ, Presbyterian, or Catholic?" Virtually everyone claimed Christianity as his or her religion, even if they were not particularly religious people.

My childhood years in Texas profoundly impacted my life in a number of ways. During those years I learned the importance of family, that people of colour were in essence, below the white population, and I learned to identify people according to their religion. However, the most powerful events of my childhood were far more tragic. I was the elder of two sons. When I was six years old, we moved to another West

Texas town called Brownfield. The name was very fitting, as the area was brown, and all cotton fields. My father was the manager of a cotton gin, an industry that takes raw cotton, combs it, and bales it.

I was in the second grade and had been taken by my mother to the physician for a check-up before school the sunny morning of October 18, 1973. As we left the doctor's office, we heard the screaming sounds of the sirens of police, fire trucks, and ambulances. Not an uncommon sound for a city, but in that small West Texas town it was unusual, and a bit unnerving. Inevitably we would either know or have some relationship to the person or persons for which the emergency vehicles responded. I begged my mother to follow the emergency vehicles so we could see what had happened. She insisted I needed to get to school. An hour later two of my mother's friends came to my classroom door and knocked. The teacher met them outside and I noticed as they talked that they would glance at me through the window in the door. My teacher called me and said I was to be taken home by the two ladies. I knew something was terribly wrong, and I remember sitting in silence in the back seat of their car all the way to my home.

When we arrived I noticed several cars parked in front of our house. As we entered, I saw our pastor, a policeman, and some others I did not recognize. My mother sat crying on the sofa with one of the pastors from our church. As I approached her, the pastor sat me on his knee and said, "Kent, your daddy has gone to heaven to be with Jesus." I squirmed from his arms, ran down the hallway and dove onto my parent's bed, crying. The sirens we had heard that morning were the emergency vehicles responding to an accident at the gin where my dad had been electrocuted and fell two stories to his death.

The impact my father's death had upon me and my entire family was intense and the shock waves can be felt to this day.

Resounding questions continue to echo through the years as I contemplate how things would have been different if he had not been killed.

Following my father's death, my mother, brother and I returned to Floydada to live near my grandparents, and my mother eventually remarried. My brother and I spent every weekend at my grandparent's home. My father had been the youngest of four children, and the only child to stay in town, therefore we had an especially close bond. My grandfather began drinking alcohol in order to help him cope with the death of his youngest son. Eventually he became an alcoholic. This caused a great deal of stress and turmoil in our family. One Friday evening, my mother refused to allow my brother and me to go to my grandparent's home, for no apparent reason.

That evening the phone rang and the Sheriff told my mother that my granddad had committed suicide by shooting himself. Suicide has been called the most selfish act a person can perform. The pain of my family was magnified by questions like, "What did we do wrong," or "What could we have done to prevent this?"

My great-grandfather lived next door to my grandparents. He was an important figure in my childhood as well. He lived to be ninety-two years old. Pa lived a rich and fulfilling life and passed away within a couple of years of my grandfather's death. Within a very few years, all significant male figures were stripped away. This is with the exception of my new stepfather. It has been said that when a boy loses his father at a young age, he spends the rest of his life trying to win his approval. It is my presumption that when a boy loses all male figures in his life at a young age, this phenomenon is compounded.

The events of my early childhood no doubt played a significant role in my choice of occupations. A common axiom is that counsellors go into counselling because they need counselling. I propose that a similar truth would be asserted when considering the professional pastoral ministry as well. I have continually sought the approval of men who have been teachers, pastors, Scout leaders, and coaches.

At a young age I felt a desire and a calling to become a pastor. I have often reflected how my choice to become a pastor and counsellor, may have been to some degree a result of needing to feel that others, including God, approved of me. Insecurity has been a constant theme throughout my life, and I can even attribute an element of my continuing education to an attempt to fulfil that insecurity and need for approval.

My early teen years brought the move of my family from West Texas to Southern Louisiana. From the comfortable and familiar to a culture I had only seen in the movies or on television. In the media, African-Americans were the gangsters, robbers, murderers, and the violent drug addicts of society. I distinctly remember driving through the streets of New Orleans for the first time. As a teenager I literally sat on the floor of the car out of fear of the countless African-Americans on the sidewalks. The African-American population was not limited to the city in general, but was reflected within the schools as well. I had been literally thrust from a school of only a handful of African-Americans, (who had assimilated into the white culture as much as possible), to a school system where the African-American population rivalled, if not outnumbered the Caucasian. Walking the corridors of the school in fear, I decided the only way to keep "them" from robbing me, or worse, was to try and make friends. I began hanging around "them" occasionally at lunch and, at times, specifically tried to sit near "them" in class. I suppose I was unconsciously trying to "keep the enemy close".

As I began to befriend these people of another colour and culture, I began to realize there were not as many differences as I had presupposed. My new friends had many of the same interests, problems, and goals as I. I would not say I was transformed during that period, but a new light had begun to dawn on my understanding of the "other". It was from that point I began to attribute more of a sense of equanimity to those of a different colour.

While I was still working on my undergraduate degree, my mother and stepfather moved to Frankfurt, Germany. I had travelled to Europe on two previous occasions, but now I had the opportunity to spend my summers there. The opportunity to be in another culture for extended periods of time was another step in my journey of personal evolution. It was in Europe that I first began to see, on a regular basis, couples of mixed races. My first responses were sharp, but with time, I began to pay little attention. I had begun to be desensitized to inter-racial relationships and this went against what I had been taught in elementary school by my grandparents. The children of these couples were not zebras.

The colour of skin is not the only prejudice that has plagued my evolution to a more enlightened individual. In addition, socio-economics, religion, and sexual orientation have been significant, and quite probably more significant barriers by which I have found transformation blocked. These prejudices are less tangible. In general, religion, sexual orientation, and socio-economic status are not as readily identifiable as the colour of skin. However, attitudes toward people in the "other" category within these domains have surfaced as powerful factors. Religion has risen as a pronounced factor in differentiating groups of people, most significantly Christians and Jews from Muslims. In context of the present research project, I will examine my personal attitudes and beliefs toward other religious faiths, or the lack thereof.

In her book, Encountering God: A Spiritual Journey from Bozeman to Banaras (2003), Diana Eck chronicles her spiritual journey which in many ways parallels mine. However, we are at different points in the story. Her book examines her fundamentalist Christian, Western, beliefs in light of her experiences with the "other". From Bozeman, Montana to Banaras, India is a long journey geographically. However, as with me, it is a much longer journey spiritually and emotionally. As she experienced and developed relationships with the "other", her own prejudice was revealed and she was forced to choose to respond. She chose to allow her own paradigm to evolve rather than rigidly grasp the traditional views she had held. Speaking of religious beliefs, Eck (2003) states:

> For many people religion is a rigid concept, somewhat like a stone that is passed form generation to generation. We don't add to it, challenge it, or change it; we just pass it along. But even the most cursory study of history of religions would undermine such a view. Religious traditions are far more like rivers than stones. Like the Ganges or the Gallatin, they are flowing and changing. Sometimes they dry up in arid land; sometimes they radically change course and move out to water new territory. All of us contribute to the river of our traditions. We don't know how much we will change the river or be changed as we experience its currents. (p. 2)

Rigidity is an appropriate descriptor of my religious world view. Simply critically examining my view of God and religious beliefs in writing the present chapter generates a sense of guilt. I feel as though asking questions and embarking on the present transformational pursuit is heresy. I am in constant flux between two dichotomous voices. One says, "God is big enough for you to ask questions and to allow you to have an open mind." The other cries out, "Stop! You are headed for trouble. You cannot question your beliefs or open your mind to a new way of perceiving the 'other'! You are in danger of loosing your salvation!" It is therefore out of sheer discipline and resolve that I heed the voice of the former and continue in my pursuit.

In 1987 I married Tonya Lynn Lee. She was born in Hood River, Oregon where she lived until her early teen years when her family moved to South Texas to be missionaries. Tonya's parents hold strongly to fundamentalist Christian teachings. She went to a Christian high-school and her father had strict guidelines for watching television and style of dress. Although Tonya came from a very strict background, she is decidedly open-minded and extremely logical. She is very solid in her Christian faith, yet is open to discussion and debate. Tonya is stable, level, and remains rational in the most difficult and trying of times. She is a very strong supporter of my continued education and my transformational journey. A personal desire for growth and enlightenment has been her hallmark since we married, and she has been my partner throughout most of my adult life. Toni and I married while attending a very fundamentalist Christian college. Following some unfortunate events surrounding the administration of the college, I decided not to complete my degree, and to accept a position as an associate pastor in Gallup, New Mexico.

Gallup is in the heart of the Navajo Indian Reservation. I was thrilled because my great-grandfather had been one-half Comanche Indian and lived for a number of years on the Navajo Reservation. Throughout my childhood I had longed to be an Indian and now I had the opportunity to learn from the culture and serve a people I had for so long admired. My enthusiasm was not necessarily reciprocated by all Native Americans I met. I found that I was considered the outsider and because of my skin colour I was cast into the category of the white-man. The white man who took their land, destroyed their culture, and broke the promises they made. This was very disheartening to me. However, my eyes were opened a little more to the pains of stereotyping people because of an attribute they may have in common with someone else.

This time I was the "other." I was approached outside of stores and on the streets by Native Americans who propositioned me for money, since I was white and I took all they had. My experience as a white person in Indian country is not unique, but it serves two purposes in my story. First, I experienced the pain of wanting to be accepted and, at least by some, was kept on the outside. Secondly, I learned not to stereotype all Native Americans as having prejudice because of my experience with a few. I had equal numbers of positive and enriching experiences on the reservation. I was invited into homes and I made some very dear friends.

While living in New Mexico, I experienced the devastation one nation can cause to another. The Navajo language is a dying language and the culture has been infused with so much from the outside that it has been almost lost. The most painful truth I have experienced in my exposure to the American Indian saga is that its cultural devastation was done at the hands of supposed Christians, and in the name of Christianity. The early settlers and pioneers came with missionaries in order to civilize a pagan and barbaric society. They took the children and placed them in missionary schools, cutting their hair, clothing them in European dress, and forbidding them to speak their language or practice their customs.

Within a generation the ancient cultures became almost extinct. This brings a great amount of sorrow to me. I identify strongly with the American Indian because of my great-grandfather. I am pained even more to know that this conquering was done in the name of the religion I profess.

My wife and I moved from New Mexico to Florida, and then to Washington State. These moves exposed us to a broad assortment of American sub-cultures, yet I still had very little contact with those of other religious faiths. In moving to Seattle I became acquainted with my brother-in-law, who is from Iran. He is Muslim. Our first meeting I felt intimidated because all I knew of Muslims was what I had seen on television. I assumed Muslims hated Christians and Jews, and I believed their religion bred terrorism. My prejudgments were revealed as erroneous once I developed relationships with Siamac, his family, and his Iranian friends. Although I enjoyed a level of friendship with my Muslim acquaintances, I nevertheless possessed a degree of an attitude of "otherness" towards them.

Following the tragic events of September 11, 2001, I recognized a familiar prejudice arise within me. For me, along with many in our nation, the anti-Muslim sentiment seemed to swell feverishly as the media and various Christian leaders began focusing on the evils of Islam. There has been a steady outcry from many Christian fundamentalists and to some extent the secular media as well, about the impending onslaught of Muslims. In recent days I have heard, on several occasions, how the purpose of Islam is to annihilate Christianity, especially in the United States. This view and message has become a rallying cry of some Christians against a common enemy. Virtually all Muslims were placed into the same category as the hijackers of the American Airlines jets and Osama Bin Laden.

The 9-11 attacks birthed a new dragon against which we as a nation and especially as Christians could join forces to fight. There was an immediate call to unity and nationalism that seemed to be what our nation needed. This common foe brought a country with many different philosophies and political agendas together. Many believed the phenomenon of unity would have a positive effect on our national psyche. I found myself in alliance with those who viewed all of Islam as a common enemy. Concurrently, I found myself asking how I could perceive all Muslims with this view and at the same time love my brother-in-law and his family. If all Muslims were out to destroy Christianity, and in the process me, would not my brother-in-law be a part of the scheme?

The recognition of these dichotomous views was instrumental in the early stages of my journey reaching the symbolic London in my story. Approaching London required a willingness to examine my world view, and a willingness to evolve. The pivotal point of arriving in London was my matriculation into the University of Buckingham. I had originally been drawn to the University because of a great admiration and connection with Dr. Lessem. However, upon arrival to the campus and meeting my fellow colleagues and the various professors, I realized a greater purpose than simply attaining a Doctor of Philosophy. The trans-cultural context of the University is unlike any I have ever experienced. My first hour on campus I met a student from Afghanistan, a professor from India and one from Iraq, and a minister in the government of Bangladesh. The students in the program in which I am enrolled are from Bulgaria, Jordan, China, and the United Kingdom. In a very real sense, my experience at the University of Buckingham has been a personal renaissance. The difficult task of de-constructing, and re-constructing my perspectives is presently being addressed in the "London" phase of my journey.

At this point I have been forced to look as objectively as possible at the foundational document of my religious faith, the Bible. The Bible is literally the supposed basis for all my beliefs and world view. Several years ago I began to understand, to a small degree, that even though a belief is taught as Biblical, it may in fact be in error. As a young person, I was taught, in one particular setting, that black people were that colour because God cursed them. It is easy to comprehend how white Christians could justify slavery and devaluation of blacks in light of this erroneous doctrine. Another example of how some have used the

Bible and Christianity in a manner I find completely inconsistent with my world view is the Crusades. Charles Kimball, in his book, When Religion Becomes Evil (2002), gives many examples of how the name of God has been invoked to conduct atrocities upon mankind. He not only addresses these acts in the name of Christianity, but also Islam and other religions. The beginning examination of my personal beliefs and views required the conquering of an extremely defensive attitude. I have only on rare occasion been willing to confront the doctrines I have been taught. However, it is an imperative in the course of my transformation.

As I stated earlier, this type of questioning comes with an element of guilt. The presence of this guilt has become an intriguing subject throughout this chapter. I have spent a significant amount of time examining why I should feel guilty about questioning my religious and spiritual foundations. I have found that some of the guilt is imposed from teachers in my past who demanded blind faith and taught to simply believe, do not question. This, in reality, is erroneous since I truly believe a faith that cannot withstand questioning cannot stand. This illuminates the difference between my feelings and my knowing.

I have discovered it is important to examine why I feel what I feel, and ask whether that feeling is logical, rational, or even Biblical. Dr. Albert Ellis (1973) developed Rational Emotive Behaviour Therapy which deals directly with the conflicts between feelings and rational thoughts. As a Counselling Psychologist I have studied this theory in-depth, yet I am still finding areas of unconscious irrational thinking. Another origin of my guilt is fear. This is not something I readily or easily admit, yet it is undeniable.

Fear can be dangerous. In speaking of man's relationship to animals, but equally applicable to other human beings, Native American Salish Chief Dan George (1974) said, "If you talk to the animals they will talk with you and you will know each other. If you do not talk to them, you will not know them and what you do not know, you will *fear*. What one *fears*, one destroys" (p. 25). Fear underpins my sense of guilt because I know if I question my beliefs, I have the potential of finding answers that may conflict with those beliefs. If that were so, my entire life course would be interrupted. While I am intellectually and emotionally confident in my spiritual foundations, I understand the dramatic impact this journey will have on life. If fear, based on ignorance, is the beginning of conflict, then relationships and understanding of the "other" can bring harmony.

The present pages in the story of my life are of a journey to Mexico. Not necessarily in a physical sense, but in a psychological, emotional, and spiritual sense. I am a pastor and a counsellor. My sphere of influence includes a congregation of approximately two-hundred, a weekly television program with a potential audience of approximately one-million, counselling clients, and organizational consulting clients as well. As such, I have opportunity for influencing, potentially, a significant population. My desire is to make a significant impact not only in my immediate circles, but literally in the world. In writing this chapter, I have come to the realization that I can begin here and now.

While I still hold strongly to my Christian beliefs, I have begun a transformation. This transformation includes seeing the "other" not as an impersonal enemy agenda, but an individual. A Muslim, who is a classmate, a brother-in-law, or a neighbour, is much less of an enemy than some abstract agenda. In reflecting upon the "other" in light of New Testament Scripture, I considered the attitudes and actions of the founder of Christianity, Jesus. In Luke 6:27-39 of the New Testament, Jesus taught, "love your enemies, do good to those who hate you, bless those who curse you, pray for those who mistreat you".

This teaching does not fit with the message of angry outcries against those who are Muslim. Jesus' message was one of love, not anger, except when dealing with leaders of his own Jewish faith who were hypocritical. In Luke 20:45-47, Jesus spoke harshly against the hypocritical religious leaders.

It is when looking through a new and evolved lens, that I see Jesus himself spent most of his time with the "other". He sought out relationships with those who were different like the woman at the well in John 4, and Zaccheus, a tax collector in Luke 19.

In the story of "me," I have found the necessity of re-visiting the foundations of all I believe and what I consider truth. This investigation is simultaneously confusing, enlightening, anxiety-producing, and exciting. While considering my hermeneutical framework, I am making an effort to interpret the words and actions of Jesus with renewed understanding. I am sifting through preconceptions and previous teachings and searching for truth and meaning.

Postscript

"From Texas to Mexico via London." Texas represents the opening chapters in my story where I spent many years with a dualistic, ego-centric, religio-centric world-view. Somewhat ironically, Mexico is not all that far from where I grew up. In fact, it is estimated that in this century Texas and California will be majority Mexican-American. However, in my story, Mexico represents the "other": the Muslim, Mexican-American, African-American, Jordanian, African, Chinese, Taiwanese and the French. Mexico symbolizes people from different religious convictions, cultures, and languages who are human beings. These human beings are not all that different from me. They are

not an enemy to be feared, they are souls to be revered. London, specifically the University of Buckingham, is far from home, and it has been a long journey to this point in my story. It is London that represents the present point in my story. It is the place of transition, awakening, and evolution. I do not believe I have yet reached Mexico, but I am on the journey, and I am eagerly anticipating the next chapter in the story of my life.

The story of the ITSM began with a M.Sc. course I taught on hermeneutics at the University of Buckingham early in my Ph.D. work. Resulting from the discussions in this class, I changed the direction of my research and ultimately developed the concept of the Interpretive Transcultural Storytelling Method. The following chapter chronicles the genesis of the ITSM.

References:

Bible. *The New International Version,* (1984). Grand Rapids, MI: Zondervan Publishing House.

Eck, Diana L. (2003). *Encountering God: A Spiritual Journey from Bozeman to Banaras.* Boston: Beacon Press.

Ellis A., & Sagarin E., (Ed.). (1973). *Humanistic Psychotherapy: The Rational-Emotive Approach.* New York : Julian Press.

George, Chief Dan (1974). *My Heart Soars.* Surrey, B.C: Hancock House Publishers, Ltd.

Hofstede, Geert. (2001). *Culture's consequences: Comparing values, behaviours, institutions, and organizations across nations, 2nd Edition.* Thousand Oaks, CA: Sage Publications.

Kimball, Charles. (2002). *When Religion Becomes Evil.* San Francisco: Harper San Francisco.

Randall, William Lowell. (1995). *The Stories We Are: An Essay on Self-Creation.* Toronto: University of Toronto Press.

Chapter 8
Genesis of the ITSM

Having now provided methodological, method, literary, and researcher context of the ITSM, the present chapter provides a historical context of its development. The Interpretive Transcultural Storytelling Method is the result of an evolution of my Ph.D. work. Originally, the direction of my research was centred on leadership. This topic would be evaluated in light of great religious leaders of the world's most significant religions. As I began the research and writing, I was encouraged by my supervisors to refine the very broad topic.

The direction then modulated to how studying these religious leaders and their teachings may bring world peace. Again, this topic was extremely broad and needed to be narrowed and refined, but a new direction was evasive. Following is an orientation to the genesis and evolution of the ITSM. The names of the participants have been used with their prior consent. Frank and Jeff, however, adopted Western names while at Buckingham so those are the names by which they will be referred.

The University of Buckingham M.Sc. Module

In October 2004, I had the opportunity to teach a four day module on hermeneutics for the Masters of Science programme in Socio-economic Transformation. The programme is directed by Dr. Ronnie Lessem in the School of Business at the University of Buckingham. Participating in the module were two Taiwanese men, a Chinese woman, a French woman, an American woman, and Dr. Lessem.

This M.Sc. programme is conceptually unique as it is developed to function, in essence, as a group M.Sc. The students were expected to complete many of the assignments as a group project, rather than individually. Throughout the programme, which began in January of 2004, the students experienced a number of challenges in working together. Some of the challenges may have stemmed from personality differences, but culture played a profound role. This became even more apparent in the course of this module.

I began the module with an overview of the history, ontology, and epistemology of hermeneutics. A core concept of hermeneutics is that of a prejudiced researcher. In the more experimental and positivistic methodologies, the researcher strives for objectivity. Hermeneutics recognizes that this is difficult at best. The methodology incorporates the researcher's biases into the research. The key is for the researcher to recognize those biases. "Every act of hermeneutic understanding begins with a pre-understanding, which orients the inquirer to the text or topic.

One of the tasks of the hermeneutic scholar is to become aware of and reflexively explicate this pre-understanding in a way that creatively feeds into the process of understanding itself" (McLeod, 2001, p.23). Hermeneutics was originally developed as a methodology for Biblical interpretation, and later for researching literature. It is presently evolving as a methodological choice within the social sciences. During the module, we attempted to understand ourselves and others by considering the "self-as-a-story". Each person was to consider his or her own story. This would help engage self-understanding, a basic premise in hermeneutics.

The group participated in exercises to help the participants understand themselves. First, I asked them, "What are your dreams, or your goals in life?" Jan, an American, and Ludivine, a French woman, had no difficulty answering the question. However, Frank and Jeff, Taiwanese men, and Ying, a Chinese woman, could not answer the question. They did not understand the question. Jeff expressed that his plan was to return to Taiwan to take over his family business. I asked if that was what he "wanted to do." He replied, "That is what I am expected to do." I again asked if that was his dream. He said that he was born to take over his family's business.

After much discussion, the participants and I realized that the question was not an appropriate question for these students. The Easterner's "individual" dreams were enveloped in the context of their families and societies. The Westerners found the lack of personal dreams appalling. They argued that the Chinese and Taiwanese students had been deprived, that it was wrong these individuals could not be *individuals*.

The following exercise was the Components of the Self worksheet. The participants were asked to rate each item's significance pertaining to the composition of their personal identities. Each person, including Dr. Lessem and myself, completed the worksheet. When the group began to reveal the items rated as having the most influence, a significant distinction arose between the Westerners and the Easterners. The individuals from the West scored highest, the items relating to personal, individual factors. However, those from the East scored the societal, cultural, and familial factors higher. Among the three highest rated factors, no correlation between the East and West was revealed.

The Spectral Management Type Inventory (SMTI) (Lessem, 1993) was administered to each of the participants. This inventory correlates the individual's personality to colour spectrums which in turn identify typologies of management styles. The SMTI was used to aid the emergence of self-understanding, as well as a platform for discussion. The students had taken the inventory previously and some had changed to one degree or another. The following discussion allowed colleagues to give input to, and ask questions of, each other regarding the results of the inventory. This process, again, provided a valuable tool for investigating the self and building understanding of each of the participants.

The significance of the exercises in this module was the discussion which aided understanding of self and others, not the revelation of quantitative results. Each participant in the module had previously been keenly aware of the differences between the East and West, and the impact those differences potentially could have upon their team efforts. However, during this dialogue, the concrete revelation of those differences illuminated the root of a variety of issues the students had encountered during the several months they had been working on team assignments.

The next segment of the module involved narrative or storytelling. Each participant was asked to share a personal story that would help the others understand more about them. No participant was obligated to share, and each was encouraged to share only to the level they felt comfortable. Their story could be told using pictures, diagrams, written or it could be told orally. Each participant had a unique way of telling their story. For example, Ludivine used diagrams, Ying used pictures and metaphors, and Jan, Frank, and Jeff told their stories orally. Each story gave a transparent and intimate window into the lives of each person, allowing a greater understanding of each individual.

Frank, one of the Taiwanese men, told of an experience he had in school. His instructor hit him on the hand with a ruler, bad enough to leave a permanent scar, for not performing adequately in his studies. He told how he reported this to his father. His father, instead of being his advocate to the instructor, gave the instructor permission to continue this type of punishment if Frank did not do his best. During the story and in previous discussions, Frank referred to his father as the emperor of his family. The Westerners expressed how this comparison seemed "cold" and "un-fatherly". Their concept of a father had different connotations. That this was a cultural issue was apparent when the other Taiwanese and the Chinese students readily identified with the analogy. The Eastern students also understood the drive Frank's father placed upon him to excel in school.

The woman from China, Ying, told of how she was expected to excel in her academics as well, and how disappointed her mother had been on an occasion when she had not done her best. Ying told how she studied so much after that experience, that she ruined her eyes and now has to wear glasses as a result. All three of the Eastern students told of how they studied and went to school up to fourteen hours each day, and how demanding their parent's expectations were for them to excel. The Western students had a very difficult time understanding the pressure these students had been under. Some expressed how they felt this pressure cruel and unwarranted, but the Easterners accepted it as part of life. I was in awe of the transparency with which the students shared their thoughts and feelings. The differences of the frames of reference each person had, was illuminating. Although each of the participants had knowledge of cultural differences, the personal stories gave life to those differences, enhancing the students' interpersonal as well as multicultural understanding.

The final project for the module was a group paper which shared the personal stories of each student and the story of the evolution of the group as a whole. Each story was written incorporating each student's unique stylistic elements such as diagrams and metaphors, yet was cohesive and demonstrated the team's ability to work corporately while maintaining individuality. The paper required the students to reflect critically upon the development of their team and to work on a project which demonstrated their ability to function as a cohesive team. Within the story of the M.Sc. group, each individual surfaced in context of the group. This project ultimately demonstrated an

Eastern paradigm that individuals have meaning within the context of the collective.

Final Project of the Module

The student's project represented a synthesis of their understanding and development, both individually and corporately over the year and throughout the module. As the project began, the students spoke of the lessons learned from being stretched, comparing these lessons to suffering. In the opening lines the paper draws on Buddhist philosophy. This immediately sets the cooperative, collectivistic timbre of the project, being actually typed by Jan, the American, but representing the group's diverse philosophical paradigms.

Within the project, the students were remarkably adept at examining the thoughts and feelings of each individual, yet retaining the story of the group as an evolving entity. "It wasn't until this day in October [following the module] as we sat reflecting upon our stories, that we learned just how varied and deep our emotions actually ran. We have now formed a close friendship and partnership and have become co-creators in a way that was never imaginable to us on that first day". In this statement the students summarize their initial, individual feelings of the joint Master's programme. Each student entered the programme with different anticipations and concerns.

The group evolved from strangers to friends, partners, and co-creators. Within the empirical methodological framework, this statement by the group is immeasurable and improvable. There are no graphs, surveys, nor any other quantitative instruments which positively identify how much their partnership evolved, or the ultimate quality or efficiency of their cooperative co-creativeness. It is in matters like this that hermeneutics is differentiated from empirical methodologies. Hermeneutics is not designed to quantify the results, rather to gain new understanding. In this case, the new understanding is within the realm of a group of people who have, over a period of time, grown in knowledge of themselves and each other to become a cooperative team. Regardless of the lack of quantifiable results of whether or not the group actually performed better, the members of the group expressed their belief that real, meaningful growth had been accomplished: "In the end, we feel strong, happy, and excited to begin our next phase of our lives separately, but together".

Following the introduction, the students identified the initial thoughts each had when the programme began. Jeff, along with most of the others, was not thrilled with the idea of a programme that incorporated group work as a central theme. "Jeff was angry and felt a panic rise within him. He did not foresee that he would have any valid role within our group and frankly, he had no desire to develop such a role". Frank was also unhappy with the emphasis group work was to play within the context of the programme. Both Jeff and Frank desired to simply get a "normal" Master's degree. Jan was excited about the programme, but apprehensive about how she would be accepted as a forty year old. She also felt she would be more productive working solo. Ludivine entered the programme anticipating the community that would develop within the group, and Ying wanted to make everyone happy. The reactions of each person toward working in a group setting resulted from both cultural and individual historical roots.

Jeff and Frank were at Buckingham to receive a Western Master's degree so they could go back to Taiwan and fulfil their obligations to the family businesses, and both were also fulfilling the wills of their fathers. Jeff and Frank, within their contexts, were two men with an agenda to accomplish. The group emphasis simply added to the complexity of achieving their goals. Without understanding the context within which both of these gentlemen were grounded, an unwarranted assumption could have been made regarding their interest, motivation, or cooperativeness.

For Jan, the excitement of the programme was clouded by a bit of apprehension of her age and her ability to work efficiently in a group. She could have been viewed as resistant or stand-offish. Ludivine is culturally rooted in a very social society. Community and relationships are important to her. Ying's desire to please others is rooted from an experience she had as a child when she disappointed her mother by not doing her best in school. She vowed to never disappoint her mother again, and she realizes that this vow affects present relationships as well. Context is vital in hermeneutics.

Understanding the cultural and historical roots of others is necessary in interpreting their behaviours and words. A clear and contextual self-understanding is also important in the process of discovering new understanding. Aristotle said that all knowledge is birthed from previously existing knowledge. Through writing their individual and corporate stories, the M.Sc. group was forced to reckon with self-knowledge and its impact upon understanding the others within the group.

The first project for the M.Sc. programme was a group assignment. Jan, the most individualistic of the group, immediately began to observe the cultural and language barriers that were being transcended by the common goal and cooperativeness of the group. During their first assignment, the group recognized their co-creative synergy.

The story of the M.Sc. group progresses to a day when Dr. Lessem posed a question to the group. The students had a difficult time understanding the question, so each one averted their eyes. After a time of silence, Ludivine stepped out and attempted to answer. Utilizing a white board and markers, at Dr. Lessem's request, Ludivine began drawing charts and diagrams.

"The lines, structures, and shapes came to her brain as she visualized what was going on. For the first time, she felt that she was able to express what she was seeing in her mind". Ludivine had found her voice, a very personal and effective form of communication. When she shared this experience with her father, he told her he had recognized this gift in her even when she was young. This self-discovery proved to be a valuable asset in the continuing work of the M.Sc. group as a whole, but also provided valuable self-insight for Ludivine. This discovery is valuable because she now recognizes her visual nature and that diagrams are a viable and effective way for her to be understood and for her to understand others.

Ying's experience in identifying her personal preference for communication was equally as profound. Having studied for four previous years in a traditional Western environment, "her imaginal world had crashed with the rational, conceptual world". Ying's father trained her in traditional Chinese philosophies and the relation of man to nature. By using metaphors, Ying discovered she could communicate her thoughts more effectively.

Frank is an artist. He had attended art school as a young person, but his art gradually gave way to other studies. During the M.Sc. programme, Frank re-discovered his talent and passion for communicating through pictures. The group described this ability as Frank producing "a snapshot in time. He puts the spoken words from the group into pictures".

The identification of the communication preferences of these individuals is valuable hermeneutically because it helps them to contextualize their own communication styles and to interpret the communication of others with this knowledge. The hermeneutic axiom that there can be no knowledge without self-knowledge, applies equally to areas of styles or preferred methods of communicating. Throughout the final project, the group utilized the various preferred forms of communicating by including many graphs, metaphors, and pictures into the story of their corporate transformation. The variety of these styles within the group was recognized and the attitude was adopted that each person had a particular role to play and a particular gift to offer the group as whole.

As the story unfolds, the paper tells of Jeff's victory in winning a contract with a Dutch company and then the crushing blows of insecurities. He relied heavily upon the support and encouragement of the group and realized that even if his insecurities were justified, the opportunity gave him a chance to prove himself. Jeff realized that through the cooperative efforts of the group, "he was doing something important for his father and his family as well".

Frank, initially sceptical of the group emphasis in the programme eventually found meaning and fulfilment in the process of the group work. "Through this joint venture he felt he was doing something important for his father and his family as well". The hermeneutic implications of this statement are profound. Originally, Frank's context of the M.Sc. programme was strictly pragmatic. He desired to get his degree and move on. He gradually began to believe in the group process, and in fact, the process became as meaningful as the outcome. Frank said, "To me the unforgettable experience was not the result; it was the process of us producing the presentation."

Throughout the programme he began to find himself in the context of a group, in essence a new family, or at a minimum a new team. This cooperative programme introduced Frank to another paradigm; one in which he was part of group other than his family, his family's business, and even that of the Taiwanese people as a whole. Frank had entered into a group of people who eventually evolved into a team with a vision to have a synergistic impact upon society. Frank's experience is common across the sum of the M.Sc. participants. Each came within a particular context and focused on a particular purpose.

The group, in essence, created their own cultural context, one rooted in the cultures of each participant and simultaneously transcending those cultures. An example of the group's evolving culture maintaining the roots of individual culture is the repeated use of Chinese philosophy within the group's final project. For example, the paper begins with a quote from Buddhism. In this new culture, new roles were developed by each participant, and new ways of communicating evolved.

The communication purposefully emerged as the students recognized the innate gifts and styles of each individual. Within each project, the students relied upon each of these styles and roles to surface in a co-creating manner. The final project for this module is an example of the incorporation of the different communication specialties each student possessed. Within the context of this particular group, creating new knowledge was emphasized, for example, the students created a new model of multicultural group development, the UAACT: Understanding, Acceptance, Appreciate, Co-create, and finally Terminate.

In concluding the final paper, the students expressed a desire to continue the work they had begun in the M.Sc. programme. This mindset is bipolar to that of most of the students at the beginning of the programme. They transformed into a team with a new culture, and a vision to co-creatively impact the world, not just earn a degree.

Synthesis and Implications

Resulting from the dialogue during this module, a new understanding of each member of the team emerged. This understanding, or knowledge, was of the others in the group, the group as a whole, and the individuals of themselves. Each student expressed how valuable this module would have been at the beginning of their team M.Sc. rather than near the end. The consensus was that such a module would have enhanced their efficiency in working corporately.

Following the module, Dr. Lessem and I discussed what had transpired. We agreed a new direction for my research had been revealed. While multicultural literature and research abounds, an apparent gap exists in the present material and the application in building multicultural teams. I then decided to dedicate my research to the practice of developing understanding among teams, specifically, multicultural teams. Since hermeneutics was developed for the purpose of Biblical interpretation, evolved to incorporate all literature, and is presently evolving to the social sciences, storytelling surfaced as a natural method.

The purpose of my research evolved to the utilization of storytelling/ narrative and hermeneutic principles to assist teams in building relationships which will transcend culture and increase the efficiency with which they work. The following chapter will provide a brief review of the inception, revision, and application of the Interpretive Transcultural Storytelling Method.

References:

McLeod, John. (2001). *Qualitative research in counselling and psychotherapy.* London: Sage Publications.

Chapter 9
ITSM: Conception, Revision and Application

As stated in the previous chapter, the direction of my Ph.D. research has evolved from my initial direction on leadership. Throughout the fieldwork process, the ITSM has also undergone substantial revisions in function and form. The title of the method has been modified from the Interpretive Transcultural Method (ITM) to the Interpretive Transcultural Storytelling Method (ITSM). In the beginning, the stages or steps were primary, and the method of storytelling was secondary. Eventually, I recognized the influence of my positivistic foundations in the linear, objective nature the model originally took. Throughout the fieldwork exercises, the autobiographical storytelling proved to be the significant contribution, while the communication model became the support framework of the storytelling. Therefore, Storytelling was added to the title.

Storytelling began merely as a vehicle in which to conduct the ITSM model: In-Spection, Expression, Interpretation, Clarification, Understanding, and Emergence. In addition, each stage of the model has sub-stages of topsoil, subsoil, bedrock, and core. As the fieldwork progressed the model became difficult to track because of its subjective and cyclical nature. In addition, each workshop consisted of several individuals and the identification of where each individual was in the process became impossible to identify. In short, it did not work. While participants consistently praised the value of the communication model, the actual storytelling process exhibited the most substantial benefit to the teams. Therefore, throughout the fieldwork chapters, the evolution of the storytelling process to the primary role within the research will be detected, with the secondary emphasis being placed upon the communication model.

In practice, the participants are encouraged to become aware of where they are in the stages and topography of communication model at all times. Participants are asked to enter into dialogue with the storyteller. This dialogical process will bring the participants through the stages of the ITSM.

In summation, storytelling has risen to the primary focus of the research and the communication model has become an embedded framework for making the stories more meaningful to the team. In this chapter, I will address the conception of the ITM, which later became the ITSM, its revision, and its application. Elements from the actual fieldwork exercises will be incorporated in this chapter.

The ITSM is grounded in autobiographical storytelling and is built on a framework which, in its essence, encourages the hermeneutic process through: In-Spection, Expression, (Reception), Interpretation, Clarification, Understanding, and Emergence. The levels of communication in the model were primarily developed conceptually from a review of the developmental stages of the M.Sc. module, psychology, hermeneutics, and from the work of William Randall (1995). Following is an analysis of each stage of the ITSM.

Interpretive Transcultural Storytelling Method Model

In-Spection:
Discovering personal context. Use of Components of the Self, Trompenaars & Hampden-Turner questions to initiate self exploration and understanding
Existence: The Outside Story
Experience: The Inside story
The hermeneutic concept of Contextualization & Dasein

Expression:
The Inside-Out Story (Randall, 1997)
Telling the Story
Randall's Expression

Interpretation:
Attribute meaning to the story of another in context of self and the storyteller.
The hermeneutic process of intentional interpretation

Clarification:
Dialogue between listeners and the storyteller to clarify misinterpretations.
The hermeneutic Spiral & Dialogical Reasoning
Impression: The outside-in story

Understanding:
Storyteller and listener agree that understanding has been reached. Listener understands his or her contextual influence.
The hermeneutic Verstehen

Emergence
What cultural differences have emerged?
How can we maximize these differences within our team's context?
The new knowledge and understanding that has been developed from the dialogues revolving around each of the participants' stories results in synergistic and transformational emergence of the organization, individuals, and ultimately society.
The hermeneutic Fusion of Horizons

1. In-Spection

The initial stage of In-Spection emphasises introspection and self-knowledge. As a counselling psychologist, I was trained to be aware of my prejudice and my biases. Within hermeneutics, self-knowledge is primary to interpretation. The interpreter is to be aware of his or her preconceived ideas and to take those into account when trying to gain understanding. "Every act of hermeneutic understanding begins with a pre-understanding, which orients the inquirer to the text or topic.

One of the tasks of the hermeneutic scholar is to become aware of and reflexively explicate this pre-understanding in a way that creatively feeds into the process of understanding itself" (McLeod, 2001, p.23). In addition to a philosophical, psychological, and hermeneutic foundation, In-Spection is built upon the work of Randall's, The Stories We Are (1995). Randall presents four levels of reflecting upon our lives as stories: existence, experience, expression, and impression (p. 48).

Existence and experience rely upon introspection, or as I have termed it, In-Spection. I have chosen to use the term In-Spection to accentuate the concept of inspecting inwardly. Clearly, Randall sees the value of self reflection in the process of telling one's story. In the ITSM, I have incorporated self-knowledge as a foundation for properly interpreting the story of another as well. Within the process of the ITSM, individuals both tell their stories and hear stories from their colleagues. In-Spection, as it relates to telling your story is best reflected in Randall's existence and experience.

Randall refers to existence as the actual historical facts, or "what actually happened in the past" (Randall, 1995, p. 48). Randall states, "In general, the whole story of my life is the uninterpreted, unevaluated, unavailable totality of all the minutiae of my particular existence in time and space- in so far as that can be separated from the existence of everything else- as it might be inscribed in utter detail on some cosmic recording device, whether a colossal computer or the mind of Glover's 'objective God.' In 'objective' terms, it is the *outside* story" (Randall, 1995, p. 49).

Understanding one's life solely through facts is relevant in understanding one's own story, but hermeneutically can only be relevant to a small degree. If an individual can never truly block his or her own prejudgments, then seeking understanding by examining only the facts has limited value. Regardless of how one might try, he or she will always interpret those facts in light of bias. Randall understands that we are an accumulation of all of our previous experiences. He quotes Tennyson who said, "I am a part of all that I have met" (Randall, 1995, p. 49). Existence is highly correlated to the stage of Reception, which appeared originally in the ITSM. As the ITSM has evolved, the concept of Reception has been omitted as it is fundamentally inconsistent with hermeneutic theory.

The concept of Reception within the ITSM was built upon hearing the factual content of the story of another person without any preconceived ideas or interpretations. Having been trained in empirical and positivistic methodologies in my Master's and undergraduate education, I have continually fought the temptation to revert. A positivistic empirical methodology would encourage an objective observer blocking out personal bias and hearing a story's factual content alone.

However, hermeneutics teaches it is impossible to block out one's preconceptions. The idea that a person is able to hear a story and not filter it through his or her experience is contrary to hermeneutic methodology. (McLeod, 2001) The argument that objective events happen is inarguable, however, whether an individual is able to contemplate those events without simultaneously interpreting them is debatable. Existence, then, whether it relates to the facts of one's personal history or another's story being told, has some value, but only within context.

Randall's concept of experience is strongly correlated to hermeneutic thought. Experience is the actual interpretation of one's existence. In essence, experience makes meaning out of existence. Randall quotes psychologist Robert Kegan who states experience is "that most human of 'regions' *between* an event and a reaction to it- the place where the event is privately composed, made sense of, the place where it actually becomes an event for that person" (Randall, 1995, p. 50). For Randall, then, and for the process of the ITSM, existence is the event, and experience is the attribution of meaning to the event. Within this context existence and experience can be seen as harmonious to hermeneutics.

Ron, a Native American participant in the Family Counselling Centre (FCC) fieldwork modules exhibited the relationship of existence and experience:

> He told of how, as a child, he was called nigger, savage, and a variety of other derogatory names. This added to his reaction against his heritage. He was ashamed to be a Native American and tried to adopt the look and culture of his adopted family. Throughout his childhood and early adulthood, he maintained limited contact with his biological family, so he has always had an occasional reminder of his true ethnicity and cultural heritage. Ron shared that only in his mid thirties did he begin to explore his heritage.

Ron's existence was the hazing of children. He was called names and persecuted because he was a Native American. Ron's experience, or interpretation of the facts, was that he should be ashamed of his heritage and that he should try and remove himself from any association with his biological family and their culture. Only in his mid-thirties did Ron begin to re-interpret, or assign new meaning, to his existence and call into question his previous experience.

Within the ITSM, I have chosen to utilize a Components of the Self worksheet (Appendix 3, in the Fieldwork Packet) and some of the questions utilized in the research conducted by multicultural experts, Trompenaars and Hampden-Turner (Appendix 3, in the Fieldwork Packet). The Components of the Self worksheet has been adapted from the work of Dr. Judith Rathbone of University College London. The Trompenaars and Hampden-Turner questions are from their research.

The work of Trompenaars and Hampden-Turner focuses on the reconciliation of, specifically, seven dimensions of culture discovered in their research. Their research began with questioning whether or not the predominate American techniques and philosophies of management could be applied in other cultures. The authors begin with the premise, "It is our belief that you can never understand other cultures" (Trompenaars and Hampden-Turner, 1998, p. 1). They also set forth as a premise that the understanding of "our own culture and our own assumptions and expectations about how people 'should' think and act is the basis for success" (Trompenaars and Hampden-Turner, 1998, p. 2). This assumption is foundational in hermeneutics in which interpretation of the "other" begins with an understanding of the self.

2. Expression

Following In-Spection, Expression is the actual telling of a personal, autobiographical story. One of Randall's four levels of storytelling, Expression is the "Inside-Out Story" (Randall, 1995, p. 54). Randall (1995) cites Kaufman:

> "If the first level is the outside story, the totality of my existence, and the second is the inside story, the totality of

my experience, then the third level is the level of each individual version of my inside story that I convey to other, what I choose to call the *inside-out* story. It is 'my life' in the sense of what I present or project to the world. It is my 'life-story' as I communicate it to others. (p. 54)

Through storytelling, the teller's interpretation of his own experiences is transformed. "Just as the events of my life are changed in the experiencing, then, so the experiences of my life are changed in the expressing" (Randall, 1995, p. 55). So, as storytelling has been elicited as the mechanism for emergence of new, synergistic knowledge for a multicultural group, it is also a personally transformative mechanism for the storyteller.

Expression is encouraged, but not required of all participants within a workshop. The level of intimacy and the length of the participants' stories are at their discretion. Each person is requested to share a story lasting approximately five to ten minutes which will give the listeners a window into an event that has contributed to their personal development. Randall (1995) states:

> To qualify as a story… at least three things are required: first, a storyteller, which means a person by whom it is authored and a point of view (and thus a voice) through which it is narrated; second, a character or set of characters…; and third, a plot, which means the framework that lays out whatever these characters do, the actions in which they engage, and the situations and conflicts with which they must cope. (p. 86)

As an example, in Lisa's story (MFWI Fieldwork Chapter), we find all of the qualifications Randall sets forth. As the storyteller, it is Lisa's voice we hear and her interpretations that are presented. The list of characters includes Lisa, her grandfather, her sisters, her mother, and, to a lesser degree, her father. The plot, or story line, is Lisa's struggle to cope with the perpetual pressure her grandfather placed upon her to be the smartest and the best example to her siblings. Within the plot is a mixture of family dynamics including her parents divorce, relationships between Lisa and her sisters, and Lisa's relationships with her mother and grandfather. In telling her story, Lisa addressed some cultural implications such as the emphasis of respecting elders in the Japanese culture. When Lisa was asked by one of the listeners to elaborate on how the value of respect affected her relationship to her grandfather, Lisa said that even when she did not speak to him, she was always respectful in his presence.

3. Interpretation

In hearing the story of another, the listener is invited into a personal world and given a glimpse of a variety of elements including the teller's culture, belief system, core values, significant developmental events, and others. Since hermeneutically listening to another's story is reflexive, the listener is encouraged to continually move between what he or she is hearing and his or her own experiences. The hermeneutic process requires active self-reflection while simultaneously trying to hear the story in the context in which is being told. Understanding that the teller of a story comes from a different paradigm, the listener is challenged to find common and contrasting meanings of the teller's story.

In the ITSM workshop, the participants are asked to listen hermeneutically, which incorporates reflexively moving back and forth between the teller's context, as the listener understands it, and his or her own context. Throughout the story, the listeners are also encouraged to make notes of the topography of the expression and to cultural distinctions as well.

4. Clarification

The Clarification phase is a dialogue between the listeners and the storyteller. In this phase questions may be asked and statements made which will enable the listeners to have a better understanding of the context of the story and clarification of aspects they did not understand. In addition, the listeners are able to share similar or contrasting personal experiences. In the Clarification process, the participants are free to discuss cultural factors as well. For example, in Lisa's story, it was during the Clarification phase that a listener asked Lisa to address the Japanese value of respecting the elders and how Lisa reconciled that value with not speaking to her grandfather. Also in this stage, Lisa was asked about the emphasis her grandfather placed on her being the "best". Discussion revolved around the drive for success within the whole of Japanese society and how that compares to the culture of the United States.

This stage in the ITSM correlates to the level of Randall's (1995) Impression: The outside-in story. Impression is, "'my life' in the sense of what is *made* of me by others. It is my 'life-story' in the sense of what is *told* of me by others" (p. 56). Randall compares the outside-in story to a biography. During the Clarification phase, the participants are encouraged to tell the story they have heard in their own words and through their experiences. As these biographies are told, the original storyteller makes clarifications as needed. In considering the value of storytelling in relationships, Randall (1995) states:

> In this case, she may read a story into an event in my life that bears little or no relation to the story I read into it myself. It may be a story based on ignorance or gossip or prejudice; or a story that is largely her own, a projection of her own memories and expectations, *'storyotypes'* and biases: a variation on a particular version of- or episode

in- the story of *her* life rather than mine. ...Indeed, variations in stories constitute one of the commonest sources of conflict in human affairs on all levels, from individuals in intimate relationship to entire societies. Every side in every conflict is telling a different story. (p.107)

Of special attention in this stage is the focus of the ITSM in assisting team members to communicate and understand each other more effectively, not to resolve specific disagreements. The assumption is that development of communication techniques through the storytelling process will provide a framework in which to work through disagreements, or variations of a story, within organizations. Clarification is a cyclical dialogue which moves back and forth between self understanding, understanding of the context of the storyteller, and the story itself.

5. Understanding

As Clarification cycles back and forth, a mutual Understanding, or *Verstehen,* is ultimately, and ideally, achieved. This Understanding is based upon the listeners and the storyteller wrestling with contextual factors such as cultural, personal, and ideological. Within the context of hermeneutics rests an assumption that a pure and complete understanding of the story of another cannot truly be achieved. However, what is strived for is the best possible understanding.

In revisiting Lisa's story, the statement is made that she did not speak to her grandfather for over a year. An American listener heard this in context of his own experience. His mother and grandmother were estranged for about three years. During that time there was literally no communication. When this was shared with the group, Lisa replied that she did communicate to a degree. The Japanese value of respecting elders was important to her. Instead of rudely ignoring direct questions or being impolite, Lisa meant that she simply did not go out of her way to have conversations, or to place herself in situations where she would have contact with him more than necessary. The American and Lisa wrestled through the contextual pre-understandings to the point at which they agreed a mutual understanding had been achieved. Understanding results in the identification of new knowledge.

6. Emergence

Storytelling is utilized in the ITSM because of its transformative nature. Not only is the teller transformed through storytelling, but so are the listeners. Hearing someone else's story helps the listeners understand the teller better, and the group transforms through the dialogical, hermeneutic spiral process. New understanding surfaces throughout the ITSM process and the final stage is the intentional identification of new knowledge which will enable the team to work more cooperatively and synergistically. In this phase the questions of "So what?" and "Who cares?" are addressed. We ask, "What cultural differences have emerged?" and "How can we maximize these differences within our team's context?" The new knowledge and understanding that has been developed from the dialogues revolving around each of the participants' stories results in a transformational emergence of the organization, individuals, and ultimately society. Emergence is synonymous with the concept of "fusion of horizons" in hermeneutics. Fusion of horizons, in essence, is the bringing together of different frames of reference to a place where all parties have a picture of the same view, or where each person is looking at the same horizon. The aim of Emergence is not to diminish differences, specifically in our case, cultural differences. Rather, the goal is to assist each participant in gaining an understanding of the various differences and, as a team, identifying how those differences may in fact be assets instead of liabilities. Emergence is an intentional identification of new knowledge and ways in which application of knew knowledge can be capitalized.

In the Mukogawa Fort Wright Institute fieldwork exercise in which Lisa participated, one of the factors that Emerged stemmed from Lisa's story. Dealing with conflict in Japanese culture, as demonstrated by Lisa and her grandfather, is sometimes very different from dealing with conflict in the United States, as demonstrated by the American's mother and grandmother. With Lisa as the model, the Japanese manner is to be courteous and respectful, while the American's example was to totally ignore the other. This fusion of horizons led to a discussion of how this new knowledge would influence the group. As a team the individuals agreed that an intentional adoption of a more Japanese practice would be beneficial to building a synergistic team environment. In essence, a new corporate culture emerged from this new understanding. Emergence is consequently the application of new knowledge.

Conclusion

The communication between colleagues can be enhanced through exercises in autobiographical storytelling. In hearing the expression of others, individuals can gain insight into the behaviours, communication styles, and cultural factors that have contributed to the manner in which he or she interacts with the world. This insight can be valuable in the development of interpersonal relationships, such as within a business setting. Utilizing the Interpretive Transcultural Storytelling Method, teams can intentionally move through a framework which in essence guides them through a hermeneutic process for finding understanding, and ultimately the Emergence of new knowledge and its application.

Incorporated in the ITSM process is an emphasis on fleshing out cultural differences rather than ignoring them in deference to a common ground approach. Culturally distinct characteristics, as identified by authors such as Lessem, Palsule, Trompenaars, Hampden-Turner, and Hofstede can provide rich soil in which to grow a synergistic and well-rounded team.

The following chapter provides an introduction to the field work exercises of the ITSM. Within the chapter is an overview of the fieldwork cases and the format in which each will be written. Continuing in the hermeneutic and storytelling framework, the fieldwork chapters will be written as a story with a beginning, middle, and end.

References:

McLeod, John. (2001). *Qualitative research in counselling and psychotherapy.* London: Sage Publications.

Randall, William. (1995). *The stories we are: An essay on self-creation.* Toronto: University of Toronto Press.

Trompenaars, Fons & Hampden-Turner, Charles. (1998). *Riding the waves of culture. 2nd Edition.* NY: McGraw-Hill.

Chapter 10
Fieldwork: An Introduction

The fieldwork exercises provided a rich context for the development of the ITSM. Having begun the fieldwork with a model on which I had worked many long hours, I initially found myself resisting revising the ITSM. However, in the workshop with the Private Investigation Firm (PIF), I realized I was stubbornly trying to force the framework to take precedence over the storytelling. Changing the emphasis to storytelling and the secondary emphasis to framework was more of a paradigm shift for me than it was for the teams with which I was working. In the sessions, the storytelling naturally surfaced as primary.

Therefore, I found it necessary to modify my paradigm. This was the major revision to the ITSM. However, throughout the process, several other revisions were made as well. The following chapters chronicling the course of the fieldwork exercises will illuminate the evolution of the ITSM as well as demonstrate the practice of the ITSM in context of actual organizations.

Each of the fieldwork chapters are written in a consistent format mirroring the storytelling model: Beginning, Middle, and End (see Figure: 12:1). Although each fieldwork exercise is unique, the sub-headings in the figure below provide a general framework for each case study. This chapter will describe in more detail how the fieldwork sessions unfolded, but the following chapters on each case will provide the unique character of each of the participating organizations.

Fieldwork Chapter Outline:
1. Beginning:
    - Setting the Scene
    - Introduction of the Cast
    - Introduction to the ITSM
    - Developing the Cast- Self Knowledge

2. Middle:
    - Personal Story Telling
    - Interpreting Stories, Stages & Topography
    - The Unfolding Story of the Team
    - Cultural Elements Emerge:
        - Complimentary (common ground)
        - Contrasting (tension)

3. End:
    - Understanding of Self & Others
    - Emergence of New Knowledge- the characters recognize the value of diversity and develop a plan for working synergistically
    - Evaluation & Analysis

Each fieldwork workshop is unique because of the variety of participating organizations. The number of participants and the length and number of sessions vary with each exercise. However, the approach remains the same with each organization.

The Beginning of each workshop launches with my personal introduction and an overview of the ITSM. The Informed Consent form is then reviewed, and each person is given the freedom to choose whether or not to participate. After the participants have signed the Informed Consent form, we begin with an introduction to hermeneutics. Included in the discussion of hermeneutics are key concepts such as:

- Dasein: *being in the world*, the necessity of self-knowledge and context
- Interpretation: in context of the listener and storyteller

- ❖ Hermeneutic Cycle/ Spiral: the nature of gaining understanding through cycling between personal context and that of the storyteller
- ❖ Verstehen: *understanding*
- ❖ Fusion of horizons: mutual understanding

Also covered in the first meeting is an overview of the communication model presented in the ITSM, including cultural topography. The participants are encouraged to be mindful of the various stages and the topography throughout the sessions. Within each chapter, the ITSM stage and topography is charted by identifying different levels within the dialogue in brackets. For example: [Expression: Depth/ Subsoil] These boxes are subjectively placed, based upon my interpretation of the process. They are intended to be an example of how the participants are encouraged to be aware of the various stages and topography throughout the workshop.

To assist in gaining self-knowledge, and an awareness of dasein (being in the world), the participants are asked to complete the Components of the Self worksheet and the Trompenaars and Hampden-Turner questions prior to the next session.

The second and subsequent sessions (the Middle) correlate to the hermeneutic processes of interpretation, the hermeneutic spiral, and Verstehen (understanding), and fusion of horizons (mutual understanding). During the second session, the participants review the Components of the Self worksheet and the Trompenaars and Hampden-Turner questions. We discuss any significant differences in the Components of the Self worksheet and the Trompenaars and Hampden-Turner questions between the participants within the workshop.

Particular consideration is given to differences that may have a cultural underpinning in order to purposefully identify cultural distinctions and address how those distinctions affect the team. In addition, attention is given to the differences between the answers the participants give and those of the respondents in the Trompenaars and Hampden-Turner research. If significant differences exist between the results of the predominant culture of the present group and those of the Trompenaars and Hampden-Turner respondents, we discuss the possible reasons for those differences.

During the Middle sessions the concept of autobiographical storytelling is also introduced. We discuss the framework of stories having a beginning, middle, and an end. In addition, we discuss Randall's (1997) concepts of:

- ❖ Existence: The Outside Story
- ❖ Experience: The Inside Story
- ❖ Expression: The Inside-Out Story
- ❖ Impression: The Outside-In Story

Considering the above components, the participants are asked to tell an autobiographical story (between five and ten minutes) of an event or situation that has influenced their personal development. The participants are assured that the topographical level of intimacy at which they share, and their participation is at their discretion. The following sessions involve the telling of stories and subsequent dialogue. Often the dialogue spurs the story of another person in the group who has experienced something that compares or contrasts to the storyteller's experience. Attention is continually given to items of possible cultural relevance. When suspected, the facilitator or another member of the group will interrupt and explore the statement for cultural relevance and how it affects the group. Instead of de-emphasising differences and maximizing similarities, which is a common practice in multicultural work, the ITSM intentionally emphasises differences.

In the final session (the End), the participants are asked to discuss the new knowledge and understanding that has been discovered. This correlates to verstehen and the fusion of horizons principles of hermeneutics. Mutual understanding has been achieved and the question now is, "What do we do with what we have learned?" We identify the cultural distinctions and ask how we can maximize these distinctions to make them an asset instead of a liability.

Within the conclusion of each Fieldwork Chapter is an evaluation of the ITSM and consequent revisions to be made in following workshops. The continuum of fieldwork exercises represents the evolution of the ITSM. The following case study chapters are in chronological order.

Fieldwork Chapters:

Chapter 11: Mukogawa Fort Wright Institute (the pilot workshop)

Chapter 12: Private Investigation Firm

Chapter 13: Family Counselling Centre

Chapter 14: Pharmaceutical Manufacturing Firm

References:

McLeod, John. (2001). <u>Qualitative research in counselling and psychotherapy.</u> London: Sage Publications.

Randall, William. (1995). <u>The stories we are: An essay on self-creation.</u> Toronto: University of Toronto Press.

Chapter 11
Field Work Project 1: Mukogawa Fort Wright Institute

Beginning

Setting the Scene

The Pilot exercise of the ITSM took place at Mukogawa Fort Wright Institute (MFWI). It was established in 1990 in Spokane, WA as a branch campus of Mukogawa Women's University (MWU) in Japan. Japanese students typically attend MFWI for fourteen weeks during the Fall or Spring semester. The program is built upon a foundation of total immersion in American culture and the English language.

Introduction of the Cast of Characters

Because of the present research emphasis on transcultural communication and team building, Mukogawa provided a rich context in which to begin the field work. The participants included five Japanese students and two American faculty members. Hanna, Lori, Nina, Lisa, and Maya were selected at random from a larger group of Japanese student volunteers. Sara and Kirk were the participating Americans. The names of all participants have been replaced with fictitious names for confidentiality. The sessions lasted for one hour on three consecutive days, and took place on the MFWI campus. Imposed upon the notes of the session below are text boxes which correlate the discussion with the various ITSM stages. The identification of the stages is strictly subjective due to the qualitative nature of this research. The cyclical nature of hermeneutic understanding is demonstrated by the moving back and forth between the various stages and depths.

Session 1

The first session began with personal introductions and a brief overview of the Interpretive Transcultural Storytelling Method (ITSM). The students found it very difficult to understand much of what I said due to their limited ability to communicate in English. Their willingness and commitment were tremendous assets in light of this communication deficit. Session One revolved primarily around the first step in the Interpretive Transcultural Storytelling Method, In-Spection, (knowing yourself).

Following introductions, we discussed different ways of studying culture, and the desire of each student to fully engage the American experience while they were in Spokane. I explained to the participants that the method employed in the ITSM is specifically oriented to help people become better acquainted with one another, increase the ability to communicate and thereby build a functioning team. I also discussed the theory that an increased awareness and understanding of self and the other, including cultural contexts, would emerge.

During the first session we discussed the importance of self knowledge before attempting to understand another. The discussion of self knowledge included addressing topics such as the collectivist tendencies of traditional Japanese culture compared to the individualist tendencies of traditional American culture. The students had participated in cross-cultural courses before coming to the USA so they were very aware of the stereotypical differences between the two cultures. The American faculty had also been educated on cross-cultural issues.

I distributed a packet of handouts to the participants which included a brief overview of the ITSM, the Components of the Self worksheet (A.4), and the first three questions used by Trompenaars and Hampden-Turner (1998). Only three questions were chosen due to the limited amount of time. The purpose of this research is not to replicate or validate the findings of Trompenaars and Hampden-Turner, rather, to build upon their work by utilizing some of their material to generate understanding.

The participants were briefed on the handouts and asked to complete the Components of the Self worksheet as well as answer the three questions before the next session. Several questions were raised regarding both assignments regarding meanings of certain words, again highlighting the language barrier. After consulting a Japanese-English dictionary and with help from other students the questions were answered and the participants were dismissed.

Debriefing of Session One

Following the session, I met briefly with the American faculty who had orchestrated the on-site fieldwork. We discussed the positive feedback from the students and the excitement and eagerness with which they participated in this session. The overall assessment was that the session had been a positive and educational interaction. The first session was predominately educational with some interaction. My anticipation was that it would be more interactive with some education. Factors that contributed to the more didactic nature of the session were the language barrier and the generally new concepts introduced. Often I would notice a blank stare on the faces of some or all of the students. I would ask, "Do you understand?" and the answer would be a shy and almost embarrassed, "No... sorry." I soon became aware that using clichés such as, "Know what pushes your buttons," should be avoided.

I did not cover as much material as I had anticipated during the first session. Much time was devoted to explaining concepts that most people with a better grasp of English would understand. I came to the conclusion that in future field work, the time allotted for the ITSM would necessarily need to factor in English proficiency.

During the first session I observed some interesting anomalies. The students did not have difficulty understanding the concept of self. I compared their level of understanding to that of the Taiwanese and Chinese students at the University of Buckingham during the genesis of the ITSM. The latter had much difficulty understanding the concept of self. Multicultural literature highly correlates the Asian communities in regards to collectivism. Even the research of Trompenaars and Hampden-Turner found the Japanese to be highly collectivistic, so the readily understood self concept caused me to take note.

Another phenomenon I experienced that conflicted with my knowledge of Japanese culture was the ease with which the young, female, Japanese students interacted with the adult American faculty and me. The students freely disagreed when wrong assumptions were made and they also looked the Americans squarely in the eyes when addressing them. Multicultural literature generally says directness is not a characteristic of the Japanese culture, nor is making eye contact with elders, especially within academic settings. It should be noted that these students have only been in the USA for four months and none of them have been to the USA previous to this visit. Therefore, these apparent discrepancies cannot be attributed to the students' having become Americanized.

Middle

The second session began with much anticipation. The participants arrived energetic and anxious to begin discussion. Each retrieved the Components of the Self worksheet and the handout with the three questions. We began with a quick review of the previous session and asked if there were any questions or comments from the previous time together. Having none, we began with the Components of the Self worksheet. Immediately I observed a marked difference in the Taiwanese and Chinese students' answers (of Buckingham) and those of the present participants. There was little contrast between the answers of the American and Japanese responses.

The most highly ranked components included My Aspirations, My Body, My Education, My Will-power, My Family, My Skills, and My Experiences. We discussed the "Western" nature of their answers, pointing out that "my family" was the only component that did not directly imply a tendency towards individualism, and that there was virtually no difference in their answers and those of the Americans. [Expression: Surface/ Topsoil] The participants seemed to be surprised at this assessment. We discussed the influence of their three months in the USA. I asked, "If you had done the worksheet a year ago, would the answers have been different?" The consensus was possibly, but not probably. I also asked the American faculty, "How much influence has working constantly with Japanese students had upon your answers?" [Understanding: Depth/ Subsoil] The consensus was that there had been potential influence, but there was no way of making the determination of how much.

We concluded that the participants had been mutually influenced, to varying degrees, but that the Japanese students had a strong tendency toward individualism compared to the anticipated results. The discussion proved enlightening as it revealed much about each participant to the others as well as highlighting the commonalities shared between the presumed very different cultures. Each individual also expressed benefit from the insight they developed of themselves, not having consciously realized how fused their culture had become.

We moved, then, to the three questions derived from the work of Trompenaars and Hampden-Turner (1998). The questions incorporated in this exercise are included in Appendix 3 in the Fieldwork Packets.. The results collected by the research of Trompenaars and Hampden-Turner (1998) are compared to those found in the present research in the box following each question. The participants were not aware of the Trompenaars and Hampden-Turner results prior to answering the questions. [In-Spection: Depth/ Subsoil]

Results for question 1. Universalism versus Particularism

USA: 93% no right to expect me to testify to the lower figure- high universalism
Japan: 68% no right to expect me to testify to the lower figure

MFWI Answers:
Americans: 50 % no right to expect me to testify to the lower figure
Japanese: 50% no right to expect me to testify to the lower figure
    *90% of the total MFWI participants would not testify

Results for question 2. Communitarian versus Individualism

USA: 69% "A," demonstrating a high measure of individualism
Japan: 39% "A" demonstrating a low measure of individualism

MFWI Answers:
Americans: 100% "A" demonstrating a high measure of individualism
Japanese: 40% "A" demonstrating a low measure of individualism

---

Results for question 3. Neutral versus Emotional

USA: 43% not show emotion
Japan: 74% not show emotion.

MFWI Answers:
Americans: 50% not show emotion
Japanese: 40% not show emotion

The results of the three questions demonstrated differences between the respondents of Trompenaars and Hampden-Turner (1998) and the present participants. In regards to Universalism and Particularism, both the Japanese and American participants equally (50%) said the driver has some right to expect him or her to lie, but almost unanimously agreed they would not testify under oath. Both, the American and the Japanese participants were less Universal than Trompenaars' research.

Communitarianism versus Individualism also highlighted differences in the present participants and previous ones. The Americans demonstrated a 100%, high individualistic tendency, and the Japanese scored closely to the previous Trompenaars research as much higher in collectivism. The Japanese answers to this question demonstrated a much more traditional view of Japanese collectivism than did the Components of the Self sheet.

[Interpretation: Depth/ Topsoil] This may be indicative of the dual forces at work in their evolving cultural fusion. If so, it appears the Japanese are experiencing a greater influence from the west, than the Americans are experiencing from the east.

The question reflecting the Neutral versus Emotional tendencies demonstrated the Americans scored closely to the American respondents in the Trompenaars research, while the Japanese scored significantly lower than the previous Japanese respondents. The MFWI Japanese participants are much more likely to show emotion. The answers, once again, demonstrate the potential influence of globalization in the Japanese greater than in the Americans.

[Clarification: Depth/ Subsoil] We discussed the differences between the answers of the Trompenaars and Hampden-Turner research and those of the MFWI participants. Some of the questions that arose were, "Why do some of the answers on the previous research differ so dramatically from your responses?" "Is there is a greater western influence on the Japanese participants, than the eastern influence on American participants? Why do you suppose that is?" The students and faculty agreed that the younger Japanese generation, generally, is becoming more westernized, although they are not consciously aware of it. The Americans, because of their connection with multiculturalism have in some ways experienced a fusion of horizons, although not as dramatically. The discussion of each individual's answers provided a rich context for discourse and the group equally considered the exercise a valuable experience.

The conclusion of the session included a summary of what we had done so far and what we had learned about each other. A volunteer was requested to write a story about an event in his or her life that has impacted who he or she has become. Lisa volunteered, and her story follows in Session Three.

Debriefing of Session Two

The combination of the Components of the Self worksheet and the Trompenaars and Hampden-Turner questions provided insightful material for discussion. Both illuminated aspects that individuals found helpful in understanding themselves in context of their culture. The Japanese participants discovered how their paradigm had evolved to become more Western, without abandoning their rich culture. The Americans were able to observe how individualistic they were, and yet at the same time had also integrated some eastern cultural tendencies. The weak English vocabulary of the Japanese students proved to be the fundamental challenge. However, part of the team building that took place during the session could be attributed to the group, as a whole, working together to meet the challenge.

End
Final Session

The final session incorporated the actual model of the Interpretive Transcultural Storytelling Method. Ideally this would have begun in Session Two. However, due to the language barrier, the primary stage of "In-Spection" required more time. The group assembled one final time.

[Interpretation: Depth/ Topsoil] I observed how the interaction was much more fluid, relaxed, and comfortable than the first session. After insuring each participant had a Working Model (Appendix 2), I began with an overview of the ITSM. We discussed the first step of In-Spection and its importance. Then we addressed the following components: Expression, or telling your story, Reception, the hearing of another's story, Interpretation, the act of attributing meaning to another's story, Clarification, clarifying what has been heard, Understanding, mutual agreement of understanding and new knowledge, and finally Emergence, the application new knowledge. As the participants listened to Lisa's story, they were instructed to do so in context of the ITSM stages. In addition to the Working Model, I described the different levels of depth in conversation: Surface and Depth, and Topsoil, Subsoil, Bedrock, and Core (Lessem & Palsule, 2002). I explained that, often, communication begins and remains in the surface levels. Our goal was to move purposefully into the deeper levels.

We then invited Lisa to read her story. The group listened intently as she began to read in broken English. The following is a transcript of the story she wrote and shared with the group. [[Expression: Depth/ Subsoil]

My Life Looks Like a Roller Coaster

I have two younger sisters. My grandfather (on my father's side) is very strict toward only me, and is very kind toward sisters. He always said to me since I was kindergarten, "You must act smart, because you're oldest! You're specimen of sisters." When my sisters and I scrambled food or something, I had to endure. I hated my grandpa so I didn't want to talk with him. When I was 15 years old, my parents divorced. My sisters and I stayed with my mother, but we are living with my grandpa on my father's side. He always says, "You must do your father's role." So I exploded in anger toward him. I didn't talk with him about 1 ½ year at all! Now, his and my relationship is not so good. But my mother always supported me when I fought grandpa.

[Interpretation: Topsoil/ Subsoil] Following Lisa's sharing, I was perplexed by the disdain she had for her grandfather and my perceptions of the Japanese culture being a culture that placed high value on respecting elders. [Clarification: Depth/ Subsoil] When I asked her about this, Lisa did not understand so the group conferred in Japanese. She eventually understood the question and replied that her anger was strong and although there were times she spoke harshly to him, generally she acted respectfully. Lisa described this as a "surface" respect, with the "depth" of her feelings being hatred. This was more congruent with my perception of Japanese culture, and demonstrated a fusion of western and Japanese culture within her.

Lisa's touching story evoked the empathy of virtually everyone in the group.

[Clarification: Depth/ Subsoil] I asked the group how Lisa's story may have been different in the USA. Before the participants began to respond, I reminded them to be aware of the ITSM model, as well as the levels of depth, and to consider in what stage they were operating. Due to the transparency and personal disclosure in Lisa's story, the group immediately moved to the deeper levels of subsoil and bedrock, and at times even to the core.

[Expression: Depth/ Subsoil] Sara, an American faculty, shared the story of her relationship with her grandmother. She told how she was unkind and controlling. Sara said that her grandmother probably needed to be on medication, but refused any kind of help. Sara said her mother always told her to be polite, respectful, and to always pretend that she liked her, even when her grandmother was unkind. When she became an adult, Sara "could not take it anymore." She eventually told her grandmother her feelings. The relationship was severely impaired at that point. When her grandmother grew sick and close to death, Sara went to her and told her that she wished her well and that she did not harbour bitterness any longer. Reflecting upon her experience, she introspectively asked the question, "How do you respect someone that maybe does not deserve respect?" That was the question she struggled with for years. [Expression: Depth/ Core] Others in the group responded with affirmations, demonstrating they, too, had struggled with the same type of question.

[Clarification: Depth/ Subsoil] I drew a correlation with question three from an earlier session, "In a meeting you feel very insulted because your business counterpart tells you that your proposal is insane. What is your response?" Sara and Lisa, although one American and one Japanese, answered the question the same [Expression: Depth/ Subsoil] and both expressed the same position that even unrespectable people, especially elders or authorities, should be shown respect, even if the respect is not heart-felt. [Understanding: Depth/ Bedrock] The group's discussion revealed that this value is fairly common across the cultural divide.

In addition to the correlation between stories and question number three, I also asked the group to give feedback as to what level, topsoil, subsoil, bedrock, or core, the stories had been. The consensus was that both stories had been primarily subsoil and bedrock, occasionally moving into core when experiences were related with deep emotion and transparency. I encouraged the discussion to continue and Nina promptly spoke up.

[Expression: Depth/ Bedrock] Nina said that she had an experience similar to that of Lisa and Sara. Her parents got divorced and her mother got remarried. She and her step-father did not have a good relationship, nor did she and her step-brother. Although she did not like her step-father, she showed him respect. She also told, with great transparency, of the pain of having a step-father and step-brother with whom she did not get along, and the hurt she felt by the lack of kindness shown by each. [Expression: Depth/ Bedrock] Her story moved between bedrock and core levels, and the group listened intently and with compassion as she shared. [Expression: Depth/ Bedrock]

Kirk shared from his experience with his step-father and the difficult relationship he and his brother had with him. He told of how his father had been killed in an accident and his mother had remarried. Kirk shared how he did not treat his step-father with respect until he became an adult. When he began treating his step-father with respect, their relationship changed and now they are close. [Interpretation: Depth/ Bedrock] The other participants were attentive and receptive to what Kirk was sharing. A discussion about demonstrating respect followed. [Understanding: Depth/ Bedrock]

Becoming increasingly apparent as the session continued, was the common ground the participants shared. All had similar experiences with someone, usually an elder or some other authority figure, where the topic of respect had been an issue. The expression and clarification of these situations had revealed common ground, built intimacy within the group, and addressed the significant issue of mutual respect. Based upon a final discussion, the group emerged with a new understanding of the Japanese and American cultures, more self-awareness, and an understanding of the importance of respecting others. [Understanding: Depth/ Subsoil] The group agreed that the intimacy and understanding that was mutually developed would have a beneficial impact upon their ability to work together in a team setting.

Debriefing of Session Three

The story Lisa shared, and subsequently each of the participants shared, transcended culture. They were the stories of human beings, not Americans or Japanese. On a very basic and fundamental level, the group achieved an emergence of understanding and awareness. [Emergence] Regardless of age, gender, or culture, we all came to the agreement that there are fundamental similarities, and that an understanding of these similarities combined with our differences can enrich our personal experience as well as build a sense of cohesiveness among the group.

Although the full ITSM model was not addressed until the final session, the results were powerful. The sense when we dismissed the final session was that we were saying goodbye to dear friends, not fellow participants in a research project. Upon debriefing each participant, the consensus was that the experience had been a very positive one. I do, however, understand that Japanese culture would prohibit saying otherwise.

Conclusion

The three day module provided a valuable foundation for the beginning of the field work stage of the ITSM. Having entered into the first session with a speculation of how the sessions would actually evolve, I immediately realized the language barrier was an obstacle I had not fully taken into consideration. I was aware that Japanese was the first language of the students. However, my assumption was they would be more proficient in English. This challenge became apparent during the introduction as I had to speak slowly and define many of the terms I used. The students helped each other understand, and often referred to the Japanese/ English dictionary. In retrospect, I have learned the importance of allotting extra time for groups in which English is not the primary language, as well as the benefit of having a proficient interpreter available. As in working with any group, value lies in "knowing your audience." In future modules, advance orientation of the participants' cultural and linguistic context will be beneficial.

In addition to the language challenge, I discovered a great difficulty in participating and leading the sessions while taking comprehensive notes. On the third day I recorded the session. This allowed me freedom to take notes only when necessary and to devote more attention to the group process. The addition of a clause referring to tape recording sessions will be added to the informed consent form from this point forward. For the present project, verbal consent was given on the recording.

While this project is geared specifically toward working in multicultural settings, understanding and emergence was not limited only to the multicultural relationships. The relationships between the Americans were enhanced, as well as the relationships between the Japanese students. According to an interview during the final session, each individual gained new knowledge of the others in the group, regardless of culture, as well as new knowledge of themselves. Each participant stated they felt this experience would allow them to better cooperate within a team setting. The limitation of this information is that it cannot be validated. Since the students were in the final weeks of their time in the USA, an opportunity to have a follow-up session was not possible. If MFWI is to be utilized in the future, a module with students in the beginning of the semester would be more conducive. In addition, a group of students and faculty who would work on a joint project would allow for more reliable feedback in regards to the contribution of the ITSM in a team setting.

In a follow-up interview with the Academic Director of the University, a number of issues were discussed. In regards to the inferred "Westernization" of the students, Dr. Landa suggested that the Japanese students may have answered the questions in light of their extensive multi-cultural training. He stated the purpose of the students participating in the exchange program is to become immersed in American culture. Therefore, they may have answered, either consciously or not, the way they thought an American would answer. We also discussed the very real possibility and probability that some in the younger Japanese population may in fact be experiencing a form of cultural fusion.

However, the Japanese system as a whole will probably not experience that fusion to the same degree in the near future. This research is not predicated on determining cultural styles, rather upon helping people to learn to communicate and function effectively as a team. Therefore, regardless of the reasons behind the answers of the questions, discussions resulted that were conducive to building understanding and exposing commonalities and differences between the participants.

The three sessions with the students and faculty of Mukogawa Fort Wright Institute began with a nervous anticipation. This was the first instalment of putting into practice the model developed to increase effectiveness in communication, specifically between people of different cultures. The consensus of the participants was that this exercise was a valuable lesson in building a cohesive group with emerging and synergistic energy. In addition, the participants expressed that they found value in the communication training as well as self and cultural awareness.

The work within this group in particular, provided a unique picture of a possible emerging culture of fusion among the younger generations in which globalization is a genuine reality. The question as to why the differences between the Taiwanese and Chinese students of the University of Buckingham and the Japanese students of MFWI were so vivid, especially in regards to the concept of the self and collectivism versus individualism, may be answered based upon the level of Japanese and Chinese/ Taiwanese openness to western influence in media, advertising, or globalization in general.

My assertion is that as globalization continues to increase, a fusion of cultures will emerge. This fusion is most likely taking place unconsciously and will probably become more evident in the younger generations who grow up in a global environment. This reconciliation of cultures is precisely, either consciously or unconsciously, what Trompenaars and Hampden-Turner propose to achieve in their work on multicultural competence.

Globalization, it appears, may in fact create continually evolving and emerging cultures. If this assumption is valid, a more dynamic method for communicating cross-culturally may be in order. A method such as the Interpretive Transcultural Storytelling Method may be a valuable addition to the traditional multicultural literature.

References:

Lessem, Ronnie, & Palsule, Sudhanshu. (2002). From local identity to global integrity. Leadership and Organization Development Journal UK, Volume 23, No. 4, 174-185.

Trompenaars, Fons & Hampden-Turner, Charles. (1998). *Riding the Waves of Culture.* 2nd *Edition.* NY: McGraw-Hill.

Chapter 12
Field Work Project 2: Private Investigation Firm

Beginning
Setting the Scene

The organization participating in the second fieldwork project was a private investigation firm. The company investigates a variety of criminal and civil cases for attorneys and private clients. The firm has recently flourished by performing comprehensive background checks for nationwide companies as well as facilities like nuclear power plants. Instead of the actual company name, I will refer to the Private Investigation Firm or "PIF", to insure confidentiality. In addition, the names of the participants will be fictitious.

Introduction of the Cast of Characters

During the four sessions, I worked with eight managers and lead investigators. These individuals are all American citizens who speak fluent English. On the surface the participants' cultural backgrounds seemed homogenous, however, upon exploration we discovered that cultural diversity indeed exists. Judy is Romanian, Glenda is part American Indian, and Bruce is from the deep Southern USA. Tracy has a Ph.D. in Anthropology, and has spent years in England at University of Cambridge, Northern Africa, and Egypt. The others are Caucasians from the USA with mixed European heritages.

PIF has existed for twenty-three years and employs approximately twenty-five individuals. For the past three years the organization has experienced unprecedented growth, both in business and in the number of employees. This has dramatically changed the culture of the company and in the process created a number of issues for its leadership. The culture of PIF has traditionally been family oriented which incorporates flexible scheduling, and close interpersonal relationships.

However, as the company has grown, the leadership is finding it increasingly difficult to create a new culture which incorporates the founder's value of relationships and the spirit of family, and simultaneously provides structure and criteria for assessing job performance. I was asked to work with the managers and lead investigators to help develop communication and understanding among a team of talented individuals, yet who approach their jobs from different perspectives.

As the sessions progressed, it became apparent that many of these perspectives are culturally based. We conducted the ITSM in five sessions, each lasting between one and one and a half hours, over a three month span. The three month span was due to the increasing work load of the firm and did not appear to be a detriment in the ITSM process.

Session One

I began the first session by asking the participants to express their assessment of the firm's current morale and to address some of the matters they think should be addressed. The overwhelming responses were conflicts in relationships, deficiencies in interpersonal communication, and the "need to be on the same page." In addition to the tension caused by poor communication was the rapid pace with which work must be done because of the increase in business. I passed out the ITSM packets, and gave a brief overview of the ITSM's intended purpose of creating understanding and a synergistic team, specifically within multicultural settings. I also stated that no individual would be required to participate or even attend the sessions, and then proceeded to review the Informed Consent form.

The group as a whole listened eagerly and replied positively to the process. However, Tracy and Angie had reservations. Tracy, who holds a Ph.D. in Anthropology, began with very academic questions about my research. Her research orientation had been quantitative and empirical, so she was concerned with my sample size, reliability and validity, what my hypothesis is, and how I would test it. I had not anticipated those types of questions during the session, and the others responded nonverbally by leaning back in their chairs and rolling their eyes with looks of frustration. I explained to Tracy that I appreciated her questions and that the ITSM research was being conducted from a qualitative, hermeneutic approach, utilizing narrative storytelling method. I followed up with an acknowledgement that the others may not be interested in this topic, (to which everyone agreed) and that I would be happy to discuss her questions following the meeting if she would like. I also offered to give her a copy of my methodology and method chapters. She did stay for several minutes following the session and was content with the representation of my research approach, stating it is a different type of research method than that in which she had been trained.

Following Tracy's queries, Angie said that she was not interested in knowing everyone's stories. She suggested to Sandra, the president, that she bring in a "Leadership Consultant" to teach on leadership instead of learning "that Brent's dog or cat got ran over when he was seven years old." She continued, stating, "Business is business, and I don't care whether or not your children are sick, or that your cat or dog died… when you are at work, you do your job." This was immediately met with an angry rebuttal from a manager who has been with the company for years. Brent rose up from his chair, planted both hands on the table and leaned forward toward Angie. He stated, "If you don't care about my family, or me as a person, I certainly will not be likely to go out of my way to help you at work!" At that point the room erupted in an obvious philosophical (cultural) war. Tracy and Angie were aligned against Sandra (the president and founder), Brent, and Bob, while the others sat quietly in discomfort. I waited for an opportunity to interject.

The pandemonium subsided and I said that everyone, as I had stated earlier, was free to participate only to the level he or she desired. I continued by addressing the issue at the root of the argument. The culture of the organization was evolving. Sandra had built the business on the paradigm that employees were like family. This stemmed from her rural American routes where "neighbours helped neighbours, and everyone knew everyone else's business," Sandra said. Translating her rural philosophy to the business incorporates, for example, flexibility in scheduling, sharing personally, and spending time together outside of business hours. Viewing colleagues as family, as well as sensitivity to each person's immediate family has been the understood corporate culture of PIF. However, as new employees have come into the company, other views and practices have begun changing that culture. For example, Angie's cultural background is urban, having lived most of her life in the city where people keep to themselves and stay out of other people's business. Presently, the lack of cooperation and community is the result of this culture in flux.

The rest of the session revolved around Angie, occasionally joined by Tracy, questioning my qualifications and the relevance of my research to their "all white" (with the exception of Glenda) company. I shared with them that culture did not necessarily imply race, although that may very well be part. We discussed, as a group, the various backgrounds of each individual and how within the United States, different regions enjoy different cultural values. For example, the Southern USA and rural areas tend to have a slower pace and to be very relationship and family oriented. This topic is covered in Chapter 7 Contextualization: Macro-contextualization I.

Ten minutes after the session was scheduled to conclude, Sandra interrupted the inquisition and said that we needed to wrap up the meeting. I agreed and summarized the session, emphasising my appreciation for the freedom with which each person shared their thoughts and reminding them of their freedom to participate or not participate in future sessions. I also asked those who wished to participate to answer the questions (Trompenaars and Hampden-Turner) as well as complete the Components of the Self worksheet.

Following the session, I spoke with Tracy about her concerns about the research protocol, and then debriefed with Sandra and her assistant, Bob. They were both apologetic and frustrated about the manner in which Tracy and especially Angie conducted themselves. Sandra and Bob assured me that they felt the ITSM showed great promise for their business and that it was precisely what they needed. We then scheduled the next session. As I left the office I felt as though I had been through an hour and ten minutes of gruelling interrogation.

As we discovered in this first session, some of the managers who are relatively new to PIF did not share the opinion that a business should incorporate any elements of the employees' personal lives. This was sure to be a challenge in future meetings, and bringing personal lives into the workplace is sure to be a concern for others in other organizations.

Middle
Session Two

The second session began with much less tension than the prior had ended. I had wondered whether or not Angie and Tracy would choose to participate in the subsequent meetings, and they were both in attendance. Tracy appeared to be congenial and interested in my discourse on interpretation and the importance of self-knowledge (hermeneutics). She asked pertinent questions and took notes. However, Angie sat quietly, legs crossed, holding her notebook in front of her, and rarely looking up from her writing or doodling. Her nonverbal body language said she was there under protest and did not wish to participate to any degree. With the exception of a couple of interjections throughout the balance of the session, Angie remained silent and closed off to the group. [In-Spection: Surface Topsoil & Subsoil]

We then discussed the Components of the Self worksheet. While some initially expressed concern over the relevance of the worksheet, as we entered into the discussion they began to understand how each individual valued different components, and how these differences may relate to understanding themselves and others. Judy stated that the act of breaking the self down into components helped her to identify those components that were most meaningful to her. No one component surfaced as overwhelmingly highest or lowest. However, the components with the greatest range of difference were: My Gender (9-1), My Aesthetic Sense (9-1), My Conscience (9-1), My Education (9-1), and My Current Relationships (9-1). Within this session, the Components of the Self worksheet proved to be a good discussion starter, but of little value in exposing cultural differences as it did in the Buckingham M.Sc. class that was the genesis of the ITSM. This may be attributed to the lack of severely distinct cultures.

Within the PIF group, each individual is primarily influenced by the general American culture, and secondarily influenced by their individual sub-cultures. We allowed each individual the opportunity to share which components he or she felt most and least influenced their self-composition. [Expression: Depth/ Subsoil] Each person shared, including Angie and Terry, and the discussion led the group beyond the topsoil into the subsoil, and occasionally bedrock, as some shared their aspirations, memories, and childhood experiences. The Components of the Self worksheet may, then, be more valuable in defining differences when cultural extremes exist, however, it still holds value in assisting the participants in self reflection, or In-Spection.

Following the Components of the Self worksheet, we then moved to the Trompenaars and Hampden-Turner questions. Because of time restraints, we chose to discuss only the first four questions, the same questions discussed in the first field work exercise with Mukogawa. The questions provided a great deal of insight and energized the discussion, at times developing into heated debate.

Results for question 1. Universalism versus Particularism

USA: 93% no right to expect me to testify to the lower figure- high universalism

PIF Answers: 87.5 % no right to expect me to testify to the lower figure, 100% not testify

Results for question 2. Communitarianism versus Individualism

USA: 69% "A," demonstrating a high measure of individualism

PIF Answers: 50% "A" demonstrating a high measure of individualism
50% "B" demonstrating a high measure of communitarianism

Results for question 3. Neutral versus Emotional

USA: 43% not show emotion

PIF Answers: 87.5% not show emotion (1 &2)

Results for question 4. Diffuse versus Specific

USA: 90% A

PIF Answers: 25% A, 50% B, 25% Both

While the purpose of the preceding questions is not to statistically compare and contrast the findings of Trompenaars and Hampden-Turner, the results do provide a framework for invigorating discussion. In remaining congruent to their law enforcement and legal context, the entire group answered the first question that they would not testify to a lower figure, even though they were not quite as unanimous in stating that the individual had no right to ask for the false testimony. The first question, although everyone agreed, provided a rich discussion regarding the universalism of law. Some could not understand why it would even be a question, as it is obvious that "right is right, and wrong is wrong." However, others understood the dilemma as it pertained to different relationships and different possible results of the accident. In the end, all agreed to falsely testify is wrong.

The second question was the most pertinent to this particular group. Exactly one half of the participants answered as communitarians and one half as individualists. This split regularly emerged as a source of discussion throughout each of our meetings, and it represented the turmoil caused by the evolution of the culture of the workplace. While PIF had been highly collectivistic in its early years, and while the president highly desires it to remain that way, as the organization has grown, individuals have joined the team who have much more of an individualistic perspective. The ensuing discussion regarding communitarianism and individualism surfaced the sharp divide among philosophies. As the discussion settled, and the participants began to find common ground, Angie was the only person holding firmly to her solely individualistic perspective.

Question 3, Neutral versus Emotional, demonstrated that the team of PIF were less likely to show emotion than the US respondents in the original research. Most agreed that to react in meeting would be less beneficial than speaking to the offender in private. However, Angie and Bob were willing to show emotion when offended, and they demonstrated that several times throughout our sessions, mostly towards one another. Question 4, Diffuse versus Specific, did not provide much discussion. However, the discrepancies demonstrated by the answers of Question 2 (Communitarianism versus Individualism) were highlighted once again. Being closely related to Question 2, Question 4 revealed the tension of a corporate culture in flux.

The Trompenaars and Hampden-Turner questions stimulated discussion which helped the participants talk through and wrestle with their personal views as well as learn the views of others. In addition, the discussion helped to lay a framework for the evolving corporate culture and to highlight areas of tension, like individualism versus communitarianism. The lively dialogue accompanying each question suggested that the interaction was having a positive effect in building community.

Following the discussion of the questions, I discussed narrative storytelling with the participants. I explained that the main purpose in the previous exercises was to help each person to understand more about themselves and to reflect upon their stories. I asked each person to consider a biographical story that has had an impact in shaping the person they have become. This would be a brief story, approximately ten to fifteen minutes in length, that might help others know and understand them better. I assured the participants they had no obligation to participate, and if they chose to participate, they were free to share as little as they felt comfortable in sharing. I encouraged each to make notes of their stories on the sheet provided in the ITSM packet. After answering questions and thanking them for their participation, the session was adjourned.

Session Three

Session three began with a brief discussion of the termination of Angie's employment. The discussion was tense as Tracy was obviously unhappy with the recent events. She did not feel that Angie was treated fairly until Sandra described the events that led up to the termination. Following her explanation, everyone seemed satisfied and we moved ahead with the ITSM.

I reviewed each of the stages of the ITSM with the group, explaining what each stage represented and how the process is cyclical. I also introduced the concept of depth topography:

topsoil, subsoil, bedrock, and core. I encouraged each person to be aware of each stage as well as the levels of depth.

Brent was the first to volunteer to tell his story which lasted for approximately seven minutes. He told of his previous job as a minister in a church. [Expression: Depth/ Subsoil] He, his wife, and his young son lived in an apartment in the church, making it difficult to separate work life from personal life. He shared how the living arrangements had a negative impact on his family and then he concluded his story. My internal reaction was that the story was short, very much on the surface, and did not reveal much about Brent. However, almost immediately Glenda indicated that she would like to speak. [In-Spection: Depth/ Subsoil] She interpreted Brent's story in context of her knowledge of his background, but also in light of her own context. She had been a pastor's child and immediately identified with the impact, both positive and negative, that being in the ministry could have upon a family.

[Expression: Depth/ Subsoil] She began to share her own story as a child whose father spent countless nights away from home caring for someone in the church. Whether counselling, visiting the sick, or helping families in times of grief, she recounted how her own family often came after the others in her father's church. Judy observed the similarities in Glenda's and Brent's stories. [Clarification: Depth/ Subsoil] She asked Brent how the events of his story had affected his view of the relationship between work and family. Her insight in addressing this point was impressive. [Expression: Depth/ Subsoil] Brent replied with a robust, "I now put my family first. I learned that my role is that of protector for my family… I see myself like a knight who goes off to battle (work) to protect and provide for my family… work is just a means to an end- not the end in itself." I asked, "Is that philosophy culturally based?" [Expression: Depth/ Bedrock]

Tracy said that she did not think it was the typical American cultural philosophy, but that it could be culturally related to Brent's religious convictions and his family of origin. Brent agreed that family was important religiously and that family was primary in his home when he was a child. [Expression: Depth/ Subsoil] Judy said that family is important to her Romanian roots as well. However, she stated that often, family time was "sacrificed in order to put food on the table and a roof over their heads." Glenda, (Native American heritage), spoke of the importance of family as she began to share her story. Below is an excerpt from Glenda's story, used with permission and names changed for anonymity. [Expression: Depth/ Subsoil]

> On August 30th, 2001 I received a phone call from my mom. She told me that the Coast Guard had called her and informed her that they had found my dad's boat. At first we thought that maybe someone had taken it and then left it to drift. Within that hour we were informed that my dad and three nephews were lost at sea.
>
> The majority of our family gathered at my mom's house waiting for news. My sister and brother-in-law lived in Odessa, WA and both of their son's were with their grandpa. My brother and sister-in-law's oldest son was the third grandchild with his grandpa.
>
> Normally more of the family would have gone on this yearly fishing trip, but my daughter was going to be married on September 1st, so it was only the four of them. My dad was scheduled to officiate the wedding ceremony. On August 31st the majority of the family left to fly to Lapush using the funds that were being donated. The Coast Guard took the family to St. James Island where my dad's boat had been found and let them walk around, as well as showing them where the boat had been found upside down at high tide level.

...The bodies of my nephews were all found, but as of this day my dad's body has never been recovered. All of this occurred just days before the bombing of the World Trade Center.

The following spring the president of the company that I was employed for offered me a position at the main office just outside of Portland. He told me that they were going to be closing the regional office where I was working. He made me an offer that was hard to turn down as I would be getting more than a $5.00 per hour raise and they would assist in my husband finding work.

I originally told him that I would like to try this, as they offered to fly me back and forth during the week to see if I would like it. After two days of not sleeping well I decided that the Lord was saying that I needed to stay where I was, even though I would be without a job shortly. I felt guided to stay in the area where I would be close to my mom and two of my three kids, as well as most of my siblings.

A lot of things happened in my life prior to August 28th, 2001, including many learning experiences and stumbling blocks, but after this date my family has a higher priority. I have been blessed with my son choosing to follow his grandpa's footsteps into the ministry. As you know, all things work together for the good of those who trust the Lord! He also led Sandra to contact me and offer me a position in her company and now I believe that I am at a job where I belong.

Following Glenda's story, and the drying of eyes from tears, the group began to discuss how the concept of family affects the PIF business. [Expression: Depth/ Subsoil] Bob said that he felt the PIF is a family, and that is how the business was founded. [Expression: Depth/ Bedrock] However, Tracy quickly replied that, although she is close to many in PIF, she certainly did not equate them to her family. Most of the room seemed to agree with her assessment. Tracy reiterated the need to balance family and business, and sited a recent work picnic. She shared how she felt "looked down upon" because she had not attended. She preferred to spend that Saturday with her husband and twin babies. Tracy felt that is was unfair that she should be expected to attend a work function on her day off. She agreed that teamwork is important to the PIF, but that her workmates are not her family. Bruce stated that the discussion was part of an unfolding story of the culture of PIF.

[Clarification: Depth/ Core] He asked, "Where do we draw the line between work and home?" While, in the past, PIF employees spent much of their time off together, not all of the present employees desire to do so. [Emergence] Tracy suggested that each individual would ultimately need to have the freedom to choose when to participate in work "get-togethers" and when to spend time with family. "The differences in stages of life among the team members", she said, "has an impact on the level of outside activities they can be involved in." Tracy had made a powerful point. [Expression: Depth/ Bedrock] Sandra acknowledged that her children are now adults, and that her employees are in essence, her immediate family. She said that she understood those with small children are at a different stage of life and that their children are priorities.

[Clarification: Depth/ Bedrock] Recognizing that our time was almost gone, I asked the group, "What new understanding and/or knowledge emerged from the discussion today?"

[Understanding: Depth/ Subsoil] Bob said that Brent and Gay's stories had been insightful, but perhaps more important than hearing their stories was the discussion the stories elicited.

[Clarification: Depth/ Bedrock] I asked him to explain. [Expression: Depth/ Core] Bob stated that the differences of viewpoints of the work team and family have a major impact on the culture of the company. He stated that while lack of participation in employee parties had been frowned upon, the new insight of life stages and priorities had helped him understand why certain individuals did not regularly participate. What had been viewed as a lack of employee team spirit was now understood differently. Each person verbally agreed with Bob's assessment, and each added comments regarding the new understanding they had each received. Bruce stated that he felt it is possible to have a family style workplace and have boundaries. He said that the team needs to allow for individual preferences and that the family concept allows for differences in levels of participation. The consensus was that the discussion of the day had been a benefit in the purposeful evolution of the corporate culture of PIF. The group appeared to have a positive and up-beat demeanour as we dismissed.

End
Session 4

The final session began with an exploration of whether or not the previous session had an impact on the workplace during the interim between our sessions. Tracy said that she felt others now have a better understanding of her desire to be with her family than they had before the last session. On one occasion she had needed to go home early to take care of her children. Instead of feeling like she was letting the team down, she said that she felt comfortable knowing that everyone knows where her priorities lie, and why. Brent said that he felt like the communication in the office had been better because of the relationships that had been further developed during the previous sessions. Sandra expressed how utilizing the ITSM process had helped her to communicate with Judy during a conversation that seemed "to be getting nowhere." They referred back to expression, reception, clarification and eventually reached an understanding. Others said that they had remembered to use the process or parts of the process during certain conversations with fellow employees and some with clients.

I asked if anyone would like to share their story, and immediately Sandra volunteered. Sandra, as the president and founder of PIF plays a significant role in determining the culture as well as the atmosphere of the workplace.

[Expression: Depth/ Core] Sandra began describing a painful experience that took place about five years prior. She had hired a middle-aged woman who had professional qualifications, yet struggled with depression. Because of Sandra's history as one who "is always responsible for those around her," she felt obligated to not only overlook this woman's professional shortcomings, but to invest in her personally and emotionally. As a child, Sandra's mother held her responsible for everything that happened to her little brothers, and for everything her little brothers did. This feeling of responsibility for others remained with Sandra throughout her life, and now into her business. After several attempts, the woman finally succeeded in committing suicide. Sandra's husband found the body when she did not report for work. Sandra felt responsible. She had intervened and rescued her employee on three previous attempts, and this time she failed. To compound the guilt, the woman left a suicide note blaming Sandra for driving her to the point of suicide. Sandra has struggled with this incident for the past five years. While she knows that she cannot accept responsibility for another's actions, she still feels guilty.

Sandra's story was moving and very emotional. Most of the participants in the workshop had no knowledge of the events Sandra had described. For a moment the room was silent.

Eventually Tracy offered her condolences about the suicide and assured Sandra that she could not prevent someone, who was determined, from committing suicide. Sandra graciously accepted Tracy's statement. [Clarification: Depth/ Core] Tracy asked if Sandra's history of "being responsible for all those around her," and whether her former employee's suicide may be significant factors in why Sandra has a tendency to micromanage her employees. Sandra's micromanagement has been a contentious issue on numerous occasions at PIF.

Judy said that she could now see why Sandra would micromanage after hearing her story. [Expression: Depth/ Subsoil] She proceeded to express that she had felt Sandra's micromanagement style was a sign that she did not trust her employees and that she thought they were incompetent to do their jobs. Others agreed with Judy's assessment. [This is a representation of the hermeneutic spiral. The conversation is cycling back and forth from Sandra's specific story, to its effects on the whole group.] [Understanding: Depth/ Subsoil] Sandra agreed that her micromanagement tendencies very well may be a reflection of her lifelong feelings that she is responsible for the actions of those around her, and that after the suicide, those feelings were compounded.

[Expression: Depth/ Subsoil] Sandra continued, speaking of her internal battles of when to step in and micromanage and when to allow an employee to work out problems on his or her own. She said she understands that an employee needs to be allowed to try to solve problems and work out situations without interruption. However, she also knows the delicate nature of their business, and that a mistake could cost PIF a client's business.

[Interpretation & Clarification: Depth/ Subsoil] Judy suggested that the management team should work together to discuss solutions that would incorporate each of the managers being available for accountability and checks-and-balances. She then suggested that Sandra seems to have a difficult time differentiating the "friendship/ family philosophy from business." She suggested that Sandra and the management team jointly produce a set of expectations by which general job performance can by gauged. The group agreed that a common understanding of expectations would be valuable in addressing some of the issues PIF is presently facing because of the growth.

[Understanding: Depth/ Subsoil] Sandra acknowledged that PIF culture needs to intentionally evolve. Presently, the lack of structure and the "we're all one big happy family" philosophy is causing confusion and dissension. [Understanding:: Depth/ Subsoil] Bruce expressed his desire to keep the "close-knit feel," but he agreed that changes in structure needed to be made.

I asked the group, "What new knowledge or understanding have our sessions produced?" [Emergence] Judy expressed that the chart outlining the ITSM process had been helpful in her understanding of how to communicate with others. Several verbal agreements followed her statement. "Another interesting insight has been hearing each other's stories. Although we didn't get to hear everyone's, the stories and the following discussions were very eye-opening," said Glenda. Bruce expressed how the consensus that "we can have a family oriented workplace and simultaneously have different boundaries and preferences is valuable."

Summarizing our final session I addressed the evolving corporate culture of PIF. This evolution is inevitable and the managers expressed the desire to make it intentional. Creating a set of expectations and guidelines for gauging work performance will decrease stress and confusion, as well as potentially decrease Sandra's tendency to micromanage. The Managers mutually agreed that they like the idea of perpetuating a flexible yet structured family friendly culture at PIF.

Noting that we were out of time, I thanked the group for their participation and dismissed them. Following the session, the group lingered and talked among themselves while Sandra expressed her desire to have a follow up session in following months to evaluate the evolution of PIF culture and possibly allow an opportunity for those who were not able to tell their stories.

Conclusion

Although the PIF participants seemed overwhelmingly Anglo-American, obvious cultural differences emerged throughout the sessions. Differences in life stages, individual preferences, and cultural views of the workplace were a source of contention among PIF managers. Developing an understanding of different definitions of family and a family oriented work culture proved to be a valuable result of the ITSM.

The ITSM, according to the participants, was valuable in identifying stages of the communication process. According to Judy, referring to the process during discussions outside of the sessions proved valuable. She said she was able to identify the point within a discussion in which the communication was breaking down.

Overall, the Components of Self worksheet and the Trompenaars & Hampden-Turner questions proved to be of some value in aiding the process of self-knowledge accumulation and identifying cultural differences within the group. It may be important to utilize these as means to an end rather than the end.

Although not every participant was able to tell his or her story, the stories shared initiated rich discussion and insight. While in the In-Spection stage, the participants gained further self-knowledge. In telling the stories, the participants helped others understand more about them and their context. However, perhaps as significant as the story was the resulting discussion.

One participant said, "The stories are a catalyst for discussion and emergence." This is in congruence with the MFWI workshop as well. The stories are not only valuable in themselves, but also in the discussion that follows as participants go through the ITSM stages cycling back and forth between the teller's story, their own interpretation and story, and the story of the group as a whole.

During this workshop, I realized the vital role the facilitator plays. My knowledge of counselling psychology and group dynamics was invaluable many times throughout the sessions. Understanding the different stages of group development, identifying common, divergent, or recurring themes, and the ability to field the myriad of complex emotions telling stories and having intense discussions can produce are some of the skills a facilitator will need. For replication of the ITSM a rigorous training for facilitators will be necessary.

The PIF workshops proved valuable in the development of the ITSM. Gaining a sense of the amount of time needed for each story was one of the primary revelations. Each participant told their story within seven to fifteen minutes. However, the resulting discussion which includes the ITSM stages can take as much as forty-five minutes. This means that getting to the story telling earlier in the workshops may be necessary. Less discussion and time spent on the Components of Self and questions may be required. Another possibility, as we did with PIF, is to have only a limited number of participants tell their stories.

The Topography was not used but a couple of times within conversation by the participants, but it helped in my evaluation of the discussion as well as in the writing up to determine how deep the participants were willing to go in self-disclosure. The level to which participants within MFW and PIF have been willing to disclose has been notably bedrock and core levels.

Rural versus urban, southern versus northern, and western versus eastern can reveal distinct cultural differences. While PIF participants included a Native American and a Romanian, the most significant differences surfaced among the geographic regions from which participants came and whether they were reared in the country or city. Differences were revealed during the ITSM, but the stories and discussions created an atmosphere in which the participants could emerge with knowledge that transcended those differences.

References:

Lessem, Ronnie & Palsule, Sudhanshu. (1997). *Managing in Four Worlds: From Competition to Co-creation.* Oxford, UK: Basil Blackwell.

Chapter 13
Field Work Project 3: Family Counselling Centre

Beginning
Setting the Scene

Family Counselling Centre is a fledgling organization within its first months of operation. The centre offers services to families and individuals, including children, teenagers, and adults. FCC, as a firm, is still in the early stages of development, and the participants expressed a level of frustration with fellow employees. The fundamental source of frustration was difficulty in communicating due to a variety possibilities, including, personality styles, cultural backgrounds, and personal histories. Each of the participants appeared willing and eager to work through the ITSM, motivated by the desire to learn to communicate better and build a more cohesive team.

The FCC workshop was divided into two sessions, one week apart. The first session spanned six hours. The discussions were suspended for a one hour lunch break. The second session lasted for two hours. Although this schedule was different from previous one hour sessions, it proved to be of equal value and in many ways superior to the more elongated time frames of previous workshops. In the present workshop, the flow from one phase to the next was more fluid, the time was utilized better because of the lack of review, and important dialogues were not interrupted due to the ending of the hour. In the present workshop, the outline used in previous workshops was adhered to less stringently, allowing us to work conceptually rather than linearly. This allowed for a more intentional and productive use of the hermeneutic cycle since previous discussions and statements were more contextually recent and relevant.

Introduction of the Cast of Characters

The FCC group consisted of Tom, a twenty-five year old Caucasian of German and Italian heritage, Ron, a thirty-six year old who is Native American, but was adopted as a child by second generation Norwegians, and Rene of German and Native American ancestry. Doug, a fifty year old Caucasian and Wayne, a forty year old Caucasian with a mix of Native American heritage were also participants.

Session One

The first session began with welcoming, expressing gratitude for the group's participation, and an overview of the purpose and general process of the ITSM. I reviewed the Informed Consent form and invited questions or comments. I asked the participants for their evaluation of the present group dynamics and overall workplace morale. It was here that the participants expressed their assessment that communication was an issue. Tom said that he had a difficult time communicating with Wayne, specifically, because Wayne had a tendency to "beat around the bush." When I asked him to explain, Tom said that often when he asks Wayne for his opinion or other input, Wayne gives a long drawn out example or story for an answer. Tom said that he usually walks away saying, "What in the world did he just say?" This is very frustrating to Tom who is "black or white, yes or no... very definitive and direct" in what he says. Tom said that Wayne is "always gray and indirect in his communication." Wayne agreed that the two seem to be "on different wave lengths."

Internally, I registered that this difference in style possibly has a cultural foundation. Another frustration, Rene noted, was that Ron "sometimes seems to be too lackadaisical in his work." She said that he performs well, but does not appear to give more than required to his job. Rene made note of Ron's consistently late, or "just on time" arrivals at work, his slow pace at work, and his lack of participation in many of the extracurricular activities.

I made a mental note of Ron's dark skin and black hair. Assuming he was not of Northern European descent, I assumed he was Mexican or Native American. If so, his view of time could also be a cultural distinction. Making notes in my notebook, I asked if there were any other topics of relevance. After a moment of silence, we continued the discussion by addressing the participants' cultural backgrounds.

I asked the participants to share their cultural history. Stating this could include subjects such as national, religious, racial, ethnic, socio-economic, and regional background. Tom began by stating that he "does not have a cultural background." He said that he is "American and White... pretty much a mixture of a bunch of different cultures." I assured him that this in itself is a culture and that it has probably had a profound impact on shaping the person he has become. I probed deeper, and Tom said that his father is third generation Italian and his mother second generation German. I made another note in my journal that the German and Italian roots may reflect on Tom's directness.

Rene stated that she is generally Northern European, but that her great-grandmother was Native American. She said that her Native American heritage had probably not affected her culturally since she had not been close to her great-grandmother. She suspects that her personality style has been shaped more by her Northern European heritage because she is very orderly, not spontaneous, and does not show emotion too readily.

Doug said that he is "a mutt... just a plain old WASP, White Anglo-Saxon Protestant." Ron stated that he had been born on the Indian Reservation and that his father had deserted his family. He and his brother were adopted by a White Norwegian family. His adopted family celebrated, and still celebrate, every Norwegian festival and holiday, and Christmas is celebrated in Norwegian style as well. I mentally noted the apparent extreme dissonance between Norwegian and Native American cultures, and wondered how this had affected Ron's development. Wayne shared that he, too was a "WASP, but also 1/16 Native American." He said that he had always desired to be more Native American and that he had always strongly identified with Native American culture. He said that although he considered himself a Christian, he also found some Native American philosophy and religious beliefs comforting.

I introduced the Components of the Self worksheet and allowed approximately ten minutes during the session for its completion. [In-Spection: Surface/ Topsoil] Upon completion, Doug said that he felt the worksheet helped him better understand himself by forcing contemplation of each area. We discussed each of the participant's answers and found some components common to all and some unique to individuals.

The most significant factors common to all five participants were, My Family and My Spirituality. Four out of the five participants chose My Conscience and My Religious Beliefs as significant. One of the distinct differences was My Gender. Wayne scored gender as one of least significant factors (1), while Rene scored it as one of the most significant (9). Culturally, Wayne and Rene are of similar backgrounds, an obvious difference is gender. Gender has not visibly surfaced as an extreme differentiating factor in any of the previous workshops, so I noted it, and we continued.

Interestingly, each participant marked My Nationality and My Culture as unimportant (1). I inquired as to the reason each individual would believe nationality and culture to be insignificant. While each participant expressed appreciation for the USA, none felt being American had a profound influence in making up the self. In addition, when queried about the low scores on culture, the respondents expressed that they simply did not identify themselves as having a culture. Ron, a Native American, spoke of the dissonance between his heredity and his environment. [Expression: Depth/ Subsoil] As a Native American growing up in a Norwegian-American home, he felt like an "outsider." "I felt left out at the Norwegian celebrations. I never fit in, and my brother and I were always outsiders," Ron said. In addition, Ron's exposure to Native American culture was limited.

None of the participants listed My Relationship to Society as a significant component. [Interpretation: Depth/ Subsoil] I knew from previous experience and research that this is a major component in traditional Native American society. [Clarification: Depth/ Subsoil] I questioned Ron, and the others who claimed a degree of Native American influence, on this topic. Ron, again, emphasised that he had little exposure to the Native American culture. The other participants agreed that this component had little significance due to the primary culture in which they were reared.

As several of the participants have a strong Christian foundation, the role of religion played a significant role in defining self. However, this religious correlation does not prescribe that each person holds identical interpretations. For example, in the Components of the Self worksheet, Wayne identified My Relationship to Nature as a top component (9), while Doug and Tom said it didn't have any role whatsoever (1). Wayne expressed that his view is based upon his religious conviction. Doug and Tom agreed that religion is significant in the identification of components, as well. All three share the same belief system, but its influence differs with each.

The Components of the Self worksheet provided a rich platform for discussion. Ron asked questions such as, "Why are certain factors important to me?, and why are other factors important to others?" During a time of discussion, the group agreed that childhood experiences were very significant in personal development. [In-Spection: Depth/ Subsoil] Ron, Tom, and Wayne changed My Childhood Experiences to number nine, very significant. Originally each had this factor listed, but relatively insignificant.

Following the Components of the Self worksheet, we began with the discussion of the Trompenaars & Hampden-Turner questions. In the interest of time and consistency between the previous workshops and the present, we covered Universalism versus Particularism, Communitarianism versus Individualism, Neutral versus Emotional, and Diffuse versus Specific. The participants did not have the questions in advance, so I read the questions aloud as they followed along in their packets. After reading each question I allowed two to three minutes for reflecting and answering. We then discussed each. The questions provided the back-drop for intense and reflective discussion. Trompenaars and Hampden-Turner did not include Native Americans in their research, so the dialogue was enlightening. [In-Spection & Expression: Depth/ Subsoil]

Results for question 1. Universalism versus Particularism

> USA: 93% no right to expect me to testify to the lower figure- high universalism
>
> FCC Answers: 40 % no right to expect me to testify to the lower figure, 100% not testify

Results for question 2. Communitarianism versus Individualism

> USA: 69% "A," demonstrating a high measure of individualism
>
> FCC Answers: 60% "A" demonstrating a high measure of individualism
> 40% "B" demonstrating a high measure of communitarianism

Results for question 3. Neutral versus Emotional

> USA: 43% not show emotion
>
> FCC Answers: 60% "1 & 2" not show emotion, 40% "3 & 4" show emotion

Results for question 4. Diffuse versus Specific

> USA: 90% A
>
> FCC Answers: 100% B

Contrary to the 87.5% in the previous PIF workshop, the first question received only 40% who said the pedestrian had no right to expect him to testify. The discussion revolving around this question made apparent that these individuals are in the helping profession versus law enforcement, as PIF. FCC participants discussed the reasons a friend might have the right to expect one to falsely testify on his behalf. Difficult to ascertain, was whether the participants were more open to this possibility because of cultural or professional reasons. As helping professionals, the participants are ethically committed to their clients and to the ethics of unconditional positive regard and being non-judgmental. Their professional practices may have influenced their responses. Regardless of whether the participants felt the person in the question had the right to ask, they unanimously agreed that they would not falsely testify. The difference between this group and PIF is that more than half could at least understand how the individual could ask for his friend to lie, even if they believed it was wrong.

Ron stated that had he grown up on the reservation his view would have been much more particularistic. He stated that the Native American culture valued loyalty to friendship and family and that loyalty would have probably taken precedence over the law. As he was reared by Norwegians, this cultural trait was pre-empted by universalism.

The second question, Communitarianism versus Individualism, spurred a lively discussion. Initially, three out of the five participants favoured communitarianism. However, the clause, "even if it obstructs individual freedom and development," forced them to unanimously choose individualism. The group struggled with answering individualistically because they highly value the communitarian principles. However, they do not value those principles as they infringe upon the rights of individuals. Ron and Wayne again addressed the differences among Native American society. They discussed how in the distant past, Native American culture was highly communitarian. However, as Native American culture was influenced by the intrusion of the European settlers, it mutated. Today, while still more communitarian than the overall American culture, it has generally grown much more individualistic.

Question number three, Neutral versus Emotional, demonstrated that three out of the five would not show emotion during a meeting. The general consensus was that demonstrating emotion would be less beneficial than handling the situation privately with the individual. The FCC answers correlated highly with the Trompenaars and Hampden-Turner findings and the PIF answers as well. However, Tom answered that he would show emotion "so that my counterpart gets the message. I believe the clarity of my message will allow me to control even greater emotional upset in the future." I asked Tom if his father and mother had demonstrated that freedom of emotion while growing up. He said they had been emotionally demonstrative, and his understanding is that it is in sync with the Italian and German cultures. After some discussion, we concluded that Tom's willingness to express himself probably had cultural foundations.

The fourth question, Diffuse versus Specific, demonstrated an interesting discrepancy between this group and the results of Trompenaars and Hampden-Turner. FCC participants answered that they unanimously view "a company as a group of people working together. They have social relations with other people and with the organization. The functioning is dependent on these relations (B)." This is highly contrasted to 90% of the USA respondents in the Trompenaars and Hampden-Turner research who answered A. In the previous PIF workshop, 50% of the participants answered B. The FCC group correlates much higher with the diffuse countries like Mexico, South

America, Japan, France, and Catholic Europe. I asked the group to what they might attribute the difference from the findings of USA respondents, and the correlation with the results of Asia and South America. The group discussed the possibilities and concluded that the heavy Native American influence was a significant factor. In addition, their roles as helping professionals probably has an influence on their very holistic views, identifying more with the whole person across settings and valuing social relationships with co-workers.

After a brief break, I reviewed the concept of autobiographical storytelling. Each person had been briefed on storytelling prior to the workshop and came prepared with a story to tell. Ron began the session. [Expression: Depth/ Subsoil] He told of how his mother had become pregnant at the age of fifteen. While he was still a toddler, his father divorced his mother and they had very little contact. His mother eventually placed Ron and his brother up for adoption. It was at this point he and his brother were adopted. Ron's adopted parents are Norwegian and very ingrained in the Norwegian culture. Ron expressed how he and his brother felt very out of place during the many traditional Norwegian holidays. [Expression: Depth/ Subsoil] He spoke of sitting in the corner and observing, never feeling connected to the family during the times of celebration. Ron shared how he did not blame his adopted family. Rather, he blamed his father for abandoning him. He decided at a young age to never be like his father. In many respects this included identifying with his Native American heritage. Although this reaction against his father drove him to all but disowning and forgetting his heritage, the children at school were not so inclined. [Expression: Depth/ Bedrock] He told of how, as a child, he was called nigger, savage, and a variety of other derogatory names. This added to his reaction against his heritage. He was ashamed to be a Native

American and tried to adopt the look and culture of his adopted family.

Throughout his childhood and early adulthood, he maintained limited contact with his biological family, so he has always had an occasional reminder of his true ethnicity and cultural heritage. Ron shared that only in his mid thirties did he begin to explore his heritage. He now has children of his own, and he has vowed to be the "father he never had." He expressed how his family is the priority of his life. He is very careful that work and outside activities never detract from time with his children and wife.

Ron now recognizes the value and richness of his Native American heritage and he desires to re-connect with that culture. His desire is for his children to have a sense of roots and heritage. While Ron said he does not envision adopting the Native American culture, he does expect that he and his family will explore and gain knowledge of that culture. He said, "I feel, in many ways, that I have come – or am coming- full circle."

Following Ron's story the group sat silently. [Interpretation] The looks on their faces demonstrated that his story had been very moving and had caused introspection. After a moment, [In-Spection/ Expression: Depth/ Subsoil] Wayne said it was somewhat ironic that he has spent most of his life trying to find an identity with the little Native American heritage he has, and Ron has spent most of his life trying to disassociate with it.

Wayne shared that once he had contacted the tribe from which his family had come. He had inquired about becoming enrolled in that tribe. He was told that his ancestry would have to be traced back to someone in the tribe who had been given land by the government. The tribal representative told him that this would be a difficult task because during that time, Native Americans were heavily discriminated against. Most Native Americans simply relinquished their land in order to dissociate with the tribe. They would then claim to be Mexican. [Expression & Clarification: Surface/ Subsoil] Wayne noted while that was in the mid 1700s, apparently not much had changed. He and the others seemed to be very surprised that racism and prejudice against Native Americans is still practiced. Ron assured them that it does still exist.

Doug told Ron that he appreciates his commitment to family. [Expression: Surface/ Topsoil] He said, "It is refreshing to hear someone say family comes first. That's not normal today." Tom agreed. . [In-Spection/ Clarification: Depth/ Subsoil] Rene asked Ron if his family's priority could negatively impact his job performance. Ron sated that he does not believe so. [Clarification: Depth/ Bedrock] Doug asked Rene if she was stating that Ron's performance is hindered by the commitment to his family, or if she was asking. Rene responded that she was asking, but that she could see how that type of commitment might affect job performance at times. Rene said that she is very committed to her family, but that she also understands she gets paid to do a job. She stated there must be a balance between the two.

Rene volunteered to present her story. . [In-Spection: Depth/ Topsoil] She began with childhood memories of cutting her "blonde curls off one side of her head" the day before Easter. Easter was an important holiday in her family of origin, and they always dressed up in their finest new clothes to go to church. Appearance was very important to Rene's mother, and she was quite distraught when she saw Rene's hair cut. This memory was significant to Rene because she was always told she should look her best. In addition to appearances, her father would tell her, "If you are going to do something, do it right." Rene's heritage is mostly German and to a small degree Native American. [In-Spection: Depth/ Bedrock] She reflects that it is the German culture that had the most significant impact. The will to succeed was also instilled at a young age. Rene summarized that appearance, excellence, and success were recurring themes in her childhood. She said, "Whatever I did, I had to do right the first time... even if I had never done it before. This is probably where my caution and contemplation began. If I was going to do something, I better have all my ducks in a row before I ever started... Spontaneity is something I find hard to enter into, and I probably miss a lot of unexpected pleasures because I feel compelled to be the responsible one." Wayne, who is very spontaneous, chuckled and said, "Wow! That's where that comes from!" [Expression: Depth/ Bedrock] Rene continued:

>Probably the most defining experience, and most difficult to discuss in a cold factual manner, has been the journey thus far with MS (Muscular Sclerosis). Knowing what I know now, I realize I have been dealing with varying symptoms for the past nine years. Unfortunately, during all those years I didn't have a doctor who knew enough about it to recognize the seriousness of the symptoms I kept complaining about. [Expression: Depth/ Core] MS has demanded a slow giving up of the things that have been an expression of who I am: being able to go out on a beautiful spring day and just take off walking for the sheer joy of movement; sitting down at the piano to play something I hear in my head; tackling a home decorating project by myself because I want to express something creatively; shopping for clothes that express who I am as a woman. What it has given me in return is muscle fatigue and weakness, irreversible nerve damage, a feeling of not knowing how to express my feminine nature in a body that feels like the Hunchback of Notre Dame, and a feeling of sometimes being a burden instead of being the one to 'do' for everyone else. I've had to

learn to quietly mourn each loss as it comes, and then gently put it away and not go there again.

Rene continued her story by addressing how the traits of success and excellence have been important factors in her challenge of facing MS. She attributed her perseverance and will to "make the best of her situation" to her parents and her faith in God. She also spoke of how the emphasis on appearance has been difficult for her to overcome. Her disease has greatly affected the manner in which she moves, what she wears, and what she does. As she rested from her narrative, the group sat visually stunned in silence. [In-Spection: Depth/ bedrock] Doug broke the silence with, "What do you say after a story like that? I appreciate how transparent you have been." [Expression: Depth/ Bedrock] Wayne shared that he used to think Rene was just slow, maybe even lazy. At times he said he felt annoyed that she would not do certain tasks, or that she did them so slowly. He said that he now has a completely different perspective of Rene, and how this disease has virtually robbed her. Tom said that he would be willing to help her anytime she needed, and the rest of the group joined him in his offer. Ron, Tom, and Doug agreed to help Rene whenever possible, especially with the more physical tasks.

I thanked Rene for her story and asked for someone else to share theirs. Tom volunteered. [Expression: Surface/ topsoil] He began telling about his father who now lives in Panama. He said that his father had been physically and verbally abusive to his mother, his brother, and to him. In addition to being abusive, his drive to make money kept him away from his family much of the time. Tom said that his father and mother had divorced when he was nine years old. Because of his parent's divorce and his father's absence a great deal of the time, Tom had very little positive male reinforcement. This has impacted Tom throughout his life. He said that he has always had an inferiority complex, and that he has never felt comfortable speaking to adults, especially men.

Tom said that he finds it very difficult to show his feelings, demonstrate affection, and have intimate relationships. [Expression: Surface/ Subsoil] He said that as he was writing his story, he realized he shared many characteristics with father. As he said this, he looked down at his paper with an introspective expression. [Interpretation: Depth/ Bedrock] This acknowledgment seemed to make Tom uncomfortable, even troubled.

After a moment of silence, Rene asked, [Clarification: Depth/ Bedrock] "How does this affect you, and how do you see yourself responding to this new awareness?" [In-Spection: Depth/ Bedrock] Tom sat quietly in thought. After a moment he said, [Expression: Depth/ Bedrock] "I have spent my life trying not to be like my dad… seeing myself in this way makes me want to change. I want to take a new direction." I realized we were moving towards a counselling atmosphere, rather than team building which was the objective. Again I noted that a facilitator of the ITSM will need to have a strong foundation in group dynamics as well as specific training in ITSM facilitation. In an attempt to reframe the discussion, I asked Tom, "How does this awareness affect you here at work, for example, your relationship to your colleagues?"

Tom looked up, and the atmosphere lifted and returned to one more appropriate for a business setting. [Clarification: Depth/ Bedrock & Core] Tom acknowledged that he has a tendency to be task oriented, not relational. This made him feel like an outsider many times, because the other members of the firm are very relationship oriented. He said that he had always felt insecure, and at times terrified of Wayne and Doug, since they are several years his seniors. He also recognized that because of this, he rarely expressed his feelings to them, unless it was in a rare, explosive and inappropriate manner. Tom stated that he has a "hot temper," and that he would work on expressing himself in a healthy and productive way. Tom continued, stating that because Wayne and Doug were older than he, he often looked to them for approval.

Wayne said that he understands how Tom feels. He said that his father had died when he was seven years old. Wayne said that he heard a psychologist on television say one time, "When a boy loses his dad at a young age, he spends the rest of his life seeking to win his approval." It was at this point that Wayne realized he had been doing just that for most of his life. [Clarification & Understanding: Depth/ Bedrock] Wayne and Tom continued to dialogue about the impact the loss of a father can have on a boy, and the man he becomes. [Emergence] They agreed to work together on finding healthy ways to express themselves.

Recognizing that the time for the first session was almost exhausted, I began to conclude the day by asking if there were any elements of cultural significance to either Ron's, Rene's or Tom's stories. Beginning with Ron's story, the group agreed that many cultural factors had significance. [Understanding: Depth/ Bedrock] "Ron, a Native American, being adopted and reared by a Norwegian family has had a tremendous cultural impact upon Ron", Rene stated. Wayne said, "He is almost like a man without a country." Doug mentioned how the effect of prejudice has surely had an influence on Ron and his perception of others, especially Whites.

Turning the discussion towards Rene, Ron said that he respects her for her perseverance and her good attitude. [Clarification: Depth/ Bedrock] He wondered whether or not she was demonstrating a very western, maybe Northern European concept of individualism. He said that she seems determined to "make it on her own." Rene acquiesced that she does have a very strong sense of, "I am going to make it on my own." The group briefly discussed the nobleness of this attitude, as well its liabilities. [Emergence] The consensus was that Rene can "let her guard down, and rely on her team at work for help when she needs it." The group unanimously concurred that the collectivist philosophy would suit their organization, especially when considering matters of health or family.

I then asked how culture might be a factor for Tom and Wayne in dealing with the loss of their fathers. [Expression: Depth/ Subsoil] Wayne said he is sure that if he had grown up in a traditional Native American family, the extended family would care for him. For example, his uncles or grandfather would have filled the role of father figure. Ron expressed that in more traditional tribes, in earlier times, or in some families this may be true, however, in his case that did not happen. Wayne agreed that the fabric of the traditional Native American culture is compromised. Regretfully, I noted that our time had expired. I thanked the group for their participation, said we would get to the rest of the stories next session, and dismissed them.

Middle
Session 2

The second session began with a brief review of the ITSM process, including the topographical outline, to ameliorate the participants' awareness of the stage and depth of dialogue. [Expression: Surface/ Topsoil] As Doug began his narrative, he expressed reservations because his story was "pretty basic and simple, compared to everyone else's." He said that he had grown up in a typical middle-class, White, Christian, American home. His father and mother had a good marriage until his father died a few years ago. He stated that his life has been very normal, and that his greatest obstacle has been fear of failure. Because of this fear, Doug did not go to college until late in his adult years.

Upon completion of his undergraduate work, he entered a Master's programme. He withdrew from the programme in the final stages of his internship and worked as a custodian for several years. With constant prodding by a friend to finish his Master's, Doug ultimately re-matriculated and not only completed the original Master's degree, but began a second in counselling. [Understanding: Depth/ Bedrock] Doug's religious convictions have been a significant factor in his life. These convictions are in no small way, a factor in his pursuit of a Master's degree in counselling. His passion is to work with married couples because his conviction is that marriages are "under attack of the enemy (the devil)." While Doug's religion plays a seminal role in his purpose for pursuing counselling, he assured the group that his convictions will not have a significant impact on his counselling practice.
[Clarifiaction: Depth/ Bedrock]

In light of hermeneutics, and the principle of the non-objective observer, I asked Doug if he really expected to disengage his religious convictions during counselling. Following discussion with the whole team, he came to the conclusion that hermeneutic principles could prove valuable in training as a counsellor. [Expression: Depth/ Bedrock] Doug stated that he was unsure as to whether he would be able to block his personal convictions. He said he thinks there is value in having a clear understanding of what his convictions truly are and how they may impact his counselling. [[Clarification: Depth/ Bedrock] As discussion of Doug's story continued, Rene asked if his fear of failure could be related to culture influences. [Expression: Depth/ Bedrock]

After reflection, Doug stated he thought may be a possibility resulting from the cultural drive for individual success. [Clarification: Depth/ Bedrock] I asked if the group thought this "drive for individual success" may be culturally distinct or if it is universal. [Understanding: Depth/ Bedrock] Ultimately, the discussion settled that a universal drive to success exists, but the individualistic nature and high value placed on personal success is probably a more Western paradigm. After allowing for more questions or comments, I asked if we should move on to the next story. Wayne said that he was the only one who had not told his story. He said he had received a phone call that morning that one of his grandparents was about to pass away and that he would prefer to not tell his story. I assured him he was under no obligation, and that he had transparently contributed a great deal to the prior discussions. The group expressed their sympathy and graciously allowed Wayne a moment to continue processing this new information before we continued.

End

In concluding the final session with FCC, I asked the group to discuss what new knowledge or understanding had surfaced in our time together. Rene said that she had appreciated hearing the stories of her co-workers. She said that she feels she can relate to them better since she knows more about their history. Tom expressed how his new self-knowledge and the ITSM skills help him better communicate with others, especially with Wayne. Ron stated that his "In-Spection had been a powerful experience." He said he was beginning to understand that, even though he was reared by Norwegians, his foundational culture is Native American. Discussion continued on the asset self-knowledge. The group agreed that this was a powerful new insight. In addition to self-knowledge, Doug said that the stories shared had been "powerful tools in helping to humanize" his co-workers. I asked him to clarify his statement. He said that his co-workers had been "simply people who had jobs in the same office. Now they had a human side... I feel more connected to them."

I asked the group to concisely state the core of the newly acquired knowledge and what impact that knowledge could have upon the organization. [Emergence] After a period of discussion, the group read the following statement: "Understanding ourselves helps us to understand others better. Understanding others better, helps us have a more cohesive and productive team." We discussed how the group could continue to practice the ITSM skills set, and how they could practice telling their stories as a normal part of their organizational culture. Each of the participants desired to continue working together on communication and Doug asked if I could return in six months for a review and follow-up session. I agreed, and thanked each for his or her participation. We then dismissed.

Conclusion

The FCC workshop provided a great platform for practicing the ITSM. The participants were actively engaged in the entire process, and everyone, except for Wayne, shared his or her stories. Wayne abstained from telling his story due to personal reasons, yet he transparently shared and interacted in the discussions throughout the workshop. The In-Spection phase seemed to have profound impact upon the group. It appeared to me that this group responded to looking inward at their personal stories more profoundly than the previous ones. Specifically, Ron and Tom encountered intense revelations during the In-Spection stage.

The Components of the Self worksheet revealed some valuable information into the differences among the group, as well as helping the participants in evaluating the components in respect to personal importance. One of the valuable insights the worksheet gave, was the differences in the value of nature to people from, supposedly, the same religious convictions. The Trompenaars and Hampden-Turner questions also introduced valuable insights and productive dialogue. On Universalism versus Particularism, forty percent of the respondents answered that they could understand why the offender could expect his friend to lie, but one hundred percent said they would not lie. Communitarianism versus Individualism, produced a vigorous discussion. Initially, most of the participants favoured communitarianism, however, after some discussion they changed their answers to fit closely with individualism. This was due to the phrase, "even if it obstructs individual freedom and development." As a group, FCC participants highly value communitarian principles, as long as they do not infringe upon the rights of individuals.

Regarding Neutral versus Emotional, FCC participants generally agreed demonstrating emotion would be less beneficial than handling the situation privately with the individual. Tom answered that he would show emotion "so that my counterpart gets the message. I believe the clarity of my message will allow me to control even greater emotional upset in the future." Tom ultimately said that he believed his answer reflected a degree of his German & Italian cultural heritage.

The fourth question, Diffuse versus Specific, marked a divergence from the results of Trompenaars and Hampden-Turner. The FCC team unanimously viewed "a company as a group of people working together. They have social relations with other people and with the organization. The functioning is dependent on these relations (B)." The FCC group correlates much higher with the diffuse countries, likely due to the strong Native American influence and their roles as holistic helping professionals. As in previous sessions, the Components of the Self worksheet and the questions produced lively discussion.

Almost unique to this session, the cultural differences were highlighted and explored.

In previous sessions, the tendency has been to highlight cultural similarities and de-emphasise the differences. However, one of the goals of the ITSM is to assist groups with cultural differences not become homogenous, rather to identify differences and dialogue about them. The Mukogawa group, for example, focused mainly on the similarities found between the Japanese students and the American faculty.

The student's story of not talking to her grandfather for a year was met with similar stories from virtually all the participants. The group acknowledged many similarities between the students and faculty, contrary to the vast divergence of traditional Eastern and Western cultures. Within the PIF group, culture was somewhat de-emphasised as well, in favour of common ground. In the FCC workshop, cultural differences were not de-emphasised. As the sessions commenced, I intentionally listened for possible cultural nuances. At times, investigation into those possibilities returned void. In many instances, though, the query developed into a valuable dialogue.

During the Components of the Self as well as the questions, culture was discussed and as participants told their stories, often cultural distinctions surfaced. For example, I asked Doug if his fear of failure could have a cultural foundation. In actuality, I did not expect much insight or discussion from this question. I asked almost as a routine. The discourse revolving around the probe ultimately revealed that the group believes a cultural bias towards individual success does exist in the West.

Throughout the FCC workshop, cultural distinctions were explored. Instead of the tendency to disassociate from those who are different, the team actually drew closer in intimacy. According to the feedback from the participants, the goal of developing understanding and fostering emergence appears to have been met. In this session I gained new insight into asking probing questions about clues that might possibly reveal cultural distinctions.

Many statements that can be taken as, simply personality styles, for instance, may ultimately unfold into attitudes, values, or behaviours with a cultural foundation. Asking simple questions like, "Is that statement culturally based?" can quickly be dismissed, but when probed deeper may very well reveal a cultural bias. Uncovering cultural dimensions can be revealing and productive both to the individual as well as the group. In understanding personal components that have cultural relevance, an individual may be more equipped to make changes to behaviours or attitudes if necessary. In addition, this same knowledge shared with the group may help team members have a better understanding and appreciation for that same person. To this point in the fieldwork, the ITSM has been utilized to help teams find common ground as well as identify cultural distinctions. Both have been valuable in building an environment where understanding and ultimately emergence can occur.

In the final session with FCC, I asked the group to produce a concise statement of what new knowledge had been gained and how emergence has occurred. This exercise produced a powerful statement the management has posted in their staff meeting room. This statement has given the team a reminder and a goal for future reference. I will incorporate this exercise into the ITSM process.

The format of the FCC workshop proved to be beneficial in the continuity of dialogue and thought. It also provided for a more spiral or circular movement in the discussion, enhancing the hermeneutic spiral concept. Although each workshop format is negotiated with the organization, this type may be more conducive than the previous styles of one hour, once a week, for several weeks.

The FCC participants expressed favourable responses to the ITSM and we have scheduled a follow-up session in six months. In conclusion, the FCC workshop has been valuable in developing the ITSM. For example, asking probing questions to identify cultural distinctions. The addition of the final exercise of concisely defining the Emergence should be valuable in future workshops as well.

Chapter 14
Fieldwork Project 5: Investment Group

Beginning
Setting the Scene

The Investment Group is a team of five individuals who invest in residential and commercial real estate in the greater Seattle area. For approximately six years the Investment Group (IG) has bought and sold properties resulting in significant profit. The group has no team leader, resulting in each individual having equal input. Some primary sources of conflict revolve around the equanimity of the members. For example, all invest the same amount, but some members may work on improving a property while others do not. This leaves the workers feeling somewhat cheated. Another dilemma is when some members insist on selling and the others do not. Other frustrations relate to poor communication and possible cultural differences.

The workshop consisted of one four hour session with two short breaks. This worked well because the flow of dialogue was uninterrupted, allowing for more productive use of time. As in the FCC fieldwork, this workshop was fluid and dialogues were not cut short because of time constraints.

Introduction of the Cast of Characters

The Investment Group consists of three Iranian and two American partners. Hormoz, moved to the United States from Iran in his mid-twenties. He is a successful software developer in addition to his participation in the IG. Hamid immigrated to the United States approximately twenty years ago from Iran. Siamak, also an immigrant from Iran moved to the United States several years ago to attend university. He and Hamid are also co-owners of two grocery stores. Joe, born in the United States, is a nurse. James is also from the United States and works for a computer security company.

Session

The session began with a welcome and introductions followed by an overview of the informed consent form and a brief introduction to the ITSM. Immediately Hormoz asked, "There are many books on communication, what makes you think yours is better?" I immediately felt defensive because of his tone and his blunt question. Before responding I managed to practice hermeneutic interpretation. In a matter of seconds I placed his tone and style of question in context of other Persian and Arab men I have known. Hormoz had asked his question consistently with my experience and I realized he was not being rude or accusatory, simply curious. I explained to him the hermeneutic and application process of the ITSM and he appeared satisfied.

Each person in the group recognized culture and communication as issues which have adversely affected the group's functioning in the past. Although the participants had a degree of understanding of the other's culture, most saw significant room for improvement. The participants also believed their communication had been, at times, negatively affected by cultural differences. Although all participants presently live in the United States, the Iranians have a well established sub-culture in the Seattle area. Families join together and celebrate Iranian holidays, and they were presently preparing for the Iranian New Year celebration. The Iranians in the group travel to Iran almost yearly and still have many family members residing in Iran. They have adopted an element of Americanization, but hold to many traditional Iranian customs, language, holidays, and food.

Beginning the ITSM, I provided an overview of the purpose and method of the model. I then presented the hermeneutic principals foundational to the ITSM process. Each participant appeared to grasp each concept and eager to continue the process.

[Ins-Spection: Surface/ Topsoil] I asked the participants to take a moment and complete the Components of the Self worksheet. When everyone had finished, I asked them to begin sharing the top components identified. The most significant components had strong correlations between the Iranian participants. For example, My Pleasures, My Family, My Relationship to Nature, and My Successes were all rated as eight or nine. The American participants scored the same components as having only medium value. For the Iranians, My Culture was scored nine, seven, and nine. However, the Americans scored My Culture five and three. The dialogue following the Components of the Self worksheet appeared to be most valuable when the participants looked at the scores of the others. Often making statements like, "I knew you would answer that way!" and, "Why did you answer so low on this one… I thought it would be higher?" The Components of the Self worksheet sparked compelling dialogue and appeared to be somewhat valuable as an In-Spection tool.

Following the Components of the Self worksheet, we took a short break to allow time for answering the Trompenaars and Hampden-Turner questions. [In-Spection: Surface/ Topsoil] As in the previous groups, we answered only questions one through four. When each had answered the questions we proceeded with exploring the answers. The results are as follows.

Results for question 1. Universalism versus Particularism

USA: 93% no right to expect me to testify to the lower figure- high universalism

IG Answers: 60% some right as a friend to expect me to testify,
           40 % no right to expect me to testify to the lower figure; 60% testify

---

Results for question 2. Communitarianism versus Individualism

> USA: 69% "A," demonstrating a high measure of individualism
>
> IG Answers: 80% "A" demonstrating a high measure of individualism
> 20% "B" demonstrating a high measure of communitarianism

Results for question 3. Neutral versus Emotional

> USA: 43% not show emotion
>
> IG Answers: Each different: 1=3, 1=4, 1=2, 1=1

Results for question 4. Diffuse versus Specific

> USA: 90% A
>
> IG Answers: 60% B, 40% A

None of the answers were unanimous, and none of them were highly correlated between members of the same cultural backgrounds. Therefore, the revelation of stereotypical cultural responses did not emerge. The exercise had value, however, as an

In-Spection tool as it was apparent in the discussion that each participant had wrestled intimately with his answers. The discussion of the answers provided insight into the other participants as well. Of significance among the answers, in regard to culture, was question 1. Compared to the results found by Trompenaars and Hampden-Turner, the Americans in this project were not Universalists in their responses. Both Americans said they would testify that the friend was going the speed limit.

Two out of the three Iranians said they would not testify. Interestingly, the Iranian who said the friend had no right to ask him to testify responded that he would testify to the lower number. His reasoning was that his friend did not have a right to expect him to lie, but that he would in order to help his friend. This was the first such answer I had observed in any workshop I have performed. While the Iranians, in particular, expressed their opinions candidly and with fervour, the discussions revolving around the answers to the questions was not as heated as in some of the previous workshops. I gave the participants an introduction to storytelling and allowed time during a break to identify a brief story that would help other members of the team understand them and their culture better.

Middle

Upon reconvening, I invited a volunteer to begin. Siamak quickly volunteered. [Expression: Surface/ Subsoil] He began by telling of his childhood in Iran. (Siamak had scored Childhood Memories a nine on the Components of the Self worksheet.) He vividly remembers walking through the streets of his Iranian village as a child with his grandfather. They came upon a camel. As he stood their staring at this giant animal, Siamak remembers the camel standing two stories tall. He said he remembers the feeling of awe as he stood looking at this huge animal.

As he grew older, Siamak said he came upon many camels, but none could validate his memory of a camel that stood two stories tall. He said that this experience taught him the significance of perspective. The camel was not two stories tall, Siamak was simply a small child. He shared that we all have perceptions that colour the way we view the world, and sometimes those perceptions cannot be validated. As Siamak concluded his brief story, I sat in awe at the remarkable picture he had painted of a land so foreign to me as to have camels in the streets.

I was also enthralled by his wonderful example of the concept of prejudice that is such an integral component of hermeneutics. [Clarification] Joe asked, "What was a camel doing in the street?" This was an interesting question because it did not actually clarify the meaning of Siamak's story, but illuminated the diverse cultural context of the group. The question was never answered. Dialogue continued on the subject of perception and how it impacts our view of the world. I emphasised the importance of perception or prejudice in hermeneutic interpretation. [Clarification/ In-Spection] I asked for other examples of how our perceptions influence our interaction with others. [Expression: Depth/ Subsoil] James spoke of how his religious background influenced his view of Muslims and others who are not Christian.

He said he grew up believing people who are not Christian are bad people. From his adult experience with people other than Christians, he has learned this paradigm is erroneous. [Expression: Surface/ Topsoil] Hormoz spoke of how perception of age is a prejudice he deals with as he gets older. He said he was recently talking to someone about an older person he had met. The person he was speaking of was forty years old and

Hormoz is fifty-one. James said, "I have something that is on a totally different subject... something that has affected me greatly...but not really a cultural prejudice."

[Expression: Depth/ Bedrock] James said, "When I was a toddler, the first memory I have is being at my grandmother's and my dad had a seizure and broke his back. He spent many years recovering. My mom had to get a job. She was someone who had, years ago, received a scholarship to medical school and turned it down to get married and have kids. So she got a job as a teacher, never living up to her full potential. As I was growing up, I got the message that I should never be dependent on anyone... because you never know when you are going to have to take care of not only yourself, but someone around you. Those who know me know that I don't depend on anyone... I am pretty self-reliant. When it comes to seeing how you discriminate against others... when I see people who aren't self-reliant, who don't support themselves, I don't have a lot of respect for them. I question their value... what are they contributing?" [Expression: Depth/ Bedrock]

Siamak referred back to the Components of the self worksheet component of "Childhood Experiences." He said, "That is why I marked it as a nine... because those childhood experiences really impact the way you look at things... it's almost like you don't have a choice." [Clarification: Depth/ Bedrock] James interrupted quickly, "But you do have a choice..." Siamak spoke over James and said, "For me it was the camel thing, and years later when I realized the camel wasn't really that big, the impact of it subsided... we can become aware of those experiences and how they affect us so that we can react, maybe, a little bit different... to truly *see* what we are seeing." [Clarification: Depth/ Bedrock]

Joe asked James if he thought this was a "good thing to have happen [to him] as a child." [Expression: Depth/ Bedrock]

James said, "In some ways it was very good because it drove me to be a successful person... and in many ways it was bad. I won't let people help me... I won't reach out, and maybe for that reason I am not as successful as I could be... because I won't let anybody support me." [Clarification: Depth/ Bedrock] James replied, "But... you are able to see both sides of it, and some people cannot." [Interpretation/ Clarification: Depth/ Bedrock] Hormoz broke in and said, "On the Childhood Experiences, I put a three... I think they may be important, but where is the balance? Ok, you know that this happened to you as a child, but at what point do you say... ok, I will lean on you... let you help me. You know, learn from it and not get stuck in it?"

[Interpretation] I began looking for signs of cultural differences in the discourse. James, an American, had expressed that due to childhood experiences, he was very self-reliant. This is a trait closely related to individualism, a strong American characteristic. [Clarification: Depth/ Bedrock] Hormoz is from Iran, and although each of the Iranians scored somewhat individualistically on the Trompenaars and Hampden-Turner questions, I inquired if there were cultural differences involved. [Expression: Depth/ Bedrock] Siamak said that Iranian custom is to care for the family. If a father dies or is injured, the oldest son cares for the family. If the son is unable because of age or for some other reason, the duty is passed to another person. Perhaps an uncle, brother, or father-in-law will take the responsibility of care.

Siamak said that when he moved to the United States, he sent money home to his brother, sister, mother, and father to help care for them. Eventually all of his immediate family moved to the United States and Siamak provided housing, jobs, and other necessities for them. He did this without expecting anything in return. [Clarification: Depth/ Bedrock] I compared this to James' story of self-reliance and asked, "How might James' situation be different had he been Iranian?" Hamid spoke out for the first time. As he began, he was quickly moved to tears. He stopped speaking and said someone else should go. Hormoz insisted that he should feel free to speak. After a moment of silence, Hamid began to share his story.

[Expression: Depth/ Bedrock] Hamid said when he was twenty-one years old, his father died. "At that point I was expected to begin caring for my family. Although I am not the oldest son, my brother was unable to care for them financially." Hamid accepted this responsibility and has been taking care of them, especially financially, for over thirty years. When he moved to the United States and became successful in his business, he felt even more obligated to care for them. He said that by now his father would have naturally been too old to provide financially for his family, and his siblings would have begun to care for themselves and share the responsibility of caring for his mother. However, since he had been successful, his family continued to rely upon his money being sent back to Iran monthly. This was a very emotional subject for Hamid and he had tears in his eyes the entire time. He said that his story demonstrates how Iranian culture differs from James'.
[Expression: Depth/ Bedrock] Joe said that there should be a balance somewhere between these two extremes. Hormoz replied, "In general, we do not learn... or we do not want learn, to capitalize on our experiences to find a balance. We Iranians are a people of extremes... we love extremely, and we hate extremely... it is hard, especially for us to find this balance!" Hormoz said he would like to tell the story he had chosen to share.

[Expression: Surface/ Bedrock] Hormoz began. "I am going to give you a short story. The first time in my life someone told me about women's rights, I could not understand it because I am not from a family that understands women's rights or man's rights. After I learned about women's rights, I began to stand up for it." Hormoz expressed how difficult this was in Iran. "When I tried to talk to my aunt about women's rights… to tell her she has rights not to have to cook or do things she did not want to do. She had a very hard time understanding what I was talking about… she did not understand, and many other people did not understand. So any way, I came to the United States and got the shock of my life… in Iran women were not educated and did not have opportunities like here… so I came here, and went to Bellevue Community College.

At that time I was very vocal, so I started talking about women's rights… and I had all of these papers I was distributing. This girl came in the middle of the school and started arguing with me about how wrong I am. I was so shocked that I went home and told my sister what happened. I said that I can understand why a man would argue with me, but I don't understand why a woman would argue with me. She was like twenty-one years old and she was telling me that a man has to be like this, and a woman has to be like that… and I just froze. I never thought I would hear that in this country.

From then on, I decided that I could shout what I believe, or I can start from their level… to see where they are… so I can understand where they are coming from instead of telling them what I think they need. So I realized that we are all living together, and everybody has their own way of thinking. We are a community and we need each other, but like James was saying, we also need to be able to take care of ourselves. So maybe there are some people who do not agree with us… if we come to their level and try and understand them, maybe we will have a better society… where we can rely on each other and still take care of ourselves." [Interpretation]

Hormoz had inadvertently illuminated some significant hermeneutic concepts. He spoke of his own prejudice (advocate for women's rights] and the importance of understanding the context of the other person ["coming to their level"]. In addition, the understanding achieved by understanding himself and the context of the other is congruent with a hermeneutic fusion of horizons.

[Expression] Hamid said that all of the stories, "even though they are different, fit together with common themes." [Clarification] I asked, "What have you identified as a common theme?" [Understanding] His response was finding balance between self-reliance and interdependence, and that our experiences influence how we view the world. At this point the hour was late and the participants were visibly becoming weary. I recognized Hamid's statement to be a natural segue to the emergence phase.

End

I acknowledged the late hour and suggested we begin the final stage of the evening. I asked the group, "What new knowledge has emerged throughout this workshop?" Joe replied that having an opportunity to hear the stories of the other members had helped him "have a better understanding of why they may act the way they do." James said that understanding the importance of each person's world-view had been valuable. Siamak said that the theme of interdependence had "stuck out as important" to him. I asked the group to compose a statement that would reflect a practical application of this new knowledge. James to the initiative to write down the comments, and eventually the statement had reached consensus. [Emergence] "We can work better together by working as an interdependent team."

I expressed my appreciation for each person's participation in the workshop. Each person appeared to have a favourable response to the session, and each expressed how valuable it had been to have a different level and style of conversation.

Conclusion

I took a moment to reflect on the workshop and make notes. I continued to marvel at the simple story of a two-story camel in the streets of Siamak's home town. Siamak had painted such a vivid and practical picture of how our perceptions culminate from our experiences. The stark contrast between James' response to his father's death, and the experience Hamid had following his father's death resonated deeply. Hormoz had discovered the value of trying to understand the context of another person, or as he had stated it, "getting to their level." He recognized that in order to communicate effectively, individual's need to strive to understand the other before trying to be understood by them. In the midst of the turmoil and the stand-off between the Iranian government and those of the USA and Britain, this final workshop provided me with an element of hope that storytelling can positively impact relationships. The following chapter will provide a summary of the fieldwork exercises.

Chapter 15
Fieldwork Project 4: Pharmaceutical Manufacturer

Beginning
Setting the Scene

The Pharmaceutical Manufacturer (PM) is a subsidiary of one of the largest multinational pharmaceutical manufacturers in the world. Locally, the PM employs over five-hundred individuals making it one of the largest employers in the Inland North-western United States. In addition to being one of the largest employers, the PM is also one of the area's largest employers of multicultural individuals.

The organization has a high level of security so detailed information about the company's operations is restricted. Generally, the organization consists of management, research scientists, manufacturers, and ancillary personnel such as maintenance and security. Quality of communication between and within each job category is imperative.

Barriers to communication consist of the stereotypical personality style differences between the different types of employees as well as different cultural backgrounds. The purpose of the present exercise is to enhance "inter" and "intra" departmental communication. The ITSM workshop consisted of three sessions lasting for approximately one hour and thirty minutes each.

Introduction of the Cast of Characters

The PM workshop included four participants. David is American. His mother is Japanese and his father is African American. Lynda is of Portuguese descent and was born and reared in Hawaii. She has lived on the U.S. mainland for about fifteen years. Rudramurty is Indian and has lived in the United States since 2003. Majid is from Pakistan and moved to the

United States in 1990. The group was assembled by the human resource director because they work together daily and they represent the multicultural/ multinational character of the organization. I was told there are no present problems, but the desire is the ITSM will enhance communication and the cohesiveness of the team.

Session 1

The first session began with a brief explanation of the ITSM project and its intended purpose. Each participant made personal introductions and shared briefly about their cultural background. Rudramurty introduced himself as an Indian from a middle income family. He said he has lived in the USA since 2003. He came to the USA to pursue his master's degree. He is married and travels to India often to his parents and siblings. Rudramurty said that he is a Hindu and follows idol worship. However, the closest temple is in Seattle so he does not go to the temple very often. Majid said he came with his family to the United States in 1990.

None of them spoke English, and yet he immediately began to work in a fast food restaurant. He said that he was grateful for the opportunities in the USA. Within two years he and his siblings could speak English. He graduated from high school and attended college and graduate school. Majid said he is Muslim and that his religion has a significant role in his life. Lynda followed Majid. She said that she was of Portuguese descent and is Hawaiian. She spoke of the difference in Hawaiian culture and the culture of the continental USA. Specifically, Lynda shared how the "pace of life is significantly slower in Hawaii." She said she is Catholic, but does not practice her religion.

David said that he is American, and that his mother is Japanese and his father is African American. He shared how difficult it is to live in Spokane where so few people of colour reside. In addition, he told of how he has serious concerns about travelling to nearby Northern Idaho because of the large population of white supremists. He said that this group had chased his father off a lake where he was fishing. David said that his wife is "Caucasian with blonde hair, and that really makes those guys mad... it's like I stole one of their women or something."

David shared that his grandfather had been a Baptist minister and that he had grown up in a Baptist church. However, once he went away to college, he began exploring his mother's Buddhist philosophy and presently adheres to elements of both religious expressions.

Following the introductions I began with an overview of hermeneutics. The participants all have advanced degrees and they quickly grasped the methodological principles. The concept of Prejudice sparked dialogue regarding how each person in the group has come from very different backgrounds. I introduced the Components of the Self worksheet and the Trompenaars and Hampden-Turner questions. I explained how the purpose of In-Spection is to reflect upon these prejudices and to help each person to have a better understanding of self. In closing the first session, I expressed my gratitude for each person's participation and asked them to complete the worksheet and questions for the following day.

Middle
Session Two

We began the second session discussing the Components of the Self worksheet. Interestingly, none of the ratings were significantly different. Each person rated My Memories, My Childhood Experiences, My Conscience, My previous Emotional Attachments, and My Culture as a seven or higher. My

Relationship to nature was rated eight or nine by everyone except Lynda who rated it five. The only components rated one or two were My Socio-economic Class, My Regrets, My Heroes, My Habits, and My Differences from Other People. The discussion revolving around the Components of the Self worksheet revealed that each person had not initially expected the exercise to yield much insight. However, the participants unanimously agreed that the worksheet helped set in motion the process of In-Spection. Following the Components of the Self worksheet we began discussing the answers to the Trompenaars and Hampden-Turner questions, numbers one through four. The results are as follows.

Results for question 1. Universalism versus Particularism

> USA: 93% no right to expect me to testify to the lower figure- high universalism
>
> PM Answers: 100% no right to expect me to testify to the lower figure,
> 75% not testify, (Indian- possibly testify/ undecided)

Results for question 2. Communitarianism versus Individualism

> USA: 69% "A," demonstrating a high measure of individualism
>
> PM Answers: 100% "B" demonstrating a high measure of communitarianism (Indian- "B" AND "A")

Results for question 3. Neutral versus Emotional

> USA: 43% not show emotion
>
> PM Answers: 75% "3" clearly show emotion, (Hawaiian "2" not show emotion)

Results for question 4. Diffuse versus Specific

> USA: 90% A
>
> PM Answers: 50% B, 25% B (Hawaiian), 25% A & B (Indian)

The PM participants answered the same on each of the four questions. The only exception was Rudramurty, an Indian. He answered primarily the same as the other participants on questions one, two, and four, but included "and" or "both." [Clarification: Depth/ Subsoil] When questioned by Lynda, he could not give an explanation. [Interpretation/ Clarification] I asked him if his answers might be related to his Indian frame of reference. [In-Spection/ Expression] Rudramurty thought for a moment and said he would suspect his answers do reflect his Indian mindset. [Expression: Depth/ Bedrock & Core] Rudramurty continued reflecting on the nature of Indian philosophy as incorporating the "both"/"and" concept.

The PM participants each answered highly Universal on question number one. [Clarification: Depth/ Subsoil] I asked if the answers were reflective of their culture of origin or of the adoption of American cultural norms. [Expression] Lynda said she was "brought up to know right from wrong", and Majid concurred. Rudramurty said that his family had taught the importance of honesty, but there may be exceptions to any rule. It was the groups conclusion that their tendencies toward Universalism were based primarily upon their training and that their training reflected their culture of origin. David agreed that his family had taught him to be truthful in all situations.

Question number two revealed a unanimously high degree of Communitarianism in the PM group. David has a Japanese mother. Lynda said that Hawaii is very populated by Japanese and Pacific Islanders and their since of community permeates the Hawaiian culture. The group is greatly influenced by Eastern and Middle Eastern culture, therefore contributing to the high degree of Communitarianism. [Expression] David shared of a situation where a competing drug manufacturer had recently decided not to produce a certain drug because it would not make them enough money. The group began to discuss the nature of individualism and its relationship to capitalism. They said that, while capitalism has some good qualities, it generally produces a greedy, self-centred approach to business. The PM group agreed society would be better if each person would care for his or her fellow man.

The third question revealed the majority of participants preferred to express themselves in order to "allow me to control even greater emotional upset in the future." [Expression] Lynda said she usually behaves in accordance to answer two, but that often she would like to act like numbers three or four. Majid stressed if his business partner used such a strong word as "insane" that he would definitely act like number three. The whole group ultimately agreed that number three would probably be the best course of action in most situations.

Question four sparked much discussion. While David and Majid answered "B", Majid recognized that "A" is important as well. [Expression] Rudramurty agreed that both are important and should be the norm. [Expression] David said that having a Japanese mother strongly influenced his "B" answer. David said he operated according to answer "B" when he owned a business in the past. He stated that he his employees were like family. All agreed that both ways of approaching business have value, but that capitalism has strongly influenced the general acceptance of the philosophy found in answer "A." [Expression] Majid said, "It's all profit driven now!"

He revisited the earlier example of the competing drug company that chose not to develop a drug because of market. Rudramurty said that some people "achieve success by putting their foot on somebody's head… this reflects the nature of answer 'A'." [Expression] David said that there is a large salary gap between most senior managers and the workers. He believes this reflects the managers' philosophy of answer "A." [Expression/ Clarification] Lynda said, "So the people who own and run the companies are 'A's" and the people who work for the companies are 'B's'… See what I have always found very interesting is that companies are nothing more than collections of individuals… and if each of us as individuals are 'B's,' how come all of a sudden the companies are 'A's?" [Expression] Majid said that companies that have at least an element of "B" will probably have more sustainability because the workers will have more loyalty. Lynda said, "I think the people who would answer 'A' would say that if the workers are performing their duties, then the company would be sustainable."

Following the discussion of each of the questions, I reviewed the elements of storytelling. I asked each person to prepare a story to share with the group for the following meeting.

End
Session Three

As we gathered for the final meeting, I asked for a volunteer to share his or her story. David began. [Expression: Surface/ Subsoil] He said that his father, an African American, had been in the Air Force and that his family had moved often. However, they lived for the greater part of his childhood in Spokane. Since Spokane has such a small non-white population, David said that he "grew up white." He shared of his recent experience of applying for another position within the company. The position was in Atlanta, Georgia. He had already passed the pre-interview phases and was flown to Atlanta for a personal interview. [Expression: Depth/ Subsoil] When he arrived, he was greeted warmly, but he said he sensed they were surprised that he was "black."

Later, he met with a (white) real estate agent who drove him around to look at houses. David said that she kept trying to steer him towards houses in the part of town where the African American community resided. Ultimately he decided not to accept the position. [Expression: Depth: Subsoil/ Bedrock] He said that while he has been the victim of racism, he has also experienced racial prejudice against African Americans. He said that when he visits cities with large African American populations, he stays "away from the black part of town."

David also spoke of how he often feels divided in his world-view. He said that often he would view the world through a Japanese lense, as reflected in many of his answers to the In-Spection tools. He also has a strong desire to contribute to society he credits to his mother's influence.

[Expression: Depth/ Subsoil] Lynda shared that she understands feeling split in her world-view. She said, for example, that her parents are Portuguese and they wanted her to date and ultimately marry "her own kind." However, Hawaii is a very tolerant and accepting culture. Many marriages are culturally mixed. She said it was sometimes difficult to live in a Portuguese home in the Hawaiian culture because of the dissimilarities. [Expression: Depth/ Subsoil]

David said he understands the mixed marriage dilemma. His father had also encouraged him to marry an African American. I noted how his father's wishes were not congruent with his marriage to a Japanese woman. David's father told him to expect a variety of difficulties if married outside of his race. David ultimately married a Caucasian woman with blonde hair and blue eyes. This has been a source of racism in a variety of settings throughout marriage.

Rudramurty volunteered to tell his story. [Expression: Surface/ Subsoil] He began by sharing how his family moved often and that they were not wealthy. Rudramurty began to speak of his religious experience. He said India has many different sects of Hinduism and religious expression. Some Hindus are vegetarian and some are not. Within his family, his mother is vegetarian, but she will cook meat for others in the family. [Expression: Depth/ Subsoil] Majid interjected and said that Rudramurty's mother must be "pretty open minded." He shared how his Indian friend is a vegetarian and "he does not even want you to eat meat around him."

Rudramurty then began to tell of the different classes of people in India. He said that the caste system was outlawed, but in essence is still practiced in some cases. He said that many times people will ask, "What class are you from?" At that point you are not obligated to tell unless you want. Rudramurty's family are from the working class community. He described the different classes as follows.

    Working Class/ Dalits/ Scheduled and Backward Class- Approximately 70%

    Business Class/ Vaishyas/ Forward Class

    Political & Fighting Class (the protectors)/ Kshatriyas/ Forward Class

    Brahmins/ Knowledge Base/ Religious

Rudramurty's description was quite insightful for me. I had heard of the different classes in India, but had never had it set forth as he had. Rudramurty said the constitution recognizes three classes, the business and Political/ Fighting as one class. He said that in the more progressive and modern cities, the class system is virtually obsolete, yet in the smaller communities it is still fairly prevalent. [Clarification] I asked him if the class system affects him in any way. Rudramurty replied, "No… it is really a perfect way. It is a very good formula. I respect the way the categories are laid out, like Brahmins, Kshatriya, Vaishya, and the Dalits… that is the perfect classification I would say. Any society, any village, needs somebody who teaches, somebody who takes care of things, somebody who does business, somebody who produces things. How much emphasis you place on the classes:… that's what matters. Just because someone is in that lower category, do you really have to treat him differently? That's where the line has to be drawn. But, the categories are very good… to have the right compilation of society." [Understanding] I said, "I guess in some ways every society has this same type of class system?" Rudramurty said, "Yes, it is just that in India it has been formalized."

    While the story Rudramurty told was not deeply personal, it opened a door into the Indian society that the Westerners in the group had not been able to look through before. This understanding of Indian culture was illuminating to me, personally. I had always assumed that the caste system was a form of bondage, and in many ways it appears that it has been and may be in some cases. However, one thing I realized is that most societies operate on this level to some degree. The group discussed how even their own organization had its own informal class system. Because of the shortness of time, I asked if someone else would like to volunteer to share their story. Majid said he would be next.

[Expression: Depth/ Subsoil] Majid was sixteen when he came to the USA. "My father's name was selected in the lottery, and since all of us children were all under twenty-one, we got to come with him. I originally wanted to go to England to play cricket for the national team. I am glad I didn't pursue that goal because I could not have made it. Since I have been here, I noticed my mother's focus has always been education. Here brother and uncle were educated as a lawyer and doctor. My father was not into education… his family had land… farmers. My parents are two totally different people… sometimes I wonder how they are still together. Every time education comes up, my father's family would say, 'Why don't they just go to work like you did?'

My father never interfered with our education… but, he never told us to go and get an education, either. My childhood was always focused on education. My mother was not educated because the women in Pakistan were not usually able to go to university. Her main thing was that we needed an education in case they were not there tomorrow… we would be on our feet. When we came to the USA, I got a part-time job at a fast food restaurant after about two weeks. That's where I learned English… in six months. I wanted to go to medical school, but I needed to provide for my brothers and sisters so I cut it short and got an engineering degree. Although I had just learned English, I did ok… sometimes I was up until three in the morning to do my homework. When we moved here, my cousins had already lived here for a while, so we moved in with them for a few months. When I would be up late studying and doing homework, they would make fun of me, like, 'Look at Majid, he thinks he's going to Harvard or something.' That made me mad, so I would turn off the light and wait until they were gone and get up again and study some more. I thought, 'I am going to show them!' So I guess part of the reason I did well in school was that initial burst of anger that made me want to succeed. After a year and a half I got accepted to Georgia tech, which was number two or three in the nation in engineering. I didn't go there because it was too far from my family, and we had just moved to the USA so it was too much change for me. I chose to go to New Jersey Institute of Technology and started my Master's which I haven't completed, yet. Although the Pakistani culture is different from this culture,

I appreciate that I can be thrown out there and have the opportunity to succeed. In Pakistan, I was babysat… people take care of you and tell you what you need. One thing I don't like about this country is that I became very individualistic… it became all about me. All of my siblings are successful and educated… but they are very individualistic. Our family is not as close as it were. We became successful, but lost part of our culture… what is important to us. So now we make an effort to see each other more. I travel to New Jersey very often to see my family. With a little bit of effort, we can bring everything back. Life is constantly evolving… we have lost some of our traditions, but all in all everything has worked out very good for us. When we need each other, when someone is hurt, we are all there."
[Expression/ Interpretation: Depth/ Bedrock]

Lynda spoke of the class system in India. She suggested that Majid and his siblings had crossed the invisible barriers between the classes, but at a cost. The cost was the loss of some traditions and other cultural elements. Majid said that she was correct. [Expression: Depth/ Subsoil] "We used to go to parties with other Pakistanis who were educated, and we would feel very intimidated because our family was not educated. But the cost is... now that we have crossed those barriers, we no longer have time to go to the parties to associate with those people! In our culture we have something like the caste system... one of the first questions people ask is, 'What does your father do?' In the states many Pakistanis care about what you do or who you are. But in Pakistan it is still the old way." [Expression: Depth/ Subsoil] Rudramurty said that this was actually a valid question. He said that in order to know someone, you need to know their background. Rudramurty said, "I don't know how it is in Pakistan, now, but in India, arranged marriages are still common. My marriage was arranged. The way we get into this arrangement is they will look for someone with a similar background and then ask questions about a couple of generations back. What types of people are in this person's background? What types of health issues? What did their ancestors do?" [Clarification/ Understanding: Depth/ Subsoil]

I said this sounds similar to the concept of context in hermeneutics and the ITSM. Rudramurty said, "Yes, if you know someone's context, you can know them better." [Clarification: Depth/ Subsoil] Lynda asked Majid, "Are arranged marriages common in Pakistan?" Majid replied that they are, but his was not a traditionally arranged marriage. He said that his family strongly encouraged him to marry his "own kind, just like David and Lynda. My sister signed me up on an internet site that helps Muslims all over the world meet other Muslims. I met my wife on the internet, and then I had to go to Pakistan to meet her in person. There, I met her family."

I thought how amazingly ancient tradition had been assisted in this modern day by technology. Majid and Rudramurty agreed that the parents sometimes give the children the choice in the arranged marriage process. We continued to discuss the concept of arranged marriages and the pros and cons of both arranged and choice marriages.

Majid yielded the floor to Lynda. She said, [Expression: Depth/ Topsoil & Subsoil] "Growing up in Hawaii certainly shaped my perspective. Hawaii isn't perfect, but I am grateful for the underlying philosophy of tolerance. Hawaii is a small little rock and people accept other people. Not that everything goes, but the assumption that other people want to be accepted. I have come to the realization that this concept is ingrained in my perspective. I treat people like I want to be treated… I want to be accepted, and I think they do also. Underneath all of our differences, we are all the same. I went back to Hawaii recently and I was stuck by how cohesive the people are… we are very collectivistic in Hawaii. I miss that. I was also reminded of how openly affectionate the people are… hugging and kissing all the time. That is something I had to be careful with when I came to the mainland…" [Clarification: Depth/ Subsoil]

Rudramurty asked about demonstrating affection and friendship with the opposite gender. He said, "In India, you are not supposed to be friends with the opposite sex because it always leads somewhere." He noted how the US culture is different from his own in this regard. Dating is another issue Indians face when moving to the USA. Since arranged marriages are still common in India, dating is not accepted. Rudramurty said that the Indians have a saying, "Eating a hamburger does not make you an American… if you are a true American, you can let your daughter go on a date and sleep peacefully at home."

The time allotted for the session had been exhausted and we moved to the Emergence stage of the ITSM workshop. I asked the group to identify some of the themes that had arisen throughout the workshop. [Emergence] Lynda noted the theme of "differences, and how differences can be integrated. You evolve, but like Majid, you can come full circle back to your foundation." The different classes indentified in the Indian society were also discussed. It was suggested that the different classes work together to perform the functions of society. The Emergent statement for the PM group was, "Within differences lies the basis of working together." This statement reflects the collectivistic nature of the group and the wide variety of cultural experiences represented.

Conclusion

The Pharmaceutical Manufacturing firm provided an extremely rich context for the final case study of the ITSM. With participants from India, Hawaii, USA, and Pakistan, the cultural variance was vast. While none of the stories were deeply personal, the cultural insight proved to be valuable. Again, as in the other cases, the concept of differences and the contribution they could make arose as an important theme throughout the workshop. This is probably due to the emphasis placed upon identifying differences rather than common ground in the ITSM model.

I asked the participants to share their reflections on the ITSM workshop. Each expressed that it had been an enjoyable experience, and that it had helped them better know their workmates and their cultural backgrounds. They also shared that the In-Spection was beneficial for examining some of their own prejudice. Some concern was raised over how well the ITSM might work in an environment where the participants did not know each other well. Majid said he thought they may not be as open to telling their stories if they had little previous contact. I agreed that it may be a factor to consider. Rudramurty said he thought the ITSM would be difficult with a larger group. I believe he is correct and that is why I have intentionally kept each case below eight participants. In conclusion, the ITSM workshop achieved the goals of team building, enhancing group communication, and building synergistic relationships within the context of differences. The management and human resource director have expressed favourable views of the ITSM process as well. The following chapter will provide a summary of all of the case studies performed throughout the ITSM research.

Chapter 16
Summary of Fieldwork
Beginning
Setting the Scene

The three fieldwork exercises spanned the course of fourteen months, and with each exercise I gained insight in the development of the ITSM. The workshops took place in organizations based in Spokane and Seattle, Washington, and each organization was represented by varying degrees of multiculturalism. Although the methodology of the ITSM is hermeneutics, which is cyclical in nature, I initially found myself unconsciously operating in the linear positivistic and quantitative mindset of my previous graduate training. Although I understood the cyclical nature of hermeneutics, I began my work with organizations from a linear frame of reference. Storytelling was simply the means to practice the ITSM model of Inspection, Reception, Interpretation, Clarification, Understanding, and Emergence.

As the fieldwork progressed, I became keenly aware of the stifling effect being bound by a linear frame of reference had upon dialogue. Although the model proved beneficial in aiding the communication process, the storytelling process proved to be the highlight of each workshop. One of the first adjustments made to the ITSM was to place the emphasis on the storytelling and to encourage participants to be aware of the movement from one stage to the next. Therefore, the original name of the Interpretive Transcultural Method (ITM) was changed to Interpretive Transcultural Storytelling Method (ITSM) to emphasise the role of storytelling. Although the model was subjugated somewhat by the storytelling, it continues to remain a vital part of the method.

The model stages were especially valuable in dialogue when communication would break down. The participants could discuss at which stage the communication broke down and why. While the model provides a road map by which to track dialogue, it is concurrently fluid and cyclical. Rather than a linear model, the ITSM process moved through the stages and then cycled back through the stages as the dialogue intensified in its topographical depth. Also, as in hermeneutic methodology, the dialogues in the fieldwork exercises moved back and forth between the part and the whole. With this new cyclical frame of reference, the ITSM began to work more cohesively.

Another significant revision in the initial ITSM model is the use of the topography model adapted from Lessem and Palsule (1997). Originally, the participants were to track the topography of a story or conversation by making notes. The participants found it impossible to constantly analyze and track the topographical levels and simultaneously remain an active participant in the dialogue. However, as with the stages of the ITSM, the topographical levels proved to be of benefit as the participants were encouraged to simply be aware of the topography of the stories and the dialogue.

The topographical levels were valuable in the reflective follow-up discussion in the final two workshops. In the PIF, FCC, and IG workshops we noted that, consistently, if one person moved to a deeper level in his or her story, the group as a whole would gravitate to the deeper levels. However, this gravitation was not linear, but cyclical, meaning that it did not remain at the deeper levels indefinitely.

The dialogues cycled between the topsoil, subsoil, bedrock, and core very naturally. Being a work environment and not a counselling group, if the story or dialogue reached a level that was too intimate for comfort, someone would share something that would begin the cycle back to a more comfortable level. I observed that the stories and dialogue often began at the topsoil or subsoil levels, gravitated down to the bedrock level, and briefly moved into the core.

After a period of core level discussion or storying, the discussion would move very naturally back up to the less intense levels. Each individual had different topographical levels at which he or she felt comfortable sharing. The PM group did not often venture into the deeply personal realms of bedrock or core, but the dialogue was still extremely valuable in identifying cultural differences. Each group seemed to have a corporate comfort level for the depth of dialogue in which they generally moved. In my initial frame of reference, I hypothesised that the most productive discussion would take place at the core level. However, I found that the subsoil and bedrock levels are valuable as well. The natural fluidity of dialogue cycled back and forth between the topographical levels with very little intervention from me.

Therefore, the method stages and the topographical levels continue as significant concepts in the ITSM process, but operate more as scaffolding upon which storytelling and dialogue are draped. The revision of the ITSM is also addressed in Chapter 9, ITSM: Conception, Revision and Application.

Introduction of the Cast of Characters

Mukogawa Fort Wright Institute (MFWI) was the pilot project of the ITSM fieldwork. MFWI is a branch campus of a Japanese women's university. During the three session fieldwork pilot, I worked with five Japanese students and two American faculty members. The sessions lasted for one hour on three consecutive days, and took place on the MFWI campus. The next workshop was in partnership with a private investigation firm. The company investigates a variety of criminal and civil cases for attorneys and private clients. During the four sessions, I worked with eight managers and lead investigators. The third fieldwork exercise was conducted with a counselling firm, fictitiously known as Family Counselling Centre (FCC) for confidentiality.

As a relatively young organization, FCC has experienced the growing pains of building new relationships and identifying roles. The FCC participants included a Caucasian of German and Italian heritage, a Native American, who was adopted as a child by second generation Norwegians, a lady with German and Native American ancestry, a Caucasian, and a Caucasian with a percentage of Native American ancestry.

The Fourth exercise was conducted with a real estate Investment Group (IG) in Seattle, WA. The IG has experienced cultural and communication oriented conflicts in some of their investment dealings. The group consisted of three Iranians and two Americans. The final case study was performed with a multinational Pharmaceutical Manufacturer (PM) in Spokane, WA. The PM is a large organization and employs a very multicultural staff. The employees work inter-departmentally and intra-departmentally. Quality communication and good working relationships are essential. The group included an Indian, a Hawaiian, an American with an African American father and a Japanese mother, and a Pakistani.

Initial Sessions

Each of the fieldwork exercises began with an introduction to the ITSM and an overview of the ITSM packet consisting of an informed consent form, an overview of the ITSM model, a Components of the Self worksheet, the questions used from the work of Trompenaars and Hampden-Turner, and an introduction to hermeneutics and storytelling. In the initial MFWI pilot exercise, I immediately met with the challenges of the language barrier. Most of the participants were exchange students from Japan and not proficient in English. Each student brought an electronic interpreter to the session and began using them from the very beginning.

Introductions were even difficult as their names were very difficult for me to pronounce. As I began the introduction, we immediately met a virtual brick wall. The participants tried to help each other understand what I was saying, which was very distracting. When I began discussing hermeneutics, I had to present a very entry level description and refrained from the use of the word hermeneutics. Although the dialogue was slow and difficult, the participants responded with smiles and seemed eager to continue the process in the second session. The first session, then, took much longer than anticipated, throwing the next two off of schedule.

For the other groups, language was not an issue. However, I discovered that other issues can and will arise in the initial session. While the workshops with MFWI, FCC, IG and the PM were approached positively by all participants, some in the PIF group were not so willing to accept the notion of storytelling in a work setting. In addition, my credentials and the relevance of the ITSM were challenged by the same dissenters. Two PIF participants, Tracy and Angie, expressed a concern about the appropriateness of sharing personal stories in the work setting. I explained the research and the rationale behind the concept. Tracy eventually conceded to participate, but Angie remained fairly hostile to the concept. Angie also began an assault on my credentials as a consultant. She suggested the organization bring in someone who is qualified for Total Quality management training or something similar.

I found it difficult to not take her innuendos of my lack of qualifications personally. I presented my qualifications in more detail, including my twenty years of management experience, my graduate degree in counselling, and my experience in working with other organizations, in addition to the research that went into the preparation for the ITSM. I met the futility of trying to convince someone of something they did not wish to accept. Nothing convinced her that I could offer anything of value, and I realized she had come into the workshop predisposed to a negative attitude. In the end, Angie was let go from her position shortly after the second session because of unethical business practices.

The initial sessions with two of the three organizations demonstrates the necessity for the facilitator of the ITSM to have training in group dynamics as well as maintain an element of flexibility. This will be addressed to a greater degree in Chapter 18: Conclusions and Recommendations for Further Research.

The first session is valuable not only for introducing the ITSM, but for setting the stage for the entire workshop. The participants must, at a minimum, agree to participate in discussion, and ideally accept the notion that telling a personal story is appropriate for a work setting. I realized in the PIF discussion of this matter that settings exist in which a model of this nature may not be accepted as appropriate. However, based on the reactions of the majority of participants in the ITSM fieldwork, the concept can equally be embraced, especially within organizations where interpersonal relationships and communication are valued.

In addition to assigning the Components of the Self worksheet and the Trompenaars and Hampden-Turner questions, I asked the participants to identify a story of an event in their lives that could help the group know them better and that would give the group a glimpse into their cultural context. In each of the groups, I introduced the concept of personal storytelling and invited members to begin preparing a brief story to share with the group in succeeding sessions. For the FCC and IG groups, we took a break to provide time for these projects.

Middle

The second sessions proved to be valuable times of self examination and discussion. The Components of the Self worksheet provided a platform for evaluating those characteristics deemed important in the make up of individuals. Interestingly, there was little correlation between the Taiwanese and Chinese from the Buckingham M.Sc. programme and the Japanese students from MFWI. As well, there was little contrast between the responses of the American and Japanese participants. The most highly ranked components included My Aspirations, My Body, My Education, My Will-power, My Family, My Skills, and My Experiences.

In each group we reviewed the components each person had chosen as the most and least important. In doing this, an opportunity arose for a breadth of discussion, including why some components were more important to some people than others. During this discussion we addressed possible cultural factors which may affect an individual's choice. As can be seen in the above figure, there is little correlation between any of the groups. Whether or not the components have any cultural relevance is inconclusive due to, among other reasons, the small sample size. The Components of the Self worksheet fulfilled its key purpose within the ITSM of provoking Inspection. Of similar value for Inspection and spurring discussion are the questions used from the work of Trompenaars and Hampden-Turner.

Compared to the Components of the Self worksheet, the Trompenaars and Hampden-Turner questions revealed a more uniform response pattern between all participants in the fieldwork. Since all but the Japanese students permanently reside in the USA, this is not perhaps much of a surprise. However, I was surprised by the degree to which the Japanese students answered more consistently with the West than with the results of

Japanese respondents in Trompenaars' and Hampden-Turner's research.

My initial approach the MFWI workshop was with the attitude that the Japanese students would be grounded in traditional Japanese culture as I understood it from the literature and research as well as my experience with the Taiwanese and Chinese students in the Buckingham M.Sc. programme. However, I realized that these students did not fit the stereotype presented in the literature I had read. This experience highlights the need for an individual approach to working multiculturally. While the research of others such as Trompenaars, Hampden-Turner, and Hofstede is valuable in a broad and generic sense, the ITSM offers an avenue for working on understanding between specific individuals within an organization.

End

The subsequent sessions within each of the fieldwork exercises focused on storytelling and interpretation utilizing the ITSM model. For each of the workshops this exercise offered depth of insight and stimulated dialogue. During the first workshop, my focus somewhat naturally drifted toward finding common ground between cultures. As the workshops continued with PIF, FCC, IG, and the PM, I realised true Emergence relied upon the synergistic working through of differences. As in the first story of the PIF group, some were initially topsoil and as demonstrated by stories, such as Glenda's, some were bedrock to core. Brent's was the initial story in the PIF group. His story was at the topsoil level and very brief. However, the following discussion allowed the story to expand in depth and spurred a deep conversation about the cultural implications of the prioritization of family and work life. The theme of family versus work remained constant in the PIF workshop, and as

Glenda followed with her very personal and bedrock/ core story, the theme continued.

In each workshop the group experienced a setting of the stage with the first story. As the meetings continued, the ensuing dialogue and stories reflected, to some degree, the original theme. For MFWI the theme was on demonstrating respect to others, even if the feelings do correlate. For PIF the theme was the constant battle of reconciling family and work life, and the discussion of the PIF team as a family in itself. For the FCC, IG, and PM groups, the theme focused on identifying differences and building effective relationships that reflected the strengths of those relationships. Identifying a recurrent theme early in the ITSM process is an effective tool for the facilitator to obtain. In retrospect, regardless of the stories told, the groups naturally gravitated to discussion around themes that correlated with relevant issues for their respective organizations. Therefore, a case can be made that the ITSM not only can increase the synergy within a team, but can address relevant issues within an organization simultaneously.

As the final sessions began, each group moved strongly towards Understanding and eventually Emergence. In the final workshops, I found asking the group questions like, "What new knowledge or understanding has surfaced in our time together?" more intentionally identified areas where new knowledge and Understanding had been achieved. In the FCC group, some of the answers were being able to relate to co-workers better by knowing more about their history, and how knowing more about one's self amplifies one's ability to know others.

One member expressed how the storytelling had helped him to "humanize" his fellow workers. In clarifying this he stated, that his co-workers had been "simply people who had jobs in the same office. Now they have a human side... I feel more connected to them." In moving to the application of this new knowledge, the Emergence stage, I asked the group to formally state the core of the newly acquired knowledge and what impact that knowledge could have upon the organization. They replied, "Understanding ourselves helps us to understand others better. Understanding others better, helps us have a more cohesive and productive team."

Conclusion

As the ITSM workshop consecutively progressed, the depth of insight achieved and the level of Understand and Emergence reached progressed respectively. While the pilot MFWI workshop provided an opportunity to broadly re-evaluate the focus and paradigm of the ITSM, the following workshops provided opportunity for more intrinsic and practical evaluation and revisions. Upon evaluating the MFWI workshop, I revised my paradigm to be less linear and more cyclically focused on the storytelling and dialogue, using the ITSM model as the scaffolding to provide form and structure. In addition, I reframed my focus from discovering cultural common ground to identifying cultural variations.

Within the subsequent workshops refinement of the ITSM became more particular. Attention to diversity continued to intensify with each session and in each workshop. While my frame of reference has traditionally been to find strength in commonalities, I discovered that discovering and working through areas of difference can be an asset to a team. In each of the workshops the participants expressed the value of the ITSM model as an aid to communication. In addition, with the exception of Angie who was terminated from PIF, the participants unanimously agreed that sharing their stories and hearing the stories of others had been a positive experience and had contributed to strengthening their work relationships.

A major contribution of summarizing all five workshops is the emergence of the concept of the theme. While I generally observed and commented on the recurrent themes of each workshop, I have found this to be valuable for future practice. I followed up with the leaders from all five organizations two different times and asked three questions:

1. Have you noticed any negative results from the ITSM workshop?
2. Have you noticed any positive results from the ITSM workshop?
3. Do the any participants continue to practice any of the skills learned from the ITSM workshop?

The leaders from all organizations noted no negative effects of the workshop. An administrator from MFWI could not comment on long term effects because the students returned to Japan within a few months after the workshop was completed. However, he did share that he suspected the workshop had been of value for the students and faculty in understanding the need to not stereotype individuals based on cultural norms. The president of PIF shared that she and other participants, had used the model to work through conflicts and breakdowns in communication. She also said that she believed the storytelling has been valuable in helping her employees understand each other better by knowing each other's stories.

A participant from FCC utilized the ITSM model during a communication session for a marriage seminar he taught. The leader of FCC said that his co-workers communicate more clearly after identifying different personality styles and hearing "the stories behind the person." He said that taking time to bring the human element into the work setting had been valuable for building cohesion among the team.

In conclusion, the ITSM fieldwork has been a productive experience. Having utilized the workshops to grow through my own preconceived concepts, such as linear thinking and quantitative reasoning, I have discovered a deep value in cyclical thinking and qualitative research. Initially, I also found it difficult to critically address the original model I had produced. Eventually I realized that refinement was inevitable and necessary to the practice of research and the development of the ITSM. The ITSM has been a valuable resource for the organizations participating in the fieldwork, and I anticipate the use of such a model in the greater scheme of society.

In recent years we have observed New York's 9-11-01 terrorist attack, the war in Iraq, a war between Israel and Lebanon, and the threat of war between Iran and the West. On a BBC television news programme (August 10, 2006), a Muslim scholar was interviewed regarding the foiled Muslim terrorist attacks using liquid weapons on airliners from the UK to the USA. The scholar took exception to the phrase Muslim terrorist. He said that the terrorists' views did not represent those of the typical Muslim. He stated that the difference was in the "interpretation of the Koran." Poor interpretation serves as causes of conflict between members of organizations, religions, cultures, and nations.

Perhaps the ITSM, addressing multicultural management as a microcosm of the larger society, will be an instrument to assist interpretation so that conflict can be avoided or worked through in a constructive manner. The following chapter will address the implications of hermeneutics and storytelling in the multicultural management arena.

References:

Hampden-Turner, Charles & Trompenaars, Fons. (2000). *Building cross-cultural competence.* Yale: Yale Press.

Lessem, Ronnie & Palsule, Sudhanshu. (1997). *Managing in four worlds: From competition to co-creation.* Oxford, UK: Basil Blackwell.

Maslow, A.H. (1970) *Motivation and personality, 2nd Edition.* New York: Harper and Row.

Trompenaars, Fons & Hampden-Turner, Charles. (1998). *Riding the waves of culture. 2nd Edition.* NY: McGraw-Hill.

Chapter 17
Implications of Hermeneutic Methodology and Narrative Method in Transcultural Management

With the fieldwork cases and their summary completed, we now turn to the implications hermeneutics and narrative storytelling can have in the arena of multicultural management. In this chapter we will begin with a brief review of relevant multicultural management literature, examine the implications of hermeneutic methodology, and then introduce storytelling to the plot. In this research, storytelling does not stand alone as a method, rather, it is considered in the context of being grounded in hermeneutics (see Appendix 2).

As discussed in the literature review chapters, multicultural management is represented by a variety of works. However, these works typically address the topic in a generalised manner. Research such as Trompenaars, Hampden-Turner, and Hofstede is based on large sample sizes with participants from around the world. The information they present is very valuable for addressing general cultural nuances, but do not address the micro-scale of individual relationships among multicultural organizations. Although these authors do acknowledge exceptions apply, their research is geared towards providing a breadth of empirically generalised data spanning many different cultures. In addressing the multicultural management arena, I have utilized elements from these research projects, such as the questions used by Trompenaars and Hampden-Turner. In this manner, I have adopted a dialectical approach to social science research based on the philosophy of Brian Fay (1996).

As much of the research on multicultural management is grounded in Western and Northern cultures (Lessem & Palsule, 1997), it is positivistic and qualitative in nature. This type of research is best suited for answering such questions as cause and effect. In contrast, hermeneutics is founded on contextual interpretation which leads to understanding. Quantitative methodology is based in the physical sciences and assumes an objective world which can be studied and measured with scientific, quantitative methods.

As the name implies, quantitative research focuses on quantity and is primarily deductive utilizing statistical methods. While quantitative research is valuable in the natural sciences, some scholars believe it to be inadequate for the social sciences. The empirical approach does not allow for the nuances found when studying living, thinking, evolving human beings who do not live in a static cultural environment. The knowledge gleaned from more empirical research can be valuable as a foundation, but particular relationships within organizations require a more individualized approach. Hermeneutic methodology provides a natural fit for practicing this type of approach.

As discussed in the chapter on methodology, hermeneutics means to interpret. Inevitably, when individuals communicate, there will be misinterpretation. As demonstrated by the violence based on different interpretations of the Koran between Sunni and Shia Muslims in Iraq and the different interpretations of the Bible by Protestant and Catholic Christians in Ireland, interpretation can play a seminal role in relationships.

While misinterpretations within organizations may not result in this type of violent bloodshed, the resulting conflict can be harmful. It is my contention that simply knowing the stereotypes presented by the majority of multicultural management material is not adequate. For example, in the MFWI fieldwork, I approached the Japanese students with the paradigm that they would exhibit a high degree of communitarianism and that they would not easily grasp the concept of individualism. This was based, not only upon my experience with Taiwanese and Chinese students, but upon the literature I had researched such as Trompenaars, Hampden-Turner, Hofstede, and Funakawa. For instance, the research of Trompenaars and Hampden-Turner found approximately 70% of Japanese respondents answered with a high degree of communitarianism. (Trompenaars & Hampden-Turner, 1998) Only through the In-Spection phase of the ITSM was that belief challenged. Having placed the MFWI students in their individual contexts versus their stereotyped context I was better equipped to interpret their actions, their comments, and their stories more effectively. Following is an overview of some fundamental hermeneutic concepts and how they apply in a multicultural management setting.

Understanding

Understanding, for Heidegger, has its origin in his concept of a person's ongoing encounter with the world. He argues it is impossible to separate one's human consciousness from his or her encounter with the world. In other words, it is impossible to separate the subject from object. For Gadamer, understanding is a social activity, a "sharing in a common meaning" (Gadamer, 1977, p.292). Gadamer presents that individuals are always on the quest for understanding and that understanding comes from a dialogical process. To understand (*verstehen*) means to grasp something or to see more clearly, to integrate a meaning into a larger frame of reference.

In context of multicultural management, understanding is a powerful concept. Understanding places two or more individuals in a dynamic relationship in which understanding is developed and integrated into a larger frame of reference. This concept is the underpinning concept of the Understanding and Emergence phases of the ITSM. Within the ITSM, I have differentiated between Understanding and the application of Understanding which I have called Emergence. Emergence is differentiated in order to intentionally focus on the application of new knowledge.

Understanding and Emergence can be observed in the FCC workshop. Throughout this final fieldwork exercise, the group moved through the phases of the ITSM and came to a realization of new knowledge. The participants expressed how they had learned about themselves as well as their colleagues through the ITSM process. They shared of how telling their stories had been a valuable exercise in this process. The Understanding of one another, because of the new knowledge of each person's story, had helped to bring cohesiveness to the team. When asked to state how they could apply this new Understanding, the group presented this Emergence statement, "Understanding ourselves helps us to understand others better. Understanding others better, helps us have a more cohesive and productive team. We will endeavour to incorporate the skills we have learned in this workshop into the cultural fabric of this organization."

Interpretation

As stated above, hermeneutics means to interpret. Gadamer resisted the oversimplification of the concept of interpretation as simply a tool to aid Understanding. For him, interpretation was not a tool, but a part of the whole. He strongly resisted turning hermeneutics into a step by step method to reach an end. The inclination of methodizing hermeneutics is exactly what I struggled with in the initial phases of the fieldwork. Having re-framed my reference to more of a spiral or cycle, I was better equipped to grasp the concept of interpretation being more of an ingredient than a step.

Gadamer's approach was to utilize the concepts within hermeneutics as a holistic and cyclical philosophy, believing that making them tools would destroy the interpretation dialogue.

(Dostal, 2002) Viewing Interpretation as a conversation is a reason behind its placement in the ITSM. Following In-Spection and Expression, Interpretation then moves to Clarification which cycles back to the first two phases. This dialogical process provides an environment that encourages conversation, in our case between multicultural colleagues, which can serve as an ingredient in the acquisition of Understanding and Emergence.

An example of how Interpretation can impact relationships within an organization can be observed in the FCC workshop. Following Rene's story of having to cope with MS, Wayne expressed how he has previously interpreted her slow movement and lack of energy as laziness or apathy. Following her personal story, he realized her disease was much more advanced than he had previously recognized. Hearing the personal turmoil this disease had caused Rene gave Wayne a new perspective and allowed him to interpret Rene's actions and words in a new context. In relationships within any organization, the ability to correctly interpret the actions and words of others can improve communication and teamwork.

Horizons

A horizon is a world view, or paradigm. In context of the present research, hermeneutic methodology attempts to fuse the horizons of the listener and the storyteller. In hermeneutics, this is a fluid concept in which a person's horizons continually change as he or she incorporates the horizons of the other. Cushman (1995) writes:

> Martin Heidegger and Hans-Georg Gadamer argued that it is not possible to exist as a human being outside of a cultural context. People can exist only within a cultural framework that is carved out of the sensory bombardment of potential perceptions and possible ways of being... The bombardment of perceptions and possibilities is like a forest, and the carved out space is

like a 'clearing' in the forest. The clearing of a particular culture is created by the components of its conceptual systems and transmitted from one individual to the next and one generation to the next through their communal traditions of shared understandings and linguistic distinctions. It is only within the clearing that people 'show up' in certain shapes and with certain characteristics. The paradox of the clearing is thought to be caused by its horizontal nature: Horizons are created by the culture's particular way of perceiving... That is, the clearing is both liberating, because it makes room for certain possibilities, and limiting, because it closes off others. Horizons are thought to be perspectival, and therefore moveable. (p. 21)

In hermeneutic inquiry both the listener and the storyteller are changed as they dialogue back and forth, moving between horizons, until they are fused. As people within a team interact, a fusion of horizons occurs, in which all emerge transformed. Not only will the multicultural team emerge, the organization as a whole will potentially have a positive impact. In the MFWI fieldwork, I and the other Americans listened to Lisa's story through individualistic American ears. As I heard her tell of not speaking to her grandfather for a year, I interpreted that through the context of my own experiences, or horizons. Her story did not sound congruent with Japanese culture to me.

My horizon was based upon the severing of relationships when the types of feelings and behaviours Lisa expressed were encountered. In Lisa's horizon, not speaking to her grandfather for a year meant that she still lived with him, still acted respectfully, and still communicated as needed. When these two very different horizons merged, an Understanding was reached of how each culture viewed Lisa's story. The Emergent knowledge was that even though one may not care for another person, they can still act respectfully to that person.

Dialogical Reasoning

Each of the key concepts within hermeneutics flows back and forth between the others, therefore many have similar nuances. Dialogical reasoning is related to interpretation. Gadamer stressed the importance of reflection and conversation in knowing. Conversation assumes mutuality of question and answer (Gadamer, 1976), similar to the Expression, Interpretation, and Clarification phases of the ITSM. Gadamer proposed that through conversation with one another, understanding, that can not be predicted nor controlled, will occur. He believed that true conversation is when people are open, equally participative, and interested in achieving common understanding. Gadamer believed conversation to be an important function in crossing cultural or personal borders, leading to new discovery and understanding. In the multicultural management arena, this concept has powerful implications. As the ITSM brings a group of multicultural team members together, the purpose is to engage in dialogical reasoning which is an important ingredient in achieving Understanding and Emergence. The direction of the dialogue in ITSM sessions is not predetermined or controlled. The purpose is to provide an environment where participants can equally engage one another in dialogue intended to bring about new understanding and knowledge which will have a constructive impact upon the organization.

Among the valuable conversations in the PIF fieldwork was the topic of Sandra's tendency to micro-manage her staff. In her story, Sandra shared how she had been expected to care for her brothers when she was a child. In addition, she had an employee who had committed suicide. The resulting dialogue revolved around the unfair expectations of Sandra's childhood and her guilt of not being able to prevent her former employee from committing suicide.

The group came to an Understanding, through the dialogue, moving back and forth from Expression to Interpretation to Clarification, that Sandra most likely micromanages based upon her childhood experience and feeling as though she was responsible for the death of an employee. The Emergence arose from the mutual Understanding, and a commitment between them to work on relieving this unfair burden on Sandra, thus relieving the stress on the team from being micromanaged.

Contextualization

Hermeneutics emphasises contextualization, and in the ITSM, the contexts of the listeners and the speakers are important. Developing a mutual understanding of these contexts (or fusion of horizons) aids in the emergence of new understanding and meaning. Context involves, among other things, reflecting upon historical and socio-cultural factors. This is often addressed utilizing the hermeneutic spiral. The individual parts of context are revisited in context of the whole. "Hermeneutics is all about context, about placing the topic of inquiry into historical and cultural perspective" (McLeod, 2001, p. 56). McLeod (2001) continues, "Hermeneutics insists that we accept and embrace these realities, rather than pretending that we can achieve a knowledge of human affairs that somehow transcends culture and history. The way we can achieve useful understandings of human affairs is to enter fully into dialogue" (p. 23).

Within the ITSM, context is stressed from beginning with discovering self-context in the In-Spection phase, to striving to understand the context of the other in the Expression or storytelling phase. In this research project, I devoted a great amount of effort to my personal In-Spection or contextualization.

As demonstrated in the relevant chapters, I researched my context on a macro level as well as a micro scale. Understanding my personal prejudices, values, history, culture, and religion, for instance, is primary to any understanding of others that I may attempt. For that reason the Components of the Self worksheet and the Trompenaars and Hampden-Turner questions are utilized at the beginning of the ITSM.

In the discussion of these exercises the individuals become better equipped to place their colleagues in context as well. As individuals share their stories, the ITSM encourages the Clarification of Interpretations in order to facilitate better understanding of contexts.

Hermeneutic Spiral

The hermeneutic circle is a fundamental concept in the interpretation process. This principle suggests that understanding is achieved through iterations in a dialogical reflection. The researcher iterates between interdependent meaning of parts and the whole that they form. "Inquiry proceeds by building up an interpretation, through moving back and forth between the part and the whole. This involves: gaining a sense of the meaning of the whole text, and then using that as a framework for understanding fragments of the text; carrying out the micro-analysis if the possible meanings of small sections of text, and using these to challenge or re-interpret the overall sense of the text" (McLeod, 2001, p.27).

Transcultural teams can find this practice valuable when practiced intentionally, as in the ITSM. As an individual listens to another, he or she can practice moving back and forth between his or her own context and that of the speaker. This exercise helps the participants to engage in an iterative dialogue which has the potential for the listener and the speaker to experience a fusion of horizons. This concept could be considered similar to the expression, "walking in someone else's shoes." The listener attempts to alternate back and forth between their own shoes as well as walk in the shoes of the speaker. It is trying to understand where the other person is coming from, without forgetting where you are.

The practical use of the hermeneutic spiral within multicultural management is the adoption of a non-linear frame of reference. This may be difficult for some Westerners and Northerners to adopt. I found this concept difficult, especially in the beginning of the fieldwork. For team members to adopt this concept may require a constant reminder. I found through the fieldwork that typically cycling around also helps the dialogue to cycle down into deeper topography. As the dialogue cycles back and forth, the Interpretations and Clarifications can produce transformative knowledge and understanding. The PIF team experienced this as the dialogue throughout the workshop continually resurfaced the themes of family and work, and work as family. In the end, the team accepted the premises that one's family comes first, and that the relationships within PIF are akin to an extended family. This produced a more cohesive corporate culture for PIF.

Prejudice

"Every act of hermeneutic understanding begins with a pre-understanding, which orients the inquirer to the text or topic. One of the tasks of the hermeneutic scholar is to become aware of and reflexively explicate this pre-understanding in a way that creatively feeds into the process of understanding itself" (McLeod, 2001, p.23). Prejudice, defined by Gadamer (1976), is prejudgment. Prejudices are our preconceived notions of things, emanating from our past experience and socialization. Empirical research attempts to eradicate prejudice and obtain objectivity by bracketing. However, in hermeneutics this is considered impossible. To understand another we cannot shed our past experience, because it is this past experience that actually facilitates understanding the other. A common axiom in psychology is that we interpret the present in light of the past. For team members in any multicultural organization, understanding one's prejudice is a valuable resource.

Gadamer (1975) advocated continual striving to illuminate our prejudices. By identifying our prejudices we are better equipped to work with others. Not until I wrote my personal contextualization for this research project did I realize the prejudice towards people of colour that had been ingrained in my psyche. Prejudice can be racial, religious, gender oriented, or affected by any number of other factors. When members of an organization are aware of their predisposed attitudes, they will be better equipped to challenge those attitudes as necessary. While hermeneutics does not have a set of tools or a detailed guide, it possesses interrelated concepts which provide a fluid, yet rigorous philosophical framework.

Hermeneutics has been criticized by some because of its lack of carefully delineated steps. As a research methodology hermeneutics is somewhat ambiguous as to methods, but it is nevertheless a valuable framework when working with people. When juxtaposed to the overwhelmingly empirical methodological research, hermeneutics is a methodology of interpretation for achieving understanding.

Having been initially developed for interpreting the Bible, then literature, hermeneutics is now being utilized in the social sciences. The field of multicultural management is a natural progression for the use of hermeneutic methodology. As people from various cultural contexts are thrust together in the global economy, the generalized empirical data of Trompenaars, Hampden-Turner, Hofstede, and others provides valuable resources. However, it is through personal interaction with people from other cultures that hermeneutics can be utilized to bring about understanding and synergistic emergence. Since hermeneutics was originally developed for interpreting literature, the use of storytelling is a natural method for utilizing hermeneutics in the social science field.

Since the terms narrative and storytelling are used in a variety of forms, for a variety of purposes, and in a variety of disciplines, it is important to define them in this context. The terms narrative and storytelling are often used interchangeably, but there is a distinction. Academic literature often classifies storytelling as narrative.

In defining narrative and storytelling, Randall (1995) writes, "Narrative is the genus of which story is but one species. Accordingly, while all stories are narratives, not all narratives are stories" (p. 85). The narratives discussed in this project are specifically stories. For the ITSM and for the implications of narrative in multicultural management, the type of narrative used is autobiographical in nature. In the ITSM fieldwork, the stories told were relatively brief (approximately 10-15 minutes) snapshots of events in the lives of individuals that had some influence on their personal development. These stories provided a glimpse into the life of the teller and consequently into their cultural context. Utilizing storytelling proved valuable in the context of the fieldwork exercises. Therefore, I propose that storytelling may profit teams in many multicultural organizations.

I have met with some opposition to the concept of using personal stories in a work environment. Some colleagues as well as some participants in the fieldwork have expressed that the workplace is no place to introduce personal life. These individuals strongly support maintaining a line of demarcation between business and personal lives. This is a philosophy that may be incongruent with the concept of the ITSM. Therefore, I am not suggesting that the ITSM, specifically, nor hermeneutics and storytelling, generally, will be appropriate for all multicultural management settings. I do suggest, however, there are organizations that value the synergistic emergence the ITSM can produce. In the ITSM fieldwork, participants were free to share or not to share their stories. In addition, the depth at which they shared their personal story was their choice.

In the fieldwork projects the storytelling process was preceded by an introduction to hermeneutics. The ITSM is a model of blending hermeneutics with storytelling in order to intentionally provide a platform for Emergence. In this capacity the ITSM succeeded. Far from simply telling a personal story to allow someone to know you better, the ITSM is purposeful in identifying ways the story and resulting dialogue can positively impact the organization.

It is my contention that storytelling is a powerful method and that hermeneutics is a natural methodology on which to build synergistic relationships in a multicultural workplace. "In the process of telling our life stories, we share important truths, as we see them, and in so doing, create vital links with those who participate in the exchange. Telling and listening to life stories is a powerful experience... The life story, then, is very much an interdisciplinary approach to understanding not only one life across time, but how individual lives interact with the whole" (Atkinson, 1998, p. 3-4). William Randall (1995) suggests that people make sense of their lives by constructing a story in which they are the author, narrator, main character, and reader. The "stories we are," are the stories of our lives as we interpret them. In the process of In-Specting the storyteller is forced to re-examine an event in his or her life. In doing so, he or she is simultaneously re-interpreting that event. As one re-interprets an event, he or she assigns new meaning to that event. The expression of that event allows another forum for new meaning to arise, both internally and in the group setting. Therefore, the value of storytelling is not just for the listeners, it is also a transformative event for the teller. Randall (1995) quotes Sartre, "We live our lives *through* our stories and we understand ourselves, others, and our world in terms of them" (p.330).

In context of the present research, which focuses on intercultural relationships within organizations, Randall states, "Unless we hear each other's side of [that] story, however, and get the story straight, distrust is likely to grow, and the relationship itself unroll rather rockily, if not completely unravel" (Randall, 1995, p. 107). In developing relationships with others, Randall recognizes the importance of "getting the story straight," in other words, interpreting, clarifying, and understanding while communicating. Jack Maguire (1998) states, "Sharing real life stories [in human history] was an essential element in forging friendships, alliances, families, and communities. It brought individuals a greater intimacy with each other and, simultaneously, a stronger sense of self" (p. xiii). Maguire continues, quoting Jimmy Neil Smith, "We're all storytellers. We all live in a network of stories. There isn't a stronger connection between people than storytelling" (Maguire, 1998, p. xiii).

Within an organizational setting, storytelling and hermeneutics can assist in building stronger connections. Atkinson adds his conviction, stating, "People telling their own stories reveal more about their own lives than any other approach could" (Atkinson, 1998, p. 90). Transcultural management literature does not emphasise the value of people telling their own stories.

In much of modern multicultural management theory, the emphasis is on understanding generalities and customs. For example, is the culture communitarian or individualist or should you kiss, bow, or shake hands? Funakawa has taken the field into the practical realms of doing business, specifically between

Japanese and Americans, but does not broach building the relationships between multicultural colleagues. Lessem and Palsule have presented a humanistic approach which builds upon the enriching nature of incorporating the strengths of all four worlds.

According to Lessem and Palsule (1997), the South and East are underrepresented among modern management theories. In context of the four worlds (Lessem & Palsule, 1997), the use of storytelling and hermeneutics is consistent with the Southern and Eastern thought.

A National Public Radio news story on August 18, 2006 reported on the relationships China is developing with India and Africa. The reporter stated that these relationships are changing the face of industry and the seat of economic power. In addition, on the same day, the Charlie Rhoads Show on the Public Broadcasting System interviewed Christian leader, Dr. Rick Warren. Dr. Warren stated that the growth of Christianity is not taking place in the United States or Europe, but in China and in Africa.

Others are observing a shift in the focus of the global community from the West and North, to the East and South. Western management theory must evolve with this natural migration by incorporating a holistic four world's approach. Therefore, utilizing hermeneutics and storytelling will richly contribute to the Western/ Northern qualitative and empirical management theory by the addition of a humanistic and holistic approach.

As demonstrated in the fieldwork workshops, the ITSM, by using hermeneutics and storytelling, can provide an enriching resource for developing community among transcultural teams on a variety of levels such as:

- ❖ Enhancing communication through Expression, Interpretation, Clarification, and Understanding

- ❖ Discovery of self context through In-Spection
- ❖ Discovery of the context of others
- ❖ Helping team members understand each other by storytelling
- ❖ Incorporating a humanistic and holistic element to the work place
- ❖ Knowledge creation
- ❖ Providing a platform for Emergent transformation
- ❖ Creating a synergistic application to which the unique characteristics of each employee and his or her culture can contribute

Having performed the bulk of this research project in the midst of the post 9-11 tragedy, the war in Iraq, and the Israeli and Lebanese war, I have continually been reminded how hermeneutics can be a valuable resource for enhancing understanding between cultures. With the Middle East's interpretation of the West, and the West's interpretation of, specifically, Muslims, I am convinced that a new approach to reconciliation must be practiced.

It is my contention that the principles found in hermeneutic methodology can not only be transformative for multicultural management applications, but also on a grander scale of global peace building. The following chapter addresses the final conclusions from this research and recommendations for further research which includes the adaptation of the ITSM to the larger scale of global peace interventions.

References:

Abbey, Ruth. (2000*). Charles Taylor.* Princeton: Princeton University Press.

Blaikie, Norman. (1993). *Approaches to social enquiry.* Cambridge: Polity Press

Blaikie, Norman. (2000). *Designing social research.* Cambridge: Polity Press

Cushman, Philip. (1995). *Constructing the self, constructing America: A cultural History of Psychotherapy.* Reading, MA: Addison-Wesley Publishing Comp. Inc.

Dostal, Richard. (2002). *The Cambridge companion to Gadamer.* Cambridge: Cambridge University Press.

Dreyfus, Hubert L. (1991). *Being-in-the world: A commentary on Heideggar's being and time.* Cambridge, MA: MIT Press.

Fay, Brian. (1996). *Contemporary philosophy of social science.* Oxford, UK: Basil Blackwell.

Funakawa, Atsushi. (1997). *Transcultural management: A new approach for global organizations.* San Francisco: Jossey-Bass Publishers.

Gadamer, H. (1976). *Philosophical hermeneutics.* (D.E. Linge, Trans). Berkley: University of California Press.

Gadamer, H. (1975). *Truth and method (2nd edition).* New York: Continuum.

Heiddeger, Martin. (1962) *Being and Time.* Translated by John Macquarrie and Edward Robinson. New York: Harper.

Lessem, Ronnie & Palsule, Sudhanshu. (1997). *Managing in four worlds: From competition to co-creation.* Oxford, UK: Basil Blackwell.

McLeod, John. (2001). *Qualitative research in counselling and psychotherapy.* London: Sage Publications.

Chapter 18

Conclusions and Recommendations for Future Research

As demonstrated in the previous chapter, hermeneutic methodology and storytelling method significantly contribute to the contemporary multicultural management theory. By adding a humanistic and holistic approach, the ITSM integrates elements of the East and South to the traditional Western and Northern theory. By approaching multicultural management from a dialectical approach, the ITSM adds to the contributions of empirical scholars like Trompenaars, Hampden-Turner, and Hofstede. As the East and South become more significant in the global arena, management theory will need to be more intentionally adapted to the paradigm of these two worlds. The ITSM is but a step in that direction. In this chapter I will offer my conclusions from the ITSM research and make recommendations for future research.

As qualitative research, this project is not concerned with empirically determining the statistical effectiveness of the ITSM within multicultural organizations. Although some elements of empiricism were utilized, such as the questions of Trompenaars and Hampden-Turner, the goal of the ITSM research was to produce a framework for utilizing hermeneutics and storytelling in multicultural organizations. As such, the fieldwork was approached descriptively rather than statistically. The conclusions made regarding the ITSM research are based upon my participation and observation as well as feedback from the participants and managers of the organizations where the fieldwork was conducted.

Arguments, from some colleagues and two participants, against the concept of using personal storytelling in the workplace have validity for some organizations. In corporate cultures where personal life and work life are encouraged to remain distinct, the ITSM may not be appropriate. In organizations of this nature, the empirical works of Trompenaars, Hampden-Turner, and Hofstede and the more practical work of theorists like Funakawa may prove more appropriate. However, as discovered by the organizations participating in the fieldwork, there are corporate cultures that embrace a more holistic work place paradigm.

In the fieldwork exercises, I encountered no negative feedback following the workshops, and the follow up comments months later remained positive. During the PIF workshop two participants initially argued that the ITSM was not appropriate because of the inclusion of personal storytelling in the work place. Although some of the resulting discussion between the participants rose to a heated level, the end result was positive as individuals were given opportunity to practice communication in a manner that did not typically happen in their office. One of the dissenters was eventually terminated for unrelated reasons, and the other became an advocate of the ITSM process.

With exception of MFWI, the participating organizations are based in the United States. I would recommend that future research include organizations based in each of the four worlds. This would allow observations of how the national culture of the company affects the culture of the company, and thereby affects the application of the ITSM. For example, I would suppose that a Northern company would be less open to sharing personal stories than a Southern company.

As the ITSM is further refined and developed, other tools for gaining self knowledge may be deemed more beneficial. For example Mitchell Hammer and Milton Bennett have developed the Intercultural Development Inventory (IDI) which may prove valuable as a means for gaining self awareness. In addition, the IDI may prove a valuable tool for pre-test post-test evaluation of the effectiveness of the Interpretive Transcultural Storytelling method.

The purpose of this research was to develop the ITSM model. Future research should test it. Continuing research of the ITSM should include quantitative analysis of the effectiveness of the ITSM, both long term and short term. Questions should be asked such as:

1. Do participants continue practicing the tools learned in the ITSM workshop?
2. Does participating in the ITSM have an effect on employee turnover?
3. Does participating in the ITSM effect employee morale or job satisfaction?
4. Does participating in the ITSM assist in conflict resolution?
5. Does participation in the ITSM have a significant impact on the cultural literacy and competency of the participants?
6. Does the apparent synergistic emergence of the participating teams have long term effects?

These and other questions may prove beneficial in follow-up studies of the ITSM.

In future research, more emphasis can be placed upon the utilization of the actual model and the topographical levels. In the present research I ultimately utilized these as scaffolding under the drapery of storytelling. While this was effective, I believe it can be fine-tuned to better support the storytelling. Perhaps a graph or chart could be developed for participants to easily graph the phases and levels of the dialogue.

While Emergence is the final stage and the goal of the ITSM, it should be more intentionally derived. Future research should incorporate more emphasis on the practice of Emergence. As the M.Sc. group had a final group project, perhaps the implementation of a similar group project could add substance to the concept of Emergence. This may hold value, as well, for Northern and Western cultures as it could provide more substantive, and possibly quantifiable, results of the ITSM workshop.

In addition, a facilitator's guide or training material should be developed. Because of my education as a Licensed Mental Health Counsellor, I have had extensive training in group dynamics and therapeutic interviewing. These skills equipped me to be aware of the various stages of group development, dynamics, and intervention. I am also equipped to ask probing questions and to identify recurring themes. Some of the stories told reach core levels, and can surface significant emotional trauma. For example, Glenda (PIF) sharing about her father's death, Sandra (PIF) sharing about her childhood, and Rene (FCC) sharing about her MS. I believe it is unethical to simply release a facilitator with the ITSM packet without some training in these aspects. Therefore, future research necessitates a facilitator's manual.

My conclusion is that the ITSM is a valuable platform for building community among multicultural members of a team. However, the ITSM needs continued refinement and deserves further research. While not quantitatively defensible, qualitatively the ITSM has had positive feedback and has provided an enriched and synergistic atmosphere among participating organizations. In addition to organizations, I propose that the ITSM may have possible applications in the political and religious arena. The proposal of such a possible use of the ITSM has its genesis in my original research topics. Until the final stages of the ITSM research I considered my original proposals as unrelated. Now, at the conclusion, I am finding I have come almost full circle.

As I reflect upon the years I have been pursuing this Ph.D., I observe an evolution of topics I set out to research. My initial research proposal was to consider Biblical leaders and what made them effective at leading. I was encouraged to incorporate leaders from a variety of religious belief systems, and gladly accepted. In the earliest meetings with our Ph.D. cohort and my advisors, my topic evolved to finding common ground between religious world views in order to produce a peace building theory. In light of the September 11, 2001 tragedy and the Iraq war, this was a gripping evolution. However, I soon realized this topic was very broad and daunting. I found it difficult to grasp, yet continued to study and read.

In my second year I began focusing on adopting a methodology. I chose hermeneutics and began producing chapters on hermeneutic methodology. In the midst of my hermeneutic research, Dr. Lessem invited me to teach a module on it at the University of Buckingham. The participants in this module were French, Chinese, American, British, and Taiwanese. The hermeneutic process provided a significant contribution to the cohesion of this very eclectic team of students. During the final days of this module Dr. Lessem and I discussed a potential evolution of my research project. By the end of our meeting, I had decided to work towards the synthesis of hermeneutics and storytelling into a multicultural management approach.

I have often reflected on the total disparity between my original proposal of studying religious leaders, the intermediate proposal of common ground peace building, and the Interpretive Transcultural Storytelling Method. I eventually accepted that changing topics was part of the Ph.D. process, leaving the previous topics behind. As I began to reach the finality of the ITSM research, however, I realized how close I had come to full circle. As the conflicts in the Middle East continue to rage, I have realized that the same ITSM process that provides a platform for achieving Understanding and Emergence within organizations may have a similar potential in political and religious factions. If hermeneutic concepts can help people within organizations find a fusion of horizons, then perhaps they can be of value on a macro scale (see Appendix 2).

I propose that further research of the application of the ITSM in political and religious realms may be valuable. Shia and Sunnis continue to kill each other in Iraq, Israel and Lebanon are at war, Iran and Syria continue to threaten the West, and rumblings of North Korean nuclear weapons make up our global nightly news. In such a technologically and socially advanced world, conflicts and killing should be minimized. I contend that a model such as the ITSM process may be an asset in some fashion for developing a more peaceful world built upon the synergistic application of differences.

The ITSM process is intentional in the pursuit of transformational Emergence. Two or more very different world views In-Spect, Express, Interpret, Clarify, reach Understanding, and ultimately apply this new knowledge in Emergence. In our world of clashing perspectives, specifically the West and the middle-East, such a process may be of significant value in building peace. Although my original peace building topic was focused on finding common ground, the ITSM is focused on the identification of differences. Upon identifying differences, the ITSM then moves toward the synergistic relationship of those differences. I would propose that further research into the use of the ITSM in the realm of peace building is warranted. Therefore, not only has the ITSM potential for assisting multicultural organizations in the pursuit of synergistic emergence, there may also be application globally in the political-religious arena.

As the ITSM has evolved, so have I. My world view has been challenged and modified as I have explored my own story and stories and world views of others. Having begun the research process from a very Western perspective, I have become much more in step with the four worlds. My personal transformation is congruent with hermeneutic methodology. Within hermeneutics, the researcher is an active participant who approaches the research project with an understanding of his or her prejudices. The researcher is therefore a part of the research project, not an unbiased observer. Having participated in the fieldwork exercises, my world view has been modified significantly, and I can attest that shared empathy and trust increases when personal stories are shared and intentionally heard. The ITSM is like scaffolding over which storytelling and hermeneutics is draped. This process contributes to the cohesion of the team, and results in a co-creative milieu.

Through the ITSM, the process of In-Spection assists an individual in developing self knowledge. Knowing self is primary to knowing others. As In-Spection occurs, the inside story, the outside-in story, and the inside-out culminates into Expression. As one expresses his or her story, he or she is changed in the process. In addition, the opportunity is given to the listeners to hear a story of a situation that has impacted the development of the teller. The story also gives a glimpse into the cultural context of the teller. As the listeners Interpret the story, they subsequently Clarify their interpretations. Throughout the conversation, Understanding is achieved which illuminates new knowledge. The group then considers the new knowledge and its application as they mutually and synergistically experience a transformative Emergence.

The ITSM provides an added spectrum of theory to multicultural management. By dialectically approaching multicultural management, all four worlds can be addressed. My contention is that the empirical work of Trompenaars, Hampden-Turner, and Hofstede is invaluable and insufficient. As Funakawa, Lessem, Palsule and others have contributed to the more pragmatic and holistic literature, the ITSM provides an application for the humanistic and holistic approach.

As the global economy is dynamic, focal points are continually shifting. As the East and South continue emerging into the global economy, management theory must be inclusive of those world views. Utilizing hermeneutics and storytelling, the Interpretive Transcultural Storytelling Method adds elements of the East and South to the traditional multicultural management literature. The following and final chapter provides a hypothetical case for the use of the ITSM in further research involving a culturally diverse group within a socio-political venue.

Bibliography:

Abbey, Ruth. (2000). *Charles Taylor.* Princeton: Princeton University Press.

Adams, Jim. (December 23, 2002). For Time Magazine, Sovereignty 101(Part two of a series). *Indian Country Today.*

American Counseling Association. (2006). *Code of ethics regarding research.* Found [On-Line]. Available: http://www.counseling.org/Resources/CodeOfEthics/TP/Home/CT2.aspx

Armstrong, David. (2002). *Chief storytelling officer: More tales from America's foremost corporate storyteller.* Three Rivers, MI: Armstrong International.

Atkinson, Robert. (1998). *The life story interview.* Thousand Oaks: Sage Publications.

Barber, Benjamin R. (1995). *Jihad vs. McWorld.* New York: Ballantine Books.

Berman, Morris. (2000). *The twilight of American culture.* New York: W.W.

Bible. *The New International Version,* (1984). Grand Rapids, MI: Zondervan Publishing House.

Blaikie, Norman. (1993). *Approaches to social enquiry.* Cambridge: Polity Press

Blaikie, Norman. (2000). *Designing social research.* Cambridge: Polity Press

Blum, J., Catton, B., Morgan, E., Schlesinger, A., Stampp, K., & Woodward, C.V. (1968). The National Experience: Second Edition. New York: Harcourt, Brace & World, Inc.

Brew, Peter. (Jan. 11, 2005). Personal communication, University of Buckingham.

Brinkley, Alan. (1995). *American history: A survey volume 1 (9th Ed.).* New York: McGraw-Hill.

Buchanan, Patrick. (2002). *The Death of the West.* New York: Thomas Dunne Books. Norton & Company.

Bureau of Indian Affairs. (2003). *Orientation to the U.S. Department of the Interior: Bureau of Indian Affairs.* [On-Line]. Available: http://www.doiu.nbc.gov/orientation/bia2.cfm.

Covey, Stephen R. (1989). *The 7 habits of highly effective people.* New York: Simon & Schuster.

Cushman, Philip. (1995). *Constructing the self, constructing America: A cultural History of Psychotherapy.* Reading, MA: Addison-Wesley publishing Company, Inc.

Deloria, Vine. (1992). *God is red.* Golden, CO: Fulcrum Publishing.

Denzin, Norman K. (1989). *Interpretive biography*. Newbury Park: Sage Publications.

Dostal, Richard. (2002). *The Cambridge companion to Gadamer*. Cambridge: Cambridge University Press.

Dreyfus, Hubert L. (1991). *Being-in-the world: A commentary on Heideggar's being and time*. Cambridge, MA: MIT Press.

Durant, Will. (1953). *The story of philosophy*. New York: Washington Square Press/Pocket Books.

Eck, Diana L. (2003). *Encountering God: A Spiritual Journey from Bozeman to Banaras*. Boston: Beacon Press.

Elashmawi, Farid & Harris, Philip R. (1993). *Multicultural management: New skills for global success*. Houston, TX: Gulf Publishing

Ellis A., & Sagarin E., (Ed.). (1973). *Humanistic Psychotherapy: The Rational-Emotive Approach*. New York : Julian Press.

Fay, Brian. (1996). *Contemporary philosophy of social science*. Oxford, UK: Basil Blackwell.

Friedman, Thomas L. (2005). *The world is flat: A brief history of the twenty-first century*. New York: Farrar, Straus and Giroux.

Funakawa, Atsushi. (1997). *Transcultural management: A new approach for global organizations*. San Francisco: Jossey-Bass Publishers.

Gadamer, H. (1976). *Philosophical hermeneutics*. (D.E. Linge, Trans). Berkley: University of California Press.

Gadamer, H. (1975). *Truth and method (2nd edition)*. New York: Continuum.

Geertz, Clifford. (1973) *The interpretation of cultures*. New York: Basic Books, Inc.

George, Chief Dan (1974). *My Heart Soars*. Surrey, B.C: Hancock House Publishers, Ltd.

Gephart,Roberthttp. (Summer 1999). *Paradigms and research methods*. Academy of Management, Research Methods Division. Research Methods Forum, Vol.4. Retrieved May 10, 2004 from Http://www.aom.pace.edu/rmd/1999_RMD_Forum_Paradigms_and_Research_Methods.htm

Grondin, J. (1990). Hermeneutics and relativism. In K. Wright (Ed.) Festivals of interpretation: Essays onHans- Georg Gadamer's Work. New York: State University of New York Press.

Hampden-Turner, Charles & Trompenaars, Fons. (2000). *Building cross-cultural competence*. Yale: Yale Press.

Heiddeger, Martin. (1962). *Being and Time*. Translated by John Macquarrie and Edward Robinson. New York: Harper.

Hicks, Douglas A. (2003). *Religion and the workplace: Pluralism, spirituality, leadership.* Cambridge, UK: Cambridge University Press.

Hirsch, E. D., Jr.(1967). *Validity in interpretation.* New Haven: Yale University Press.

Hoffman, G. K., Monroe, C., & Green, L. (2006). *Compassionate listening: An exploratory sourcebook about conflict transformation.* [On-Line]. PDF Available: www.newconversations.net/compassion/.

Hofstede, Geert. (1997). *Cultures and organizations: Software of the mind.* New York: McGraw-Hill.

Hofstede, Geert. (2001). *Culture's consequences: Comparing values, behaviours, institutions, and organizations across nations, 2nd Edition.* Thousand Oaks, CA: Sage Publications.

Huntington, Samuel P. (2004). *Who are we?: America's national identity and the challenges it faces.* NY: Simon & Schuster.

Kimball, Charles. (2002). *When Religion Becomes Evil.* San Francisco: Harper San Francisco.

Koch, T. (1995). Interpretive Approaches in Nursing Research: The influence of Husserl and Heidegger. Journal of Advanced Nursing, 21, 827-836

Laverty, S. M. (2003). Hermeneutic Phenomenology and

Phenomenology: A Comparison of Historical and methodological considerations. <u>International Journal of Qualitative Methods</u>, *2*(3). Article 3. Retrieved May 11, 2004 from http://www.ualberta.ca/~iiqm/backissues/2_3final/html/laverty.html

Lessem, Ronnie, & Palsule, Sudhanshu. (2002). From local identity to global integrity. *Leadership and Organization Development Journal UK, Volume 23, No. 4,* 174-185.

Lessem, Ronnie & Palsule, Sudhanshu. (1997). *Managing in four worlds: From competition to co-creation.* Oxford, UK: Basil Blackwell.

Maguire, Jack. (1998). *The power of personal storytelling: Spinning tales to connect with others.* NY: Jeremy P. Tarcher/ Putnam.

Maloney, M. (1993). <u>Silent strength: A Heideggerian Hermeneutical analysis of the stories of older women</u>. Unpublished doctoral dissertation, Georgia State University, Atlanta. Retrieved April 2, 2004 from http://www.coe.uga.edu/quig/proceedings/Quig98_Proceedings/byrne.html

Maslow, Abraham. (1964). *Motivation and personality.* New York: Harper & Row.

Maier, Pauline (Introduction). (1998). *The Declaration of independence and the constitution of the United States: With index.* New York: Bantam Classic.

McLeod, John. (2001). *Qualitative research in counselling and psychotherapy.* London: Sage Publications.

Merriam, S.B. (1988). *Case study research in education: A Qualitative approach.* San Francisco: Jossey-Bass Publishers.

Mulick, Chris. (2003, January 8). 2 Asparagus Plants Closing. *Tri-City Herald*, Kennewick, WA.

Nabokov, Peter. (1991). *Native American testimony.* New York: Penguin Books.

Page, Jack. (2000). *In the hands of the great spirit: The 20,000 year history of American Indians.* New York: Free Press.

Palmer, Richard. (1969). *Hermeneutics.* Evanston: Northwestern University Press.

Rabinow, Paul & Sullivan, William M. (1987). *Interpretive social science: A second look.* Berkley and Los Angeles, CA: University of California Press.

Randall, William Lowell. (1995). *The stories we are: An essay on self-creation.* Toronto: University of Toronto Press.

Rathbone, June. *Components of self.* (Online), Found October 2003. University College, London. http://www.homepages.ucl.ac.uk/~ucjtjur/

Reich, Robert. (1997). *Tales of a new America.* New York: Random House.

Reissman, Catherine K. (1993). *Narrative analysis.* Newbury Park: Sage Publications.

Ricoeur, Paul. (1981). *Hermeneutics and the human sciences.* Cambridge: Cambridge University Press.

Schlesinger, Arthur, M. (1983). *The almanac of American history.* New York: G.P. Putnam's Sons.

Simons, George F., Vazquez, Carmen, & Harris, Phillip R. (1993). *Transcultural leadership: Empowering the diverse workforce.* Houston, TX: Gulf Publishing.

Singer, Audrey. (2005). *The changing face of America. E-Journal USA.* [online]. Available: http://usinfo.state.gov/journals/itsv/1204/ijse/singer.htm

Smith, Gary. (2003). *Northwest income indicators project.* Washington State University [On-Line]. Available: http://niip.wsu.edu/Washington/selwa2.htm.

Taylor, Charles. (1994) *Multiculturalism.* Princeton, NJ: Princeton University Press.

Taylor, Robert. (May 29, 2003). Elijah receives suspension for wearing religious headband. *Indian Country Today.*

Thorene, Kari. (Fall, 1998). *Compassionate listening.* Yes! A Journal of Positive Futures. [On-Line]. Available: www.newconversations.net/listening01.htm

Traubman, L. (2006). Jewish-Palestinian Living room Dialogue

Group mission statement. [On-Line]. Available: http://traubman.igc.org/mission.htm

Traubman, L. (August and September 2006). Personal communication, telephone and email.

Trompenaars, Fons & Hampden-Turner, Charles. (1998). *Riding the waves of culture. 2nd Edition*. NY: McGraw-Hill.

Webb, William J. (2001). *Slaves, women & homosexuals: Exploring the hermeneutics of cultural analysis*. Downers Grove, IL: InterVarsity.

Wells, Spencer. (2002). *The journey of man*. Princeton: Princeton University Press.

www.ingramcontent.com/pod-product-compliance
Lightning Source LLC
Chambersburg PA
CBHW031608210526
45464CB00004B/1483